THE
DRUID RENAISSANCE

THE
DRUID RENAISSANCE

The Voice of Druidry Today

EDITED BY
Philip Carr-Gomm

Thorsons
An Imprint of HarperCollins*Publishers*

Thorsons
An Imprint of HarperCollins*Publishers*
77–85 Fulham Palace Road,
Hammersmith, London W6 8JB

3 5 7 9 10 8 6 4 2

© Philip Carr-Gomm, Prof Ronald Hutton, Erynn Rowan Laurie,
Philip Shallcrass, Isaac Bonewits, Steve Wilson, Dr Michel Raoult, Frank MacEwen Owen,
Christine Worthington, Louise Larkins Bradford, Chris Turner,
Robert Mills, Madeleine Johnson, Dr Graham Harvey, Caitlín Matthews,
Dr Gordon Strachan, Dr Christina Oakley, Mara Freeman, 1996

Philip Carr-Gomm asserts the moral right to
be identified as the editor of this work

A catalogue record for this book is available from the British Library

ISBN 1 85538 480 9

Printed and bound in Great Britain by
Creative Print and Design (Wales), Ebbw Vale

Edited with Foreword by Philip Carr-Gomm

THE DRUID RENAISSANCE
The Voice of Druidry Today

PART V – FINDING OUR ROOTS
– FINDING OUR FUTURE

Philip Carr-Gomm

Foreword
THE DOOR

If you're an asker you'll be a knower:
poetry's knotty and wily –
the riddles you hear are windows,
and the door is enquiry …

GOFRAIDH FIONN O DALAIGH

Druidry is the perfect lover. You fall in love with her so easily because
she is so romantic. She whispers to you of the magic and mystery of
the turning stars and seasons. She loves trees and Nature above all
things, and you yearn for these too. She tells you stories of Gods and
Goddesses, the Otherworld and fairies, dragons and giants. She
promises secret lore – of sacred trees and animals, of herbs and
plants. She points deep into the past, and ahead towards a future
which is lived in harmony with the natural world. But just when you
are convinced you will marry her, because she is so beautiful, so
tantalizing, so romantic, she turns around and there she is, with
rotten teeth and hideous face, cackling and shrieking at your naivety.
And she disappears, leaving you with just her tattered cloak- made up
of a few strands: some lines from the classical authors, whose
accounts are probably inaccurate anyway, a few inferences drawn
from linguistic and archaeological research, which could be wrong,
with the rest of the cloth woven from material written from the
seventeenth century onwards, replete with speculation, forgery and
fantasy.

You feel a fool. You don't tell your friends about your lover. You feel
tricked and defrauded, and decide to follow something more
authentic, more established, more substantial – like Buddhism, or
Christianity, or Sufism, or Taoism – something serious. But then you

go out walking. You follow the old trackways, you come to the old places. You see the chalk gods and the stone circles, the barrows and the dolmens. You pause and open yourself to the Land, and She is there again. But this time she is even more enchanting because you can see that she is not just a pretty woman, full of romance and seduction, you can see that she is also a wise woman, who will provoke as well as seduce you, who will make you think as well as make you feel. And then you suddenly know why she has been the object of fascination for so many through the ages. She is the Muse, the Goddess behind Druidry, the bestower of Awen, of inspiration.

The articles that follow in this collection show that She is as present as She ever has been – and perhaps more so at this time. The Goddess who seduces us with romantic images of magic and mystery at one moment, and then repels us with images of the tattered remnants of past ages at the next, is trying to lead us beyond the realm of illusion to something more substantial, more enduring and more creative. Many of us have been drawn to Druidry by its evocative power – it conjures up images of wise sages, of ancient wisdom and secret lore. Others, usually the more academic, have avoided Druidry because of the dearth of substantiated facts about its history, and the plethora of fantastical speculation it has evoked over the centuries. But this collection proves that we can enjoy Druidry's evocative power, *and* we can approach its history with discernment. And this collection also shows that we can see beyond both, towards a spiritual practice that is rooted in a love of the Land and an appreciation of a heritage which is at once both rich and elusive.

Druidry is evocative and provocative, substantial and insubstantial – it is infuriatingly paradoxical. But these qualities are ideal for stimulating the creative process, and a concern for creativity lies at the heart of Druidry.

When I was asked to re-form the Order of Bards Ovates and Druids in 1988 I felt honoured, inspired and excited by the challenge of working with Druidry, but I was aware of the fact that, for many, Druidry wasn't really considered a serious spiritual path. It existed on the fringe, or even beyond the pale, for not only respectable academics but also for those seriously interested in spiritual enquiry, who gravitated towards the established religions, or towards the study of Theosophy, Anthroposophy, Sufism, or Taoism, for example. Druidry was seen by most as living at the 'lunatic fringe' of alternative spiritualities – as Stuart Piggott remarked in his 1968 book *The Druids*: 'In considering the bodies of selfstyled Druids ... we enter a world at once misleading and rather pathetic.' In many ways Piggott's conclusion was justified, because Druidry had been plagued with dubious scholarship, and it is only recently that Druid groups have started to be critical of their own histories.

R.J. Stewart in *The Complete Merlin Tarot* states that 'an indigestible mass of spurious nonsense has been written about the druids; unfounded pretentious claims from 'druid orders' derive entirely from nineteenth-century fabrication. None of these groupings may truly lay any claim to be druidic, separated as they are by at least a millenium from the last vestiges of practising druid religion.' It is true that the subject of Druidry has stimulated an enormous amount of literature, much of it being dense and having little more than curiosity value for us now. John Matthews' *Druid Source Book* attempts to relate this material to both earlier and later source texts, and presents samples of it, while the New York City library holds the world's largest collection of such literature. It is also true that many Druid groups, in common with other Western esoteric movements such as Rosicrucianism, The Golden Dawn, Theosophy, and Wicca, have presented 'creation myths' which bear little relation to the historical facts of their origins. Having said this, it is a fundamental error to believe that these deceptions, infuriating as they are, somehow invalidate their work or their message. All these groups, including Druidry, has a contribution to make to humanity's spiritual progress, and the challenge facing us, if we wish to follow one of these paths, is to use our discernment to retain that which is valuable and discard that which is deceptive or outmoded. In the past, these groups felt they had to establish a history or a lineage to be taken seriously. Today, they have a history, simply by virtue of having been in existence for many years. And at the same time, we can recognize that they are movements that are responding not only to the past, but also the future – to a vision of how we could be in the world, and of what we may become.

Both Piggott & Stewart, in common with many commentators, see Druidry as a human creation, with a gap in linear time creating an unbridgeable chasm between 'real' Druids who lived thousands of years ago, and 'fake' Druids who have lived from the eighteenth century onwards. I prefer to see Druidry as existing in the spiritual or archetypal world as a source of inspiration, energies, images and ideas. Over linear time, a number of people have responded to this source of inspiration, including the proto-Druids who built the megalithic monuments, such as Stonehenge; the Celtic Druids, known to us from classical writings; the Bards whose formal schools continued to the eighteenth century; the romantic Druid Revivalists of the

eighteenth century; and those who today might call themselves
Druids. Each group has helped to build the tradition that we now call
Druidism or Druidry.

In 1988 Piggott's book was the *only* book in print about the Druids
in the English language, but in the world of ideas and approaches to
spirituality events can move astonishingly fast. In the seven years
since 1988, Druidry has moved, in many peoples' perceptions, from
the 'lunatic fringe' to a position in which it is seen as a viable and seriously considered spiritual path, and this has happened not only to
Druidry but to a range of ideas and movements which include Wicca
and Shamanism and Paganism in general. Two things, it seems, have
been running in tandem. On the one hand, the established religions
have been failing to satisfy the spiritual needs of many, and at the
same time the mounting environmental crisis has made many turn
away from the dualism and authoritarianism of these religions,
towards more nature-centred and holistic spiritual ways. As evidence
of this, the last seven years has seen the publication of literally
dozens of books about Druidry, and the related subject of esoteric
Celtic studies. Many of these are cited in the contributors' bibliographies. In 1988 the problem was finding *any* book about Druids, now
the problem is deciding which one to read.

What has happened in these last few years is that Druidry has
begun to articulate itself, and its relevance, in a way that has resulted
in large numbers of people finding that it speaks to their own
passions and concerns. It no longer sounds archaic or eccentric. It
sounds, now, remarkably sensible and relevant to the needs of our
time.

As we develop more honesty and rigour in attempting to understand our own lives, we undertake a journey that hopefully leads us
closer to a more authentic sense of self and, at the same time, closer
to our Intuition; to our Soul. The same process applies to a spiritual
tradition. As we try to articulate and understand it, we go through a
similar process of discovering false memories, unconscious or delib-
erate deceptions, thefts and projections, that threaten our trust and
belief in the validity of the tradition itself – just as our faith in our
own selves is threatened when we undertake our own journey of self-
enquiry. But if we persevere, we come to the depths, and discover
that the journey was indeed worthwhile.

Druidry in this present age is undertaking such a journey, and this
book can be seen as a report-in-progress of the voyage. As well as a
new level of honesty and rigour in historical analysis, there are other
exciting movements that I see occurring in Druidry today and which

are reflected in this book. These include the increasing role of a psychological understanding and use of Druidry; a changing perception of Druidry's relationship with Christianity and Paganism; a growing awareness of the importance of the Feminine in Druidry; and an emerging awareness of the connections between Druidry and Wicca. Each of these movements deserves our attention.

Druidry and Wicca

The two main streams of 'British' Paganism are Wicca and Druidry. Although both traditions draw their inspiration from past ages, much of their contemporary practice has evolved very recently – from the eighteenth century for Druidry, from the 1940s onwards for Wicca. The eighteenth century saw the development of Druid ceremony, much of it articulated by Iolo Morganwg, and in the twentieth century the MacGregor-Reids and Ross Nichols gave further inspiration and form to Druid ceremony and thought, while Gerald Gardner proved the catalyst for the rebirth (or birth, depending on your opinion) of Wicca.

Since Wicca and Druidry share so much in common, it is natural to wonder whether they were originally one and the same, only developing later in different directions. Gerald Gardner, in *The Meaning of Witchcraft* (1959) wrote 'The great question is, were the witches and the Druids members of the same cult? … Personally, I think they were not; the witch cult was the religion of the soil, as it were, and the Druids were the more aristocratic religion …' At a Pagan Federation conference and then later in *The Druid Way* (1993) I asked Gardner's question again, and quoted various authors' views on the subject. Christina Oakley's article continues the debate, and her conclusion tallies with Gardner's: Wicca and Druidry have different histories. They certainly 'feel' different, as Christina Oakley mentions, and I think our Paganism is all the richer for these two vital, distinct and rich traditions growing side by side.

Many people, however, are now following both paths, combining them idiosyncratically to suit their own tastes and practises, in the time-honoured slightly anarchical way of modern Paganism. There is value in this, but also, I believe, a danger. The value lies in our being able to develop our own unique path. Paganism, Wicca, Druidry, Shamanism, the Earth Religions – all avoid the problems of the Revealed Religions, which so easily develop into personality cults and dogmatic systems. The eclecticism and anarchy of the former prevent this. And so a creative meeting of Wicca and Druidry is occurring, with some people feeling that the private focus of Wicca fulfils one need, while the more public focus of Druidry fulfils another. Christina Oakley says, 'At the heart of Wicca is the image of the God and Goddess joined in love as one'. Whilst variants of Wicca do not make the Great Rite central, she is speaking here of Traditional British Wicca, whose focus is on the act of union, just as Druidry's focus is on the results of that act: symbolized by the Divine Child, the Mabon, and expressed through the Arts and the Bardic tradition. Thus, the emphasis on the joining of male and female energy in Wicca seems perfectly balanced with the emphasis on the results of that joining in Druidry. So we can see that it is quite possible to follow both Wicca and Druidry, since each fulfils a different need and helps to express a different facet of the self. To return to Gerald Gardner's suggestion, we could say that now we can embrace both traditions because socially we are no longer so constrained, and the person of the soil and the person of culture both need feeding within us. Having said this, it is important to realize the limitations of this argument, since many Wiccans and Druids will, quite rightly, point to the completeness of their own tradition, which belies any necessity for combination with a complementary path.

Even so, the mixing is undoubtedly happening. If you were to visit a nonaligned Pagan ceremony at a festival time, you would almost certainly find yourself participating in a ritual which draws its inspiration and form partly from Wicca and partly from Druidry. Ask Wiccans if they are Druids too, and a good deal will say they are, and vice versa. The question is, are we enriching our traditions or diluting them?

While some contemporary Pagans eclectically blend Wiccan and Druid practice, research is revealing more of the connections that existed in the seminal years of modern Druidry's and Wicca's development – the 1940s and 50s. The influence of the related movements of Woodcraft Chivalry and Naturism of the 1920s and 30s, which could be seen as effectively Pagan movements, is only now being explored (see Ronald Hutton's article in *Enchanté*, (Autumn 1993) and Steve Wilson's article in *Aisling* 8 (1995)). Both Gerald Gardner and Ross Nichols, founder of the Order of Bards Ovates & Druids, were influenced by these, and we know that Gardner was a member of the Ancient Druid Order (*The Druid Way* p.57). It has also been suggested that George Watson MacGregor-Reid, Chief of the Ancient Druid Order, was also a member of the famous New Forest coven in 1939 (W.E.Liddell *The Pickingill Papers,* Capall Bann (1994)). From conversations with Ross Nichols, and from his writings, I believe that he was probably not an initiated Wiccan (although I cannot be certain of this), but I know that he was highly sympathetic to Wicca and had many Wiccan friends, including Justine Glass, author of *Witchcraft, the Sixth Sense and Us* (Neville Spearman, (1965)) and apparently Doreen Valiente. Gardner and Nichols were friends too, and as a result of their exchanges the eight-fold Pagan festival cycle was born. (Or reborn, depending on your point of view. For a discussion of the history of this central feature of modern Pagan practice see Steve Wilson's article in *Aisling 8* (1995) p.15, which is based partly on detailed research by Ronald Hutton for his forthcoming book on the history of modern Paganism, *The Triumph of the Moon*.) Following their discussions, Wiccans incorporated the Solstices and Equinoxes into their celebrations, and Druids incorporated the fire festivals into theirs. That is a tremendous example of cross-fertilisation between the two traditions, and in the last few years we have seen this happening in a wider, though less dramatic form.

I believe we can avoid a dilution or homogenization by understanding Druidry and Wicca as two discrete, separate entities, which nevertheless have much to offer each other. Some will want to work in both traditions, feeling that they complement and enrich each other. Others will prefer to root themselves firmly in just one tradition, sensing that it is complete in itself.

Druidry and the Goddess

Another development in Druidry's recent history is the increasing emphasis placed upon the Feminine in Druid ceremony and thought. This is symbolic of the re-emergence of the Wisdom of the Feminine, which, when experienced, leads us to a greater understanding of Druidry's true nature. It can be tempting to isolate spiritual movements for the purpose of analysis, treating them like museum exhibits, classifying their creeds, and comparing their dogmas. But Druidry has no creed, it has no dogma. Its mythic teachings simply flow like a river through the generations, twisting and turning, responding to the contours of the land, echoing the Spirits of Time and Place. It is forever changing and yet is eternal. The moment we try to grasp it too firmly with our analytical minds, its spirit eludes us, just as in scooping water from the river into our hands, that which we hold is no longer the river. And we cannot separate Druidry from the Zeitgeist. As Tony Grist, former vicar turned Pagan, poet and novelist, wrote in *The Guardian:* 'The archetype of the Goddess is breaking through everywhere; in feminism obviously, in the Green movement with its Gaia hypothesis, in the occult revival and the New Age religions. Even the patriarchal religions are having to come to terms with Her ... In Christianity the campaign for women priests and the recognition by radical theologians that God is also Our Mother are all signs of her insistent troublesome presence.'

The Druidry that speaks to us today has a somewhat different, more feminine, voice to that of the Revival Druidry of the eighteenth and nineteenth centuries, which was a preoccupation of an almost exclusively male group. The only female Druid of that time that I have been able to trace is Augusta, the Princess of Wales, whom William Stukeley named Veleda, the Archdruidess of Kew, apparently asking her to be the patroness of his Order. Even then, this title could well have been fanciful – the Princess probably never participated in a ceremony of Revival Druidry.

A whole body of Druidry, of the Henry Hurle lineage described by Michel Raoult on p.108, still has male-only Lodges, with a few female lodges and the occasional social function at which the sexes mingle. Some Druid ceremonies, written probably in the 1920s and 30s by George Watson MacGregor-Reid, and still used by some Orders, show an unfortunate patriarchal bias, but again these cannot be separated from the prevailing cultural atmosphere in which they were written. Over the last seven years, however, there has been a noticeable redressing of the balance in Druid ceremony, and the Goddess has taken the place for many in the Universal Druid Prayer which used to begin 'Grant, O God thy protection ...'

Since the refounding of the Order of Bards, Ovates and Druids in 1988 about four thousand members have joined, their numbers divided almost exactly between the sexes. The experience of the two largest American groups is identical, with ADF having a 51% female membership. But the deepest level of change comes as women once again begin to explore and reawaken to the tradition of female priesthood. With the introduction in 1992 of the role of Modron into the Order of Bards Ovates and Druids, it was acknowledged that women have an equal and important part to play in ceremony, in teaching, and in the tremendous task which faces us all, as we once again strive to foster the awareness of the sacredness of all life on Earth.

A consideration of the relevance of gender to Druidry has not been confined to redressing the balance of the sexes. Recently, an important debate has been carried out in the Readers' Letters section of the Order's monthly journal, *Touchstone,* in which gay and lesbian members have been questioning their position within Druidry, as a spiritual tradition which places such emphasis on gender-related symbolism. Some members have felt the need to create alternative ceremonies because they have found the gender-specific roles or symbolism problematic or oppressive. Others have not felt this, and express the belief that their 'personal identities transcend the genders of our bodies...and we can assume male/female god/dess roles comfortably.' Affinity groups for gay and lesbian members are developing, and the Golden Gate group in San Francisco regularly performs Druid rituals in the stone circle they have built next to the Grove in Golden Gate park, dedicated to those who have died from AIDS.

Druidry, Christianity and Paganism

A further big shift in Druidry's definition of itself has not yet occurred, but it is about to: this book represents the first articulation of these ideas in print outside the academic world. Up until now, it has generally been believed that, with the arrival of Christianity, Druids converted easily; developing in harmony with the incoming faith, for a few centuries, a Celtic church that incorporated the Druids' love of nature and the Bardic arts. Readers who have accepted these ideas as solid fact may be troubled by the articles in this book by Ronald Hutton and Christina Oakley; and if they follow the references given in these articles, they will almost certainly become convinced that quite the reverse was the case. It now seems clear that Druidry was persecuted by Christianity with as much vigour as Christianity dealt with any opposition, and that the Druids in their turn were determined in their opposition to the new faith: 'Two of them prophesied that a new way of life was about to arrive from overseas, with an unheard-of and burdensome teaching ...' (*Quoted in full on p.266*)

The reason why Druidry developed the myth that it had cooperated with Christianity is explained at one level by the fact that Druidry was 'revived' in the eighteenth century by Christian gentlemen, who could legitimately be interested in a pre-Christian Pagan tradition only if it could be shown that this was similar to Christianity. The myth was also fed by the eleventh and twelfth century Christian Irish writers who expressed a positive, syncretic understanding of their Pagan past, in contrast to their earlier forebears of the seventh and eighth centuries,who had conveyed a picture of Druidry and Christianity being highly antagonistic to each other. For the Revival Druids, Christianity occupied such a central place in their world-view that almost everything they perceived as being valuable had to be understood in terms of its relationship to it. The psychologist Wayne Dyer has coined the phrase 'I'll see it when I believe it,' which neatly alludes to the determining power of our beliefs,which can even affect our perception. In the myth of Druid and Christian syncretism, it seems that some of the resonances between Druidry and Christianity, such as the existence of a Druid tree-god Esus, can be interpreted as evidence of this. Revival Druidry later spawned theories that linked Druidry with Judaism, and these are discussed in Gordon Strachan's contribution.

An associated myth concerning the relationship between early Christianity and Druidry is that the Culdees, a sect of Celtic Christians, became the custodians of much Druid knowledge which was then handed down from generation to generation. The Culdees were a puritanical Christian reform movement reacting against the perceived degeneration of the Church in the eighth and ninth centuries, and a study of the ascetic doctrines of this movement shows that it almost certainly does not represent any kind of continuity from Druidry. A succinct account of the Culdees and relevant sources for them can be found in Kathleen Hughes, *The Church in Early Irish Society* (Methuen, 1966), Ch.16. For a fuller account of their history and doctrines see *The Culdees of the British Islands* by William Reeves (Llanerch 1994).

Part of a historian's job is to show us what is most likely fact and what is most likely fantasy or myth. But simple debunking of myth doesn't do full justice to our attempts to understand history or the life of the psyche. In our individual life, it is not enough to demonstrate that we've been fooling ourselves for years, we have to go on to understand why we've done this, what meaning this has had for us, and what purpose it has served. The same applies culturally. We have looked at the reasons why Revival Druids may have fooled themselves about Druidry's relationship with Christianity, but of what value has this been, if any? One of the results, which is discussed in Christina Oakley's article, is that it has helped to ally Druidry with the Establishment, so that modern Druidry has come to be seen by the public and the media as the 'acceptable (and respectable) face of Paganism'. (This is also due to the fact that Druid ceremonies tend to take place in daylight and in public and can be colourful, photogenic events. This contrasts with the apparently more secret ceremonies that take place in private, and at night, of other Pagan groups. The fact that this is a simplistic distinction is missed by the media).

Other features which ally Druidry with the Establishment are the fact that the Queen is Patroness of the Welsh National Eisteddfod, and that it is widely known that Winston Churchill was a Druid (though of a type and for a duration that indicates it was probably only a passing affair). But this is only half the picture. Although the British Establishment looks kindly on Druidry, it is also undeniable that some branches of Druidry have become vehicles for anti-establishment or, more accurately, anti-government activity. Many Druids vigorously oppose government projects, such as the major road-building programme, which threatens, or has already destroyed, sacred sites and acres of trees and countryside. As well as protesting in conventional ways, they also hold ceremonies to address the root of the problem, which lies in our disconnection from the natural world.

Robed Druids have marched against the government's repressive Criminal Justice Act, and the first legal challenge to the Act was made by the self-styled King Arthur Uther Pendragon. The government lost their case and the court found in his favour, representing a triumph for democracy and for the Druid movement, which this modern-day King Arthur supports. He is now taking his fight for the right to worship freely at Stonehenge to the European Court of Human Rights, with backing from Liberty, the civil rights group. The apparent contradiction between Druids' allegiance with the Establishment and this sort of activity is resolved when one realises that Druids see themselves as championing Sovereignty in its noblest sense – the Sovereignty of the Land and of our heritage. Legislation that attacks our rights or our land is then seen not as coming from the Establishment, but from usurpers who are abusing their power. As King Arthur said to *The Guardian:* 'We Druids believe we are here for a purpose. Until we know what that is, we will fight for Truth, Honour and Justice. If those are the precepts we serve, how can we be breaking the law? We *are* the law, which is why we won in court.'

Until about thirty years ago, Druidry was quite a staid activity. Most Druids treated their activities rather like Freemasons or Rotarians, concentrating their efforts on fund-raising for charity, or the promotion of cultural events, such as the Eisteddfodau. They probably wouldn't have considered themselves Pagan, and many would have been Christians. Even the more esoteric Druid groups, whose membership was much smaller, were strongly influenced by Freemasonry and the Golden Dawn, and prior to the founding of The Order of Bards Ovates and Druids in 1964, would only have celebrated the Equinoxes and the Summer Solstice.

But in the 1960s things changed. Druidry, as expressed through OBOD, began to celebrate the eight festivals. In tandem with this, the emergence of the counter-culture in the sixties, with its spiritual and environmental consciousness, resulted in an influx of younger people interested in Druidry. They were far less staid, considered themselves Pagan, and were more interested in opposing the destruction of the environment than in charitable work. A whole new energy came into Druidry which expressed itself in a desire to gain a deeper experience of life through Druid practice, rather than in adhering to outmoded forms. In many ways, these two Druid popula-tions have developed side by side over the last thirty years, but they are not antagonistic to each other. They have met, sometimes, within the Council of British Orders, and in such contexts as the Christians and Druids conferences held at Prinknash Grange in 1989,1990 and 1991, and at Oxford and Lewes in 1996.

It would be easy to say that this is all humbug, and that Pagan Druids should clearly separate themselves from Christian Druids, but Druids have always been peace-makers and diplomats. These skills are notoriously difficult to express without compromise and without accusations of dishonesty, but they are in essence spiritual skills or gifts, to which Druids have always aspired. Somehow Druidry has developed the ability to build bridges between faiths, so as well as finding Christian Druids and Wiccan Druids, one can find people who combine their Druidry with Buddhism or Taoism, for example. Ross Nichols was both a Christian and a Druid, yet he was in open communication with many Buddhists and Wiccans, and followers of other faiths, and he introduced more Paganism into Druidry in a decade than had been present for many years.

A major focus of Druidry is on peace: on attaining both inner and outer peace. Each Druid ceremony begins with a salutation of 'Peace to the Quarters' in which peace is envisaged radiating out from the ceremony to all corners of the Earth, and one of the main tasks of a Druid consists in creating a sanctuary or grove in the inner world, whose peaceful influence radiates outwards. If Druidry can succeed in maintaining peace and open communication within its own community, and also between itself and 'The Establishment', then perhaps it can also offer that in a multi-faith context. I remember being astonished and moved at one conference, when a Catholic priest told me that 'We believe in the importance of the Druid witness in the world today.'

Isaac Bonewits, in his article, discusses three types of Druidry: Paleopagan, Mesopagan and Neopagan. Paleopagan Druidry was practised thousands of years ago and we simply cannot recover it. Even if we could, its practices would almost certainly be inappropriate and out of tune with the Spirit of our Times. Mesopagan Druidry appeared with the Druid Revival in the eighteenth century and was heavily influenced by the monotheistic and dualistic beliefs of Christianity. Neopagan Druidry has emerged only in the last thirty years, and has been an attempt to create and build a practice which is free from monotheistic and dualistic accretions. Whereas Bonewits sees the Mesopagan influence as unfortunate, something to be entirely sloughed off by the Neopagan current, we need to ask ourselves whether this is really possible or even desirable. We can see the early Paleopagan period as Druidry's childhood, the Mesopagan period as its adolescence, and the Neopagan period as its maturity. However unfortunate our adolescence may have been, however negatively influenced by the company we might have kept, we cannot deny its formative influence and, however embarrassed it may make us feel, we need to learn and grow from it.

It seems as if many of us have come to a time in our spiritual development when we are called upon to walk in two seemingly opposite directions. On the one hand, there seems a need for us to draw eclectically from the wisdom to be found in a whole variety of spiritual approaches, religions and disciplines of personal development. But at the same time, as we reach out to the diversity of beliefs and practices that can nourish us as inhabitants of the One Earth, many also feel the need to seek a rootedness in one tradition, one that can form the basis for their world-view and spiritual practice. Hopefully, although there may be moments of tension generated by these two apparently divergent impulses, we can find that we are able to draw nourishment from being both rooted in one tradition, whilst at the same time being inspired by teachings from many different sources.

Up until recently, Druidry has tended to attract people who wish to follow a particular course of development, and who have been drawn to study Druidry as one of the expressions of the Western Mystery Tradition. But the challenge that Druidry faces now, is that there are many more people who have no desire or time to study or train in Druidry in any depth, but who nevertheless feel a great kinship with its spirit, and who would like to celebrate the seasonal festivals and Rites of Passage in a Druidic way.

Druidry and Psychology

One of the most exciting developments in modern Paganism, is the creative exchange that is taking place as a result of psychologists becoming interested in Paganism, Shamanism, ritual and magical practice, and of Pagans becoming interested in psychology. Psychologists have found that their understanding of the psyche and their practice of therapy is informed and enlivened by exploring these traditions, and the Transpersonal Psychologist John Rowan recently stressed the value for a therapist in becoming a practising Pagan. It is probably no coincidence that the two largest Pagan training groups in Britain, *The Wicca Study Group* and *The Order of Bards Ovates and Druids* are both led by psychologists – with Vivianne Crowley's work in Wicca drawing much on her Transpersonal Psychology training, and my work in Druidry drawing much on my training in Psychosynthesis. With psychological understanding, Druid practice becomes capable of a tremendous deepening, and we find in the eightfold festival cycle, a structure for worship and celebration which has a profound psychological value and elegance.

The Call of the Future

Most people think that Druidry is something that existed in the distant past, and that, in more recent times, some people have tried to re-create it from the scattered remnants that we have inherited. But if we believe in the spiritual world, then we will also believe that the source of any spiritual tradition lies in *that* world, rather than in the physical world of effects. And if Druidry's source is in Spirit, and not in a lost Past, then we can free ourselves from a concern about the origins of our tradition moving ever further away from us as each day passes.

Freed also from the preoccupation of previous generations to establish 'authenticity' (which generated such bad history) we can come to appreciate the subtler, more complex facts of our inheritance, whilst at the same time responding to a Call from Spirit and from the Future which urges us to develop a Druidry that can help us to live more profoundly and more joyfully in the world today.

Philip Carr-Gomm
Lewes, Samhuinn 1995

Suggested Reading

As I edited this collection I was struck by the variety of reading suggested by the contributors. I had imagined there would be much duplication, but in fact there is hardly any – a testament in itself to the broad sweep of interests embraced by Druidry, and the wide range of relevant literature now available. There follows my selection, which for the sake of space leaves out any books mentioned by other contributors. In addition to the books cited below, I can recommend any of the relevant works of R.J. Stewart and John Caitlin Matthews.

Webb, James T. *The Occult Establishment*, Richard Drew, 1981. For an understanding of the recent influences on Druidry and British Paganism, and a fascinating and thorough study in general of recent occult history.

Minahane, John. *The Christian Druids – On the filid or philosopher-poets of Ireland*, Sanas Press (PO Box 4056, Dublin 4, Eire), 1993. On the relationship between the early Irish Christians and Druids.

Harvey, Graham & Hardman, Charlotte. Eds, *Paganism Today: Wiccans, Druids, The Goddess and Ancient Earth Traditions for the Twenty-First Century*, Thorsons, 1996

Hutton, Ronald. *The Stations of the Sun: A History of the Ritual Year in Britain*, Oxford University Press, 1996. For the most thorough study yet of the seasonal festivals.

Carr-Gomm, Philip & Stephanie. *The Druid Animal Oracle*, Simon & Schuster, 1995. The only work, as yet, that presents much of the wealth of animal lore that exists in Druidry.

Matthews, John. *A Druid Source Book*, Cassell, 1996. Presents much of the literary source material of Druidry, including most of the classical references, traditional Celtic source material, and much Revivalist and more recent material.

Beresford-Ellis, Peter. *The Druids*, Constable, 1994. One of the best histories available.

Cowan, Tom. *Fire in the Head*, HarperCollins, 1993

King, John. *The Druid Year*, Cassell, 1994. Fascinating, but to be treated with caution, since material is unreferenced and therefore unverifiable.

Blamires, Steve. *The Irish Celtic Magical Tradition*, Aquarian, 1992

Mann, Nicholas. *Isle of Avalon*, Llewellyn, 1996

Ross, Anne. *Druids, Gods and Heroes*, Peter Lowe, 1986

Green, Miranda. *Exploring the World of the Druids*, Thames & Hudson, 1997

Matthews, John. *A Bardic Source Book*, Cassell, 1997

For further reading, see the comprehensive bibliographies in Caitlín & John Matthew's *Encyclopaedia of Celtic Wisdom*, Element, 1994, (a valuable resource book for any student of Druidry); Ross Nichols *The Book of Druidry*, Aquarian, 1990; and my *Elements of the Druid Tradition*, Element, 1991

Philip Carr-Gomm is a psychologist and writer and leads *The Order of Bards Ovates and Druids*, one of the largest international Druid groups. Living in

England, he lectures and gives workshops on Druidry in the UK, Europe and USA. He is author of *The Druid Way* and *The Elements of the Druid Tradition*, co-author of *The Druid Animal Oracle* and editor of *The Book of Druidry*. Philip studied with his teacher, the Chief Druid Philip Ross Nichols, from the age of fifteen. After taking a degree in psychology, he trained in psychosynthesis, psychotherapy for adults and play therapy for children. Apart from writing and leading workshops, Philip helps direct the experience-based postal training course in Druidry produced by *The Order of Bards Ovates and Druids* together with its Campaign for Individual Ecological Responsibility and Sacred Tree Planting Programme.

Professor Ronald Hutton

Introduction
WHO POSSESSES THE PAST?

Modern Druidry has a recorded history of over two hundred years. By contrast, the discipline of scientific archaeology, and the professional study of history, have both been in existence for only about a century, and it has been only in the last thirty years that they have achieved a true scholarly rigour based upon research systematically carried out in universities. In one sense, therefore, Druids are a special interest group within society, with particular beliefs and aims based partly upon an appeal to history. In another, they are a portion of a long-established reading and writing public which used to make most of the running in historical scholarship, and is now confronted by an academic network of novel vitality and determination, set upon achieving (and deserving) a near-monopoly of authority in the discovery and propagation of information about the past.

Two things save this situation from becoming a tyranny. One is that academe remains free from control by any single political or religious group. The other is that it is divided between scholars who are encouraged to compete and to disagree with each other, and to offer the public rival interpretations. The result is not in practice an ideal one, because different academics have wildly varying talents and resources for communicating their views; the public therefore often gets a very misleading impression of the quantity of ideas on offer. None the less, professional scholars also provide a steadily accumulating quantity of solid information, from which their readers can form suggestions and beliefs of their own. The main purpose of this introduction is to show how large, how complex, how enigmatic, and how exciting a mass of material is now available, for anybody who turns for inspiration to the religions of the ancient British Isles.

The Historical and Archaeological Evidence

These islands do not, it is true, contain much from the very early periods. For most of the Old Stone Age they were too cold for human habitation, and so they lack anything to compare with the wonderful painted caves and mobile art of the Continent. Their Middle Stone Age hunters left campfires, flints, and rubbish dumps, but nothing like the rock art of Spain. Things only changed dramatically with the coming of farming, and the advent of the New Stone Age or Neolithic, in the fifth millennium BCE. Then, however, the alteration was very impressive indeed. All along the western seaboard of Europe, from Spain curving in a huge arc round to Scandinavia, people began to build chambers of massive stones or timbers, covered in enormous mounds of piled stones or earth. In Britain they have popularly been known as long barrows, dolmens, or cromlechs. Even after so many years of destruction, over 40,000 of these structures survive in western Europe.

Since 1974 it has been possible to date these chambers accurately, and the results have been remarkable. They were built in parts of the Continent from about 9700 BCE, and in the British Isles from about 9900 BCE, which means that they are the oldest human monuments on earth, far older than the pyramids of Egypt and slightly older than the first temple platforms of Mesopotamia. Along with their great age they exhibit a tremendous variety of form and use. Of those thousands of surviving examples, not one was designed exactly like another, making a mockery of any attempt to guess common symbolism in their ground plans. Nor were they associated with a common ritual. All were based upon the idea that they would contain some remains of human beings, but the bodies or bones were prepared for burial in a very wide variety of ways; six different methods in one such monument alone, the Scottish cairn of Tulloch of Assery. The number of individuals whose remains are found in one of these structures varies from one to several hundred, but the average is half a dozen. Many remained in use for centuries, new burials being added occasionally and a few old bones selected for removal. Some of the chambers would have been large enough for meditation or initiation ceremonies, but many were too small to leave room for living humans; instead the obvious ceremonial places were the forecourts outside the entrances, which have revealed plenty of evidence of fires and feasting.

The people of the age lived in scattered farms, the buildings being constructed of flimsy materials which have usually not survived. It was the houses of the dead which were built to last, and to look magnificent, and at which the inhabitants of a small district would gather for ritual. Very clearly, however, the individuals whose remains were preserved there must have represented only a tiny proportion of the local population. Most were adult, but not all, and both genders were present in no fixed ration or pattern. We have no idea of the criteria by which they were selected – they could (for example) have been from a particular local family, or chosen by lot, or offered in sacrifice, or born with green eyes, or psychic. All that is certain is that they ended up as components of a communal religion mediated, at least partially, through the dead.

That religion, and the tomb-shrines which serve as its permanent expressions, flourished all over the British Isles for about one and a half thousand years. Then, between 3300 and 3000 BCE, things started to change. In southern and central England this was apparently a time of disruption, with much movement of population and fierce fighting. It is now realized that many of the structures which have traditionally been called Iron Age hill forts were actually mid-Neolithic fortresses, and at this time a number were stormed and burned, their charred ramparts stuck full of arrowheads. When society began to stabilize again, around 3000 BCE, the peoples of these islands had become fascinated by round shapes. It is so natural for modern Pagans to view the circle as the obvious unit of sacred space that it is easy to forget that it did not become so until this time; the mounds of the earlier tomb-shrines were more often rectangular, oval, or trapezoidal. Now, from about 3200 BCE, the circle became universal.

Its use, however, varied remarkably on either side of a line one could draw diagonally across the British Isles. In Ireland, north Wales and northern Scotland, the circle was superimposed upon the older tradition of the tomb-shrine, to produce the most splendid example of that monument: the 'developed passage grave'. This is a gigantic round mound entered by one or more straight passages leading to stone chambers; the most famous are Newgrange and Knowth in Ireland, Maes Howe in Scotland, and Bryn Celli Ddu in Anglesey. These chambers also had other novel and glamorous features, such as carved abstract art, and an occasional orientation to the sun at cardinal points, such as the winter solstice. Once again, however, generalization is difficult because the motifs of the art are so varied and most of these tombs do not have an obvious solar orientation.

Across the rest of Britain, by contrast, the tomb-shrines were not only abandoned but carefully blocked up to prevent any further use. Ceremony shifted instead to open circles. In upland regions, where boulders were plentiful, these were set on end to create rings of standing stones, which have resisted weather and agriculture well enough to become the most famous class of monument from the period. Across the lowlands, however, the circles were just as common, but were made of earthen banks which later farmers could level with fatal ease, leaving most only visible as crop-marks. As in earlier times, a selection of the dead were given special burial, but now individually and under small circular mounds called round barrows or round cairns. The ideology embodied in these seems to be opposite to that of the tomb-shrines; they were never reopened once the body was interred and did not become foci for continuing ritual. Furthermore, they were accompanied by precious goods, being very clearly the burials of high-status individuals, usually, though not always, men.

These new round monuments displayed the same constant variety of size, architecture, and funeral ceremony as the tombs had done, so that an immense creativity was still contained with a common tradition. They were also even more numerous. During the past twenty years, aerial photography and geophysical surveys have revealed thousands of them in areas such as the Midlands and East Anglia, which were formerly thought to have been almost devoid of prehistoric ritual structures. The same techniques have also transformed our view of sacred landscapes. Today, for example, the circle known as the Rollright Stones is by far the most spectacular prehistoric monument in the South Midlands. When it was made, however, it was dwarfed by the huge earthen circles at Condicote, a short way along the same ridge, and surrounded by three old tomb-shrines, all requiring much more labour to erect. The accidents of destruction and survival have left it as the survivor out of all these. In the 1970s the Ordnance Survey decided that it could not keep pace with the number of ancient sites being discovered, and so ceased to enter them upon its charts. The standard one-inch map is therefore now worse than useless as a record of the prehistoric landscape, having fossilized what was known up to twenty to thirty years ago.

The circles flourished in turn for another one and a half millennia, as the Neolithic turned slowly into the Bronze Age without any discernible alteration in society or ritual. During the time at which the transition was in progress the finest of all monuments of this class was commenced, as a small earthen ring, already up to a thousand years old, was developed into the amazing structure which we now call Stonehenge. The process started around 2100 BCE, but the destruction wrought by treasure hunters and inept early archaeologists has removed the evidence which might have told us how long it lasted, and in what order. All that we can say is that by about 1600 BCE the stages of construction and reconstruction were complete. This monument was a home-grown original, the creation of a society used to woodworking which decided to use the same techniques (such as mortice and tenon joints) in stone, and see what happened. It was also the centre of a very widespread cult or kingdom, because its construction coincided with the abandonment or destruction of all the other sacred rings across southern and midland England, as far as what is now Devon and the Peak District.

From about 1500 BCE, however, the entire culture which Stonehenge represented was itself on the skids, in an alteration far more cataclysmic than that which had ushered in the age of the circles. The building of all ritual monuments, either for assembly or for burial, began to decline all over the British Isles. By 1000 BCE burials themselves were vanishing. Instead, people were starting to throw precious metalwork, such as cauldrons, ornaments and weapons, into selected bogs, lakes or rivers flowing eastward. The time of the circles had given way to one of water deposits. Such a fundamental shift of belief systems and of patterns of worship ought logically to have been associated with other large-scale changes, and the archaeological record can find two. The first was in the weather. Hitherto it had been warmer and drier than at the present day, perhaps equivalent to the modern south of France. From about 1400 BCE, however, it grew rapidly colder and wetter, perhaps closer to the climate of present-day Denmark. This alteration hit hard at a system of farming which had already been undermined by bad ecology. Ever since the opening of the Neolithic, agriculture had been expanding by felling and burning the forests which had formerly covered these islands. The tilled soil was left without roots to bind it or to regulate the water table, and started first to blow away from the hills and then to get waterlogged as the rainfall increased. The combination of these developments left vast tracts of land forever ruined for cultivation, including the moors of Devon and Cornwall, the central Welsh mountains, the Scottish Highlands, the heaths of southern England, and the Breckland. None of these are 'natural' landscapes; all are destroyed ecosystems produced by bad prehistoric farming.

With the weather worsening, and area after area of traditional settlement becoming impossible to farm, the population must have

crashed. No wonder that a complete way of worship and belief seems
to have crashed with it. Society only seems to have stabilized again in
the last few centuries before the Common or Christian era, in what
had become the early Iron Age. Then burials began to reappear,
according to strongly-marked local traditions, and temples or shrines
were once again constructed. The latter, however, were all of wood
and mostly small rectangular, rather than circular, structures, as if to
emphasize the break with the past. A sense of this break is further
suggested by the manner in which the older ritual monuments were
now treated. During the transition from the age of the tomb-shrines
to that of the circles, the former were, as described earlier, blocked
up to prevent further use, and occasionally systematically dese-
crated. The mounds and chambers themselves, however, were
always preserved, as if still filled with a power which had to be
respected or feared. By contrast, from the time of the water hoards
onward, farmers destroyed any of the tombs, circles or round barrows
which got in the way of expanding cultivation, as if any of the monuments left over from the periods before 1000 BCE were regarded as
valueless. This is the strongest single argument against any continuity of belief or practice across the divide marked by the disasters of
the late second millennium.

Thus, what we know of the ritual practices of the prehistoric
British Isles, and what major shifts occurred in it over time, is very
complicated, as I hope this short account has made plain. Even in
space, however, the patterns could be complex. Around 4000 BCE,
for example, when Britain was still in the early Neolithic, Europe was
divided into three quite distinct ritual provinces. In Greece and the
Balkans, people lived in large, well-built settlements, worshipped
mainly in household shrines, and made large quantities of mobile art,
including many figurines. In Italy, ritual practices were concentrated
in caves, often with wall art, while all along the western seaboard
they were focused upon the megalithic tomb shrines. These three
religious cultures look utterly different from each other, and may
have had nothing in common. Nor can we be absolutely confident
about the nature of any one of them; even that in the Balkans, which
has so much realistic art, has become the subject of intense, and so
far irreconcilable, controversy. By contrast, there are only two images
securely dated to the prehistoric British Isles which might be those of
deities. One is a carved head in an Irish passage grave, so heavily styl-
ized that it is impossible to say whom it represents. The other is a
Neolithic hermaphrodite statuette found in a bog, which the excava-
tors cautiously suggested might have been a divine figure, or a

magical one, or a toy, or a joke. With such material to hand, little can be said with confidence about what, or whom, the prehistoric British worshipped, and the situation across Europe grows much more, not less, diverse after the Neolithic.

It is not surprising, therefore, that professional prehistorians have more or less lost interest in the religions of the ancient British isles, preferring to concentrate instead upon social and economic questions which can be more firmly answered from the available evidence. Nevertheless, they still continue to unearth, and to publish, evidence of ritual practices in large quantity, however enigmatic that evidence might ultimately be. It is a classic case of a situation in which the experts are feeding the public with information while leaving it free to make such imaginative reconstructions as it wishes. The intellectual and artistic freedom of this process is considerable, and Druids are particularly well placed to take advantage of it. Indeed, it is almost a duty upon their part to do so, for the more people who are involved in the work, and the broader the range of plausible pictures imagined, the healthier the situation. Once again, academics and the public can be in partnership; the former mainly as researchers, the latter as visionaries and artists and makers of ceremony. It is an approach which, after all, does justice to the tremendous creativity and individuality of the monuments themselves.

Literary Evidence

So we reach the period of historical records which appear slowly over the whole period c.400 BCE to 1000 CE, and for modern Druidry three categories have always been especially important: the early literature of Ireland, the equivalent in Wales, and the inscriptions of the Roman province of Britain. During the 1980s, the first two were submitted to the culmination of a long process of textual analysis and found to be much more complex than had formerly been suspected, and much less straightforward as portraits of pre-Christian religion and magic. It seems likely now that the early Irish and Welsh poems and stories were composed from two to five hundred years after the formal end of Paganism, and did not represent oral traditions which had been passed word for word through the passage of time between. Rather, they were attempts to recapture some of the spirit of the ancient Pagan world of their lands, by people who no longer had any clear picture of what that world had been like. These poems and stories are full of material anachronisms, so that, for example, a supposedly Iron Age hero, such as Cu Chulainn, fights with a Viking sword, or an old and abandoned

site which was actually a free-standing sacred setting of posts is imagined to have been a royal feasting hall. The poems and stories are
heavily influenced by Christian literature, most of all by the Old
Testament, but more importantly and insidiously by the Pagan literature of Greece and Rome. In about 670 the Saxon bishop Aldhelm
could complain of how young Englishmen were running off to Ireland
to study the ancient Greek and Roman mythology, because they were
fascinated by it and the Irish taught it best. Aldhelm's irritation was not
provoked by its heathen nature but by his feeling that the English
ought to be able to teach it as well!

Victorian and Edwardian scholars believed that patient source
analysis ought to be able to brush away the Christian and Graeco-
Roman elements in the stories in such a way as to be left with a
residue of authentically ancient native tradition. In practice, this task
has now proved to be impossible beyond a certain point, as the
different traditions were too tightly and neatly interwoven to be
distinguishable from each other, drawing in many cases upon
common images and motifs which had been travelling across Europe
and Asia with traders and storytellers for centuries. Indeed, such an
enterprise would probably have appalled the people who actually
composed this literature, for the writers' work was valued precisely
because it drew with such skill upon so many sources, while the
material was developed still further with a powerful infusion of new
creative talent. Kenneth Jackson, the most celebrated scholar of
Celtic literature in the mid-twentieth century, could describe early
Irish literature as 'a window on the Iron Age'. So it may be, but not in
the sense that he, with too much optimism, intended the phrase. The
window is not made of clear glass but is stained and frosted, in
gorgeous colours and patterns, and overlaid with many reworkings
and repairs. As a result, it is rarely apparent whether what we are
seeing is through the window, or wrought ingeniously into the glass,
and from the point of view of a modern Druid, perhaps this really
does not matter. The imagery and action of the literature is magnificent in its own right, and it is at least arguable that anyone who
wishes to be a true successor to those who composed it should follow
their example: to draw upon old tales and figures, but to fuse them
with current needs and preoccupations, and to employ a personal
creative talent to create new works of letters and of art which speak
to a new time. It is surely the capacity of each generation to produce
its own claim to immortality, which is the essence of that semi-divine
inspiration for which the mediaeval bards strove.

Romano-British archaeology

For purists, however, there is some consolation in the simultaneous revaluation of the Romano-British material. As more and more of this is unearthed, it is becoming patent that it provides excellent primary evidence for ancient British religion. For one thing, material from this time presents a record of a living Pagan society, represented by real people who can emerge as strongly-marked individuals. My personal favourite is Saturnina, a woman so poor that she counted a linen cloth among her most valuable possessions. Devastated when a thief made off with it, she decided to make a pilgrimage to a famous temple dedicated to a god renowned for dealing with thefts. The temple stood at the top of a very steep hill, now above Uley in Gloucestershire, and it must have been a hard trek for Saturnina. When she entered its high and shadowy interior, she would have seen in front of her a pool of water, set into the floor, and gazing at her across it a handsome young man. Naked, and nine feet tall, he was made of green limestone and had a winged helmet and wings upon his heels, and in one hand he held a rod with serpents twisting about it. Most of us would now recognize Mercury; Saturnina evidently did not. An attendant must have handed her a standard lead tablet upon which she could write her request to the god. In her distinctive cursive handwriting, she commenced an address to the god Mars. Then she realized that she was wrong, and started again, writing an appeal to Silvanus, god of the wild. This, too, was scratched out in turn. The third time she got it right and wrote the name of Mercury. Now she got into her stride, composing a passionate and moving appeal, in which she poured out all her anguish at her loss and her fury with the criminal. She handed the tablet to an official, who put it in a machine which rolled up the lead so that only the god could read it. Then it was nailed to the temple wall, along with about nine hundred other requests. With that, Saturnina walks out of history. We do not know what happened to her, nor (perhaps fortunately) to the thief. Her message remained fixed to the wall until the temple fell into ruin, and eventually was buried in the rubble. In the 1970s, however, it was dug out of that red Cotswold soil by another woman, the archaeologist Ann Woodward, and perhaps beside her the ghost of Saturnina stood and smiled.

Those in quest of ancient British traditions may well dismiss this case-study as having little relevance to them; after all, the heroine was somebody with a Roman name, appealing to a well-known Roman god. Here, however, lies a deeper significance. The temple at

Uley was built over a pre-Roman shrine, and represented a monu-
mental and expensive development of it. Mercury, to judge from
many parallels elsewhere, would have been identified with a native
god who shared his attributes and to whom the place would have
been sacred. Some of the visitors would have used the Roman name
and some the British one. The latter will probably feature on at least
one of the many lead tablets from the site which have not yet been
unrolled and read; we await further reports from the scholar at
Oxford who is engaged in this work.

To the Romans, the whole world was covered in, and filled with,
divine energy. They called it 'numen', a word from which the fiction
writer J.R.R.Tolkein took the name Numenor, for his fabulous
drowned land. They believed that this force concentrated with particular strength at certain places, and would embody itself there in
divine guardians. When they took over new land, therefore, they had
to appease the local manifestations of these guardians to reconcile
them to the Roman presence - or else suffer terrible misfortune. For
example, a dashing junior officer called Julius Secundus once killed
an enormous wild boar upon what is now Scargill Moor. He was so
delighted by his achievement (in which he may have come very close
to death) that he raised an altar there to Silvanus, as god of hunters.
He had to remember, however, that the moor already belonged to a
native deity, and so he put the name of this god, Vinotonus, upon the
other side of the altar, with equal honours. Romans who were unable
to discover the name of the local guardian would leave an offering to
her or his persona (such as 'the most gracious lady') or simply to 'the
spirit of this place'. This process means that we have records of pre-
Roman British deities for most parts of what became the Roman
province, many of them little known to a public which is very familiar
with the divine beings in Celtic literature.

There is a rich trove waiting to be uncovered by those willing to
leaf through the volumes of The Roman Inscriptions of Britain.
Residents of Swindon may be interested to know of Cunomaglus, the
dog-loving god who was honoured at a big temple complex in a valley
nearby, or that the local goddess was a woodland one compared by
the Romans with Diana. Dogs were also the sacred animals of
Nodens, who like Cunomaglus was a deity of healing. The ruins of
the temple of Nodens still occupy a ridge in a wild and lovely park in
the Forest of Dean; upon my last visit I was faced by a huge jet-black
buck with spreading palmate antlers; a most tangible guardian.
Cumberland people may like to know of Belatucadrus, or 'bright
beautiful one', the local protector, while the shining god Loucetius

strode the hills of northern Somerset. Lancashire folk have Belisima, gracious goddess of the river Ribble, and Lincolnshire knew Rigonemetis, the Lord of the Sacred Grove. The goddess Rosmerta held up her double-headed axe and offered her barrel full of food to the inhabitants of the Cotswolds and the lower Severn valley. Around Milton Keynes rode a young god who loved horses and wore a feathered helmet.

What the inscriptions and carvings reveal is, once again, a huge variety and an intense localism. Not just every district, but every clan, every trade, every hill, every well, every stream, every wood and even every household had its own spirit, which required honour. The ancient instinct for 'numen' was, unsurprisingly, very good, and most of the places at which the Iron Age British built shrines, and which were developed into pilgrimage temples under Roman rule, are still beautiful and evocative. They are, however, generally unknown to modern Druids. This is partly due to a misleading sense that Britain under Roman rule somehow ceased to be British, which has caused Druidry to neglect Romano-British archaeology. It is also, however, because most of these shrines have only been rediscovered during the last thirty years and have not left obvious remains above ground level.

Into the Roman province travelled representatives of the other peoples of the empire, bringing with them the deities of Greece, Syria, Egypt, Africa and the Rhineland. When Roman rule ended, the Anglo-Saxons invaded and brought in a completely new set of divine figures, and later the Viking invasions added a complementary group to these. All these branches of religion are of relatively little interest to Druids, although they have had considerable impact upon the culture of these islands, and have helped to inspire distinct varieties of modern Paganism. Their presence is a reminder of how very complicated the early religious heritage of the British Isles is, even when the enormous range of prehistoric monuments is left out of the picture.

Modern Druidry has, however, had a very close relationship with a completely different sort of religion, which arrived from abroad during Roman rule, and which was to dominate the whole archipelago, like the tomb-shrines and the sacred circles, for about one and a half millennia. Unlike other faiths it claimed an exclusive possession of spiritual truth, based upon an unusually elaborate theology. I am, of course, referring to Christianity, and I will look here at a version of it which has loomed very large in modern, let alone modern Druidic, mythology: the so-called 'Celtic Church'.

The Myth Of The Celtic Church

One of the essays in the present volume, that by Christina Oakley, deals with one aspect of this myth – the idea that the Pagan Druids took easily to the faith of Christ and developed a form of it which embodied the finest aspects of both traditions. Her argument is that such a view can only be sustained by ignoring a great deal of evidence, and as such is fundamentally flawed. Being acquainted with the same body of material, I must endorse every word that she writes on the matter. I would like to go on, however, to examine the totality of the myth, to ask how it arose, to see how it has been applied, to demonstrate how it has foundered amongst scholars, and to ask whether anybody really needs to suffer from its disappearance.

The notion of a distinctive 'Celtic' Church, produced by the earliest British and Irish saints, was a product of the Protestant reformation. The reformers, facing the criticism that they were over-throwing a long-established and legitimate religious tradition, struck back with the claim that the original Christianity of these islands had not been that of the Church of Rome at all. Instead, they produced an image of a purer and better Christian faith, implanted by native saints inspired by early and uncorrupted evangelists. This, they insisted, had flourished for centuries until it was crushed by the invading power of Catholicism, a faith associated with spiritual tyranny, worldly ambition, personal corruption, and superstition. The Protestant reformers could therefore proclaim that they were not heretics or innovators, but merely restoring the rightful and native religion after centuries of foreign usurpation. The Celtic Church was therefore first invented as a polemical weapon, and has endured in that form until the present. During the last few years I have often heard the Celtic Church cited as a means of berating Roman Catholicism, and used as a weapon by Christian evangelists, who have appointed themselves to attack modern Paganism on current affairs programmes. The latter have regularly claimed that the Pagan Druids converted en masse on hearing the superior message of the gospels. Nobody who takes the trouble to read the earliest works of Celtic Christianity – The Confessio and letters of Patrick and the three celebrated Vitae of Bridget, Patrick and Columba – can share that delusion.

During the nineteenth and early twentieth centuries, however, the myth was reshaped for a more positive purpose. The Celtic Church came to be represented as a kinder sort of Christianity, and one admirably suited to modern liberals; tolerant, decentralized, unworldly, intensely creative, and closely associated with nature. As time passed, it also metamorphosed into a halfway house between Christianity and Paganism, for people who were disenchanted with the established denominations and recognized virtue in ancient and modern Pagan traditions, but did not quite want to abandon a faith in Christ. Such views could be readily supported by (very) selective quotation, and were not confined to mystics working outside mainstream scholarship. One well-respected historian of early medieval Britain and Ireland, Nora Chadwick, laboured hard to produce an image of a unified Celtic Christianity full of peace and piety, a dreamworld in which troubled modern Christians might find refuge. Although she died a quarter of a century ago, her publishers still blithely reprint her popular textbook on the Celts, without any revision.

The myth only fell to pieces within academe, (and is now thoroughly defunct there), as a result of the flood of new, rigorous research which emerged in the 1970s. It has been proved beyond any doubt that the churches of the Celtic British Isles never had any single organization, liturgy, or doctrine. They produced as many ruthless and malevolent individuals as gentle and unworldly ascetics, and fought each other from the pulpit and on the battlefield. Their books of penance display a detestation of Paganism and magic and a morbid fear of sexuality. They were disunited in every possible issue, including their attitude to Rome; the famous Synod of Whitby, often cited as the great clash between the two churches, was actually a quarrel between those of Rome, southern Ireland, and Brittany on one side, and those of northern Ireland, Wales and northern Britain on the other. It is correct many of their practices differed in detail from those of Rome, but this is even more true of the churches of Spain in the same period, which were actually much more hostile to the popes. It is likewise true that they absorbed many images and practices from native Paganism, but this is much less marked among the churches of the British Isles than in those of Italy, Sicily, and Greece. To quote Wendy Davies, one of the foremost academics currently working in the field: 'These points are obvious; they are not controversial; they simply need noting by a wider readership than the relatively small company of scholars that knows them well.'

What, then, will happen when a wider readership does note these points? The concept of the Celtic Church will certainly be destroyed as a polemical weapon, but that merely means that we are continuing the process of liberating ourselves from the confessional strife which rent Europe between the sixteenth and nineteenth centuries. It will be another step towards the creation of a genuinely tolerant and pluralist society. For Christians who want to achieve a kinder, greener version of their faith, and who work best with British or Irish proto-types, it will remain perfectly possible to draw upon Celtic sources. They will no longer be able to claim that they are reconstructing a complete entity; rather, they will be finding stories to inspire them in the work to develop a form of religion which embodies their ideal. In the tales of the Celtic saints, they will discover friends who did achieve peace, love and harmony with nature, in a world which was in general just as cruel, confusing and disturbing as the one in which we live now.

In fact, the religious writings of early medieval Ireland and Wales are a treasure-house for humanity in general and Christians in partic-ular. Just for the record, here are my own three favourites. First, the tale of St Mochua, who had a pet fly which kept his place in the psalm book while he took breaks, and a pet mouse who licked his ear to awake him at the hours of prayer. Second, the legend of St. Kevin, who found that a blackbird had started to nest in one of his hands while he was in deep meditation, and then held still and watched over the brood until the baby birds had flown away. Third, the story of St. Ciaran, who managed to convert a fox to Christianity but not to vegetarianism, thereby realizing that his god had not, after all, intended everybody to conform to the same rules.

Historical Attitudes To Druids

The entire history of attitudes to Druidry has been one of selection and creative reinvention of this sort. We have, in fact, not a single source for the subject, from the ancient world onwards, which does not fall into this category. To Caesar, and the Greek geographers Strabo and Diodorus Siculus, the Druids were part of a barbaric culture, the depiction of which would help to prove the superiority of Graeco-Roman civilization and the necessity for Roman rule. To the writers of Alexandria, they were wise philosophers attached to a more noble and natural culture which could be held up to criticize the corruption of their own. The composers of early Irish literature visu-alized the Druids primarily as magicians and royal councillors, exem-plars of an exciting but deeply flawed Pagan past. None of these 'primary' authorities was ever interested in describing Druidry in any objective spirit.

The range of representation (or misrepresentation) could only increase with the passage of time. Along with opium and classical architecture, Druids represented one of the three main stimulants to the British imagination. Between 1720 and 1820, John Toland used them to attack the Church of England, by claiming that they had been practitioners of an admirable religion which had looked forward to his own belief in Deism. He provoked William Stukely to reply that they had, on the contrary, been prophets of Anglican orthodoxy. To James Thomson, they had presided over a golden age of learning and patriotism. John Martin and Charles Hamilton praised them for having produced a world of order, hierarchy and respect for authority; whereupon Edward Williams and William Owen Pughe riposted that they had been Welsh, not British, nationalists, and had stood for radical democracy. Edmund Burke represented them as a self-seeking priesthood who ruled a deluded people through fear, and Edward Ledwich held them up as prime examples of 'ignorance and barbarism'. William Blake had it both ways, dreaming of them as an order which had begun by practising the pure religion of the Hebrew patriarchs but had been corrupted into evil and oppression - by Toland's doctrine of Deism! To Blake, Stonehenge was the prime monument of this later phase, 'a building of eternal death, whose proportions are eternal despair'. The poet Wordsworth and the artist William Geller both agreed, associating Druidry firmly with superstition, blood sacrifice and idolatry.

These examples represent only a tithe of the writers and painters who treated the subject during this single hundred years; to deal with them all, and to add those who did so in Britain up to the present day, would require a large volume. Even this, however, would have no space for the many modern treatments of Druidry in France, Ireland and America. Most drew upon the already sharply opposed images of the subject bequeathed by the ancient texts, but many rested upon pure fantasy.

There is here a paradox: that a large part of the power which the Druids have always exerted over the imagination has lain in the fact that they genuinely existed, but have all the characteristics of legendary beings; for all the real information which we have about them, they might as well never have been. This may be a dispiriting suggestion for a historian, but it can be viewed in quite a different way. Ever since their own time, the Druids have acted as potent stimulants to the creative mind, every age dreaming them anew, and often in two or three markedly different ways at once. An age of British society, in particular, which fails to work creatively with the image of the Druids is one which is hardly doing justice to its own inheritance, and may easily be suspected of a poverty of imagination. The present

age, whatever its faults, can certainly not be vulnerable to that accu-
sation; the range of essays in this volume alone testifies to a remarkably healthy state of interest.

In this process of imaginative reconstruction, there is an obvious
partnership between scholarship and artistry or religion, and an
equally obvious division of emphasis. The latter have not simply the
right to be selective, but a virtual necessity to be so. They can
perceive, if they wish, only those aspects of early historic Celtic
society which appeal most to modern tastes – the marvellous
patterns of the metalwork and manuscript decoration; the dispersed
rural lifestyle which involved a very close relationship with the
natural world and the rhythm of the seasons; the tribal loyalties and
assemblies; the warrior ethic which laid emphasis upon individual
courage and prowess; the high value given to poets; the notion of the
sovereignty of the land itself (or herself); the sensation of the sacred
in trees, rocks, and waters; and the concept of an ever permeable and
shifting boundary between the realms of the human and the divine.
Or they can, as legitimately, focus upon the head-hunting, the
human sacrifice, the slavery; the constant feuding between petty
kingdoms dominated by the childish vanity of a soldier aristocracy
which feasted and brawled while the peasants laboured miserably to
support it; and the daily horrors of life in a time without any really
effective antibiotics, anaesthetics, antiseptics, or contraceptives.

Until the later twentieth century, historians and archaeologists
tended to behave in this way as well, following an immemorial tradition of using the past to assist the present by deploying data from it to
achieve particular contemporary ends. This has in itself been a large
part of the reason for their readability and popularity. Only during the
past thirty to forty years have they set about the different, and much
harder, task of trying to reconstruct past societies in their entirety,
seeking to discover the ways in which all their characteristics, those
pleasant to a modern eye and those which are hideous, wove together
to create a total mental and physical universe. It is an enterprise
which becomes more difficult the further back in time the specialist
operates, and the thinner the data becomes. This is why, paradoxi-
cally, the element of imagination has never been more important in
academe than at the present, and why it is necessary to have as many
different visions as possible operating at the same time.

Part of the present disjunction between academic and popular
views of the past is that the latter are still often coloured by the divisions so beloved of nineteenth-century scholars, between nation and
nation, race and race, class and class, faith and faith, labour and

capital, woman and man, heresy and orthodoxy. These also informed the work of many professional historians and prehistorians until the 1970s, when a new generation appeared, intent upon producing more holistic pictures of the past. One effect of these has been to make former societies seem more distant, and alien, than before. There is less emphasis upon their people as ancestors, or co-workers in particular causes. The threads which tied their two worlds together also serve as barriers between them and the present. It is harder to see ourselves as a continuation of their story.

This introduction posed the question of who possesses the past. The answer must be that nobody does, except the dead. We inherit only part of the past, and that usually in a radically altered form. We are not its masters, nor its servants. We do not need to accuse it or make apologies for it, and the lessons we learn from it are likely to have no straightforward or obvious utility in providing solutions for present-day problems. We do not control and to only a limited extent can we know it. However, we cannot take the risk of forgetting it, for it remains extraordinarily powerful, retaining the ability to inspire to affection or to hatred, to loyalty or to distrust, to acceptance or to passionate endeavour. The dead are not always quiet, and the past will never be a safe subject for contemplation. Like the Celtic Otherworld, it lies for ever upon the edge of human experience, alluring and menacing, calling for attention and often erupting into everyday affairs with terrifying force; at once part of, and yet for ever separate from ourselves. The authors of the chapters which follow are all people who have chosen to gaze across that enchanted boundary, and to attempt, in their own ways, to work with what lies behind it.

Suggested Reading

The only comprehensive overview of the evidence for the religions of pre-Christian Britain remains my own book, *The Pagan Religions of the Ancient British Isles* (Blackwell, 1991), although a wider context has now been admirably provided by Prudence Jones and Nigel Pennick, *A History of Pagan Europe* (Routledge, 1995). Since the publication of *Pagan Religions*, aspects of the subject have been treated by a lively and wonderfully illustrated series published by Batsford for English Heritage: Julian Richards, *Stonehenge* (1991); Francis Pryor, *Flag Fen* (1991); Julian D. Richards, *Viking Age England* (1991); Ann Woodward, *Shrines and Sacrifice* (1992); Barry Cunliffe, *Danebury* (1993); Michael P. Pearson, *Bronze Age Britain* (1993); Philip Rahtz, *Glastonbury* (1993); and Guy de la Bedayere, *Roman*

Villas and the Countryside (1993). Other recent books of significance on the subject have been Richard Bradley, *The Passage of Arms* (Cambridge UP, 1990); Julian Thomas, *Rethinking the Neolithic* (Cambridge UP, 1991); and Peter Salway, *The Oxford Illustrated History of Roman Britain* (1993).

Differing views of the way in which European Neolithic evidence can be interpreted are represented by Marija Gimbutas, *The Goddesses and Gods of Old Europe* (revised edition, 1982), and *The Language of the Goddess* (1989); Colin Renfrew, *The Cycladic Spirit* (1993); Lauren E. Talalay, *Deities, Dolls and Devices* (Indiana UP, 1993); and Lynn Meskell, 'Goddesses, Gimbutas and "New Age" Archaeology', *Antiquity* 69 (1995), 74–86.

The destruction of the concept of the 'Celtic Church' can be traced in Wendy Davies, 'The Celtic Church', *Journal of Religious Studies* 8 (1974–5), 406–11; Kathleen Hughes, 'The Celtic Church: is this a valid concept?', *Cambridge Medieval Celtic Studies* 1 (1981), 1–20; and Wendy Davies, 'The Myth of the Celtic Church', in Nancy Edwards and Alan Lane (eds.), *The Early Church in Wales and the West* (Oxbow Monographs 16; Oxford, 1992), 12–21. The quotation is from the last work, on p. 18.

Readers anxious to follow up my observations upon saints' lives can do so most easily from the four volumes edited by Charles Plummer and also cited by Christina Oakley. They are warned that for every charming anecdote such as those cited, they will find two which appeal less to a modern liberal taste, and often concerning the same person; thus St Brendan was equally admired as the Sinbad of medieval Irish legend and a hater of women. Readers are also warned that virtually nothing in these biographies can be taken literally, almost all having been composed by monks writing centuries after the time of the subject, and having few or no hard facts at their disposal.

A good selection of eighteenth-century British views of Druidry can be found in Sam Smiles, *The Image of Antiquity: Ancient Britain and the Romantic Imagination* (Yale UP, 1994)

Ronald Hutton is Professor of British History at the University of Bristol, and the author of seven books in that field. He is a fellow of both the Royal Historical Society and the Society of Antiquaries.

I

THE CALL OF
THE LAND

And all the times I was picking up potatoes, I did have conversa-
tions with them. Too, I did have thinks of all their growing days
there in the ground, and all the things they did hear. Earth-voices
are glad voices, and earth-songs come up from the ground through
the plants; and in their flowering, and in the days before these days
are come, they do tell the earth-songs to the wind … I have thinks
these potatoes growing here did have knowings of star-songs.

The Singing Creek where the Willows Grow – The Mystical
Nature Diary of Opal Whiteley, PENGUIN, 1994

So wrote Opal Whiteley in Oregon when she was about seven
years old.

The reason for the resurgence of interest in Druidry at the end of
the twentieth century is that we yearn, now, to hear the earth-songs
and the star-songs. We know that, collectively, we have turned away
from them for centuries, and now we want to turn back – before it is
too late.

Druidry is based on a love of the land, and of Nature. Druids make
pilgrimages to sacred sites, walk the old tracks, and study the trees,
plants and animals that were traditionally held sacred. Practically,
many Druids today are involved in environmental campaigning and
tree-planting programmes.

Erynn Rowan Laurie

THE PRESERVING SHRINE

'Three perfect immovable rocks on which are supported all the judgments of the world: poet, letter, nature.'

Senchus Mor

In Seattle, we live with the trees. They line our streets and shelter our yards. They stand in parks and urban groves, filling the city with a thousand shades of green. Hidden in a corner of West Seattle is a pocket of old growth forest, with towering cedars wider than a man is tall. A Druid learns from the trees: patience, strength, serenity, perseverance. A tree doesn't complain about the boulder beside it. It grows around the stone, gaining grace and beauty with the years, developing personality through the quirks imposed by the circumstances of its growth. The tree is a teacher. It is an embodiment of deity.

The early Celts had a deep and visceral connection with nature. They honoured and revered the world around them. The Gods themselves were identified with nature, as voices in the wind, the brightness of the sun, or the black feathers of a raven. For the Celts, the world was wilderness and wilderness was the embodied sacred. Wilderness. For most modern westerners, the word evokes a tangled wasteland fraught with the danger of lurking carnivores; bears and wolves, biting insects, poisonous snakes, deep and hazardous waters. The wilderness is experienced as dark and foreboding. How different is our grasp from the understanding of the Celts.

In the law text called the *Senchus Mor*[1] there is a haunting passage. 'What is the preserving shrine?' it asks. 'Not hard,' the answer comes, 'the preserving shrine is memory and what is preserved in it.' Again, the question is asked. 'What is the preserving shrine?' This answer is slightly different: 'Not hard; the preserving shrine is nature and what is preserved in it.' How can we appreciate the subtle message this gives? Nature and memory are one. They are the places where all things remain, luminous and intact, for future generations. They are linked in Celtic lore by tales of transformation, the hidden art of ogham letters, and the connecting thread that moves between all things.

The Irish sage Tuan preserves the memory of mythic time by living as stag, eagle and salmon, inhabiting all three of the sacred realms of land, sea and sky. His cycles of life and death in animal form provide one of the most beautiful stories in Celtic myth. Tuan is nature, and he serves as history, continuity, memory, and the transmission of lore from past generations into the 'mythic' present. Through his many lives, the genealogy of ancestors is kept so that they may be honoured by subsequent generations.

The Filidh, or poets, Aimirgen and Taliesin, identify themselves completely with their wilderness, becoming wind and water, sound and sunshine, the crest of the ninth wave that separates this world from *an saol eile*, the Otherworld. These transformations speak of the wilderness that is within each of us, waiting to be called forth. Wisdom is hidden in nature; ways of relating and ways of coping with adversity, paths leading to strength of character and creativity. This same wisdom is hidden in each of us. Taliesin tells us:

> *'I was in many shapes before I was released. I was raindrops in the air, I was stars' beam; I was a path, I was an eagle, I was a coracle in seas. As for creation, I was created from nine forms of elements. From the essence of soils was I made, from the bloom of nettles, from water of the ninth wave.'* [2]

The poet Aimirgen offers the same sense of identity:

> *'I am a wind on the sea, I am a hawk on a cliff, I am the most delicate of herbs, I am a lake in a plain.'* [3]

Because of their identification with nature, both of them know deep secrets. 'In what place lies the setting of the sun?' asks Aimirgen, and it is apparent that he knows the answer. 'I can put in song what the tongue can utter,' says Taliesin, daring to put into words the mysteries that cannot be spoken by lesser poets.

Taliesin's expression of mystery reaches into the Otherworld and brings forth song. Poetry is revealed as the only fit language for speaking the deepest of riddles. The *Auraicept na n-Eces* [4] calls this 'the great darkness or obscurity of poetry.' Taliesin's words and metaphors lead glowing fragments of truth from the Otherworld, through the interplay of darkness and light; the 'great darkness' of poetry, and the brilliant fire of *imbas*, poetic frenzy. The ancient technique of *imbas forosnai* required the isolation of the poet in darkness, a way to insulate and create sensory deprivation which allowed intense contact with the inner wilderness. Emerging from this inner forest, we re-enter the outer world and experience dark poetry as a blinding flash of light. This darkness of incubation produced Taliesin himself, whose name means 'radiant brow'. At the moment of stepping over the threshold from one world to another, from darkness to light, poetry explodes from the poet in torrential streams.

In silence and darkness we find the inner wilderness, and so the outer wilderness must likewise be approached in silence. Cormac Mac Art[5] explains this in precise terms: 'I was a listener in woods, I was a gazer at stars, I was blind where secrets were concerned, I was silent in a wilderness.'[6] The poet deliberately closes her eyes, seals her lips, and places herself in darkness so that the inner senses may reveal wonders. The human silence of the wilderness is contrasted with the human sounds of culture in early Irish poetry. Fionn Mac Cumhail and his warriors cherished this wilderness, as did the mad poet Suibhne Geilt.[7] Again and again, the belling of stags and the calling of blackbirds, the shriek of eagles or the quack of the duck are compared with the call of a church bell, and the civilized tones of bronze and iron are consistently found lacking.

Our culture imposes its civility upon us. Its urbanity stifles and conceals our inner wilderness. It gives us no silence. It substitutes rationality for intuition and believes that this is no loss. As we grow older, we forget the wilderness of childhood, forget that we are one with our world. We grow civilized and insist that we are separate from nature. But our deepest mind remembers that we are cedar, starfish and wren. It is written in our genes. Should civilization vanish, our bodies would still remember how to tell nourishing plants from poisons, and find shelter under the trees. When we begin to dissolve the artificial boundaries between human and nature, we gain a glimpse of what the poets knew. Our world is transformed. We become shape-shifters.

Modern Druids seek this wilderness within and without. We look for it in back yards and parks, in forests and amid the stones of the mountains. We pursue it with meditation and divination. We ask our Gods to break down the barriers that civilization has set forth between us and our birthright. Through the perfect immovable rock of the letter, we seek connections in the tales of Celtic tradition, and in the mnemonic device of the ogham alphabet.

For some, the ogham consists of a list of trees with their associated lore. This is but a fragment of the vast body of information associated with the letters. All the natural world is represented in these enigmatic scratches on wood and stone. The ogham alphabet is a forest of trees and poetry, populated by creatures of flesh and of metaphor. Each letter is a world of its own. Huath, for instance, is the whitethorn, but it is also a pack of wolves, a raven, an ox, a colour called 'terrible', and is as 'fearsome' as the monsters lurking within the deep caverns of the psyche.

This forest of words was created by the God Ogma to serve as a carrier of wisdom for Druids and poets. The letters of the ogham make the stave of words wielded by poets for blessing, for satire, and for the transmission of knowledge from one generation to the next. In this way, nature serves as a literal memory, for each plant, animal, river and bird has its own fragment of poetry residing within. Each colour in a stone has its own tale to tell. A complex web of meaning can be read by making a journey into the wilderness and looking for the story that each thing must tell by its very existence. The task of the Druid is to seek out the disparate threads of the tale and combine them into a coherent order.

To truly understand the preserving shrine of nature, we must seek it out. Because I live in North America, my wilderness is not that of the Irish Iron Age, or the forests and mountains of modern Wales. My wilderness lies on Puget Sound. It shares many things with the wild lands of my European ancestors; wolf and salmon, oak and eagle. But it holds many different things as well. I live with cedars and dog-tooth violets, with banana slugs and stellar jays. I live with the Duwamish river and the mountain called Tahoma. These things have as much to teach us as the rowan or the Shannon or Mount Snowdon. Because they are here, now, they speak more clearly to me and with greater power than places half a world away. They come to embody the Gods for me.

All my life, I have been a wanderer, with no native place to call my own. But the great cedar and fir forests of the Northwest have laid their claim upon me. I can no more refuse them than I can refuse my own death in the hour of its approach. The poetry of this place is implacable, inexorable. It is awe-full in its wildness. And yet between the time that I write this, and the moment of your reading, more salmon runs will become extinct and more wild forest will disappear forever under the kind 'care' of the US Forest Service.

The early Celts were wanderers too, and they understood the power of place. Wherever they settled, they opened themselves to the spirits of the land there, and became one with them. And we, as modern Celts by blood or by spirit, would do well to foilow in those footsteps. We can honour the spirits of whatever place we live in, whether that place is a cottage on a Scottish moor, an apartment in Singapore, a tract house in Seattle, or a farm on the steppes of Russia. Each place is sacred in its own right, with history and with memory. Each has its own tales to tell if we know how to listen. Each place has its own ogham of trees, animals and birds. The lapwing is the letter A of the Irish bird ogham, but what can this mean for me when I know no lapwings? How can I read the tale of my wilderness if it is phrased in words that do not exist here?

If we listen to the spirits of our own place, we need not follow a human calendar to tell us when it is Samhain or Beltain, Imbolc or Lughnasadh.[8] Nature preserves the memory of the holy days for us. The calendar of nature speaks volumes, even in the city of Seattle. When does the hawthorn bloom? That is the time of Beltain. The crocus and the cherry blossom speak of Imbolc. The first frost marks Samhain, and the blackberry season brings Lughnasadh. The sun itself marks the days of solstice and equinox, circling in its eternal dance.

The Irish law texts tell us that all things are 'connected by a thread of poetry.' It is through this connecting thread that we begin to touch the sense of the sacred in wilderness and in ourselves. In the preserving shrine of nature is kept the liquid fire of music, the poetry of a beating bird's wing, the scarlet law of wolf and hare, the genealogy of life from stone to star. Within our bodies is the pounding surf of our blood and the spinning moon of our menses. Our flesh is the flesh of every living creature. When we dissolve the artificial boundaries between human and nature, we become nature. Its poetry is ours. We reflect both nature's austerities and its excesses.

This connecting thread of poetry does not exist as words on paper. It is not, and cannot be, what we write. Analysis, like dissection, kills the beast. This poetry is instead the memory of motion and stillness. It exists in the stuttering fall of leaf to loam or the recursive eddying of a stream. It is the force of gravity that binds us to earth, and the unbearable lightness within us that happens when the sun pierces the clouds and illuminates the rolling green hills below. Poetry is the terror of the whirlwind and the sudden stillness of death. The connecting thread exists in the tension and resolution between the inner wilderness of the Druid and the external wilderness of the whirling planet.

We can perceive poetry through our senses. Sound, touch, taste, sight and scent, are spoken of as streams arising from the well of wisdom located in the heart of a hazel grove. Wisdom precedes and is the source of our senses. Without wisdom, we cannot truly see or hear, we merely go through the motions. We sleep-walk through our lives, thinking ourselves separate from wilderness. We do not understand that what we do to the world, we do to ourselves. We cannot read the connecting thread that links us to our ancestors and our children, to the stones in the garden or the snow that falls soft on our skin.

With wisdom, we act in right relationship to the wilderness. The poet becomes the world-tree. We consume the salmon of wisdom, and the spark of *imbas* strikes a bonfire in our soul. The Celtic tales and poems speak consistently of wisdom in images of nature. Wisdom is a stream, a well. It is the tide-water point where river and ocean meet and become a single turbulent, fertile estuary. It is the sweet meat of the hazel nut, and the swift, flashing salmon. Wisdom illuminates us from within until we are consumed in its fire, eaten by inspiration as the salmon is consumed by the waiting poet. We are one with nature, eaten and eater, hunter and prey.

The tale of Cormac[9] in the Land of Promise describes the well and streams. Manannan tells him:

> 'the well which you saw with the five streams flowing from it is the well of knowledge. And the streams are the five senses, through which knowledge is obtained; and no one will have artistic ability who does not drink from the well itself, and from the streams. The people of many skills are those who drink from them both.'[10]

Wisdom is preserved in nature. The comfrey root does not forget its medicinal powers. The Goddess Airmid[11] has knowledge of the healing properties of herbs, and teaches them to the careful student. The bee knows the place of the sun and the secrets of making honey. Ogma Honey-mouth, the God of eloquence, creates sweet, persuasive words that can bind the hearer. Whenever we seek diligently for wisdom, we can find it.

A Druid finds the Gods embodied in nature. The sacred tree is called a *bile* in Irish, and the name of their ancestor-God is also Bile. He has his epiphanies in birch, stag, sun and ram-horned serpent. He is the world-tree that links the sky above with the land, and the waters below. A description in the tale 'The Sickbed of

CuChulainn'[12] can give us an idea of how this God may have been seen: 'there is a tree at the entrance of the inclosure – it were well to match its music – a silver tree on which the sun shines, brilliant as gold.'[13]

The Goddess Danu[14] is ancient beyond memory. Her name is preserved from India to Ireland in the names of rivers, and she is called Morrigan, the Great Queen. In Ireland, two hills called the Paps of Anu are her breasts. She is creator and destroyer, a Goddess of life and death. Manannan Mac Lir[15] is seen in the rolling waves, and the sea-foam is the hair of his wife, Fand. The tears of Manannan created three Irish lakes, and in the Isle of Man, yellow flag irises are offered to him at midsummer as rent for his sacred island. In Ireland, it is lucky if it rains on Lughnasadh, because the rain is the presence of the God Lugh at the festival. Caer Ibormeith and Oengus Mac ind Og[16] became swans, and four birds were the kisses of Oengus. In the oral tradition of Scotland, the green land of spring is the cloak of the Goddess Brighid.

Each deity is identified with, or brings into being, some aspect of the natural world. With this as a basis for understanding nature it is impossible to treat wilderness as an impersonal other. The Gods are vitally involved in the lives of those who worship them, and their epiphanies are sacred. We cannot cut down the great ancient tree that embodies a God, nor can we dump sewage or poisonous chemicals into a river that holds our image of a Goddess. We are brought into an understanding that nothing lives outside of nature. The living world becomes a being rather than a thing, and we realize that we cannot treat this being, which is our own body, with disrespect.

Heroes and poets are one with nature through *geas,* a word that means a binding spell or ritual stricture, through poetic or literal identification. It was *geas* for CuChulainn to eat dogs, because he was himself a dog. CuChulainn means 'hound of Culainn.' The name was given to him when the young boy Setanta killed the watchdog of the smith Culainn. Setanta volunteered to serve as the smith's hound until a puppy could be raised to take his place. His fierceness ultimately led to his being called the Hound of Ulster, guardian of the province. There was no shame in identifying with the animal. In fact, this identity satisfied the demands of honour. Canine and human become one in word and deed. The hound is the emblem of a fierce and loyal companion. For Diarmuid,[17] the *geas* was against killing the Boar of Ben Bulben, his halfbrother. Boar and man shared one flesh in blood relationship. When Diarmuid violated his *geas* and killed the boar, he was himself slain on its tusks. To violate nature is a deadly business. Our own civilization is learning this lesson in a myriad lethal ways.

In early Ireland, poets were identified with the sacred tree and with the stream of wisdom issuing from the hidden well at the bottom of the sea. Their ranks were seen as places within the tree, with the highest ranks becoming the crowning branches. Taliesin claims the region of the summer stars as his place, sitting at the top of the tree.

The Irish called their poets *ansruith*, 'great stream.' The poet issues from the well of wisdom just as the streams of the senses do. Through *Filidecht*, the making of poetry, we regain our senses and express the mysteries. We take liquid language and give form to the elemental forces of emotion and epiphany. The Irish said that we need not be born into a family of poets to learn the ways of *Filidecht*. The great stream of *imbas* will wash over those who must walk the path, taking them up and carrying them, swifter than racehorses, to the well of wisdom itself.

As we reach into the darkness seeking *imbas,* we are possessed by the spirit of poetry. The poet finds the depth and true perception of the senses in the darkness of ecstatic trance. This is not the extraordinary control of spirits, as in Shamanic trance, but rather the blinding and paradoxical loss of self found in the Welsh *awenithon,* or the loa-ridden horse of modern Voudon.[18] Geraldus Cambriensis[19] tells us that the *awenithon* spoke from trance 'as if possessed', and that they uttered poetry of such intensity and powerful expression that it seemed nonsense. The *awenithon* did not remember what was said, but the inquirers found their answers nonetheless in the images brought forth from the inner wilderness.

The flash of *imbas* can be so bright that at times we are drowned in its fiery stream and cannot remember what we see. Poetry comes and is gone like echoes of a hawk's scree. We are dismembered, like Boann[20] as she ran before the rising waters of Nechtan's well. In this loss of control, we are touched by the Gods. We are subsumed by nature. We return from the experience profoundly changed.

The *Filidh* were also called *druimcli,* 'the top of the ridge-pole of knowledge.' This ridge-pole is also called the roof-tree, which supports the house, bringing the forest inside the human dwelling. It is every person's worldtree, central to their daily life. Fionn, himself a master poet, was raised in a tree by three Goddesses. From his earliest days he dwells in the midst of wilderness, sheltered and clothed in the wild.

The poem on the Yew of Ross[21] expresses the spiritual significance of trees. It calls this *bile*, or sacred tree, 'best of creatures, a firm-strong God, door of heaven, strength of a building, light of sages, spell of knowledge.'[22] Beneath trees like this, judgments were given by Druids and poets. The tree stood as silent witness to the proceedings, and all of nature was expected to respond if the judgment were false. Lugaid Mac Con gave a false judgment which Cormac Mac Art corrected. 'At that, one side of the house, the side in which the false judgment was given, fell down the slope. It will remain thus forever, the Crooked Mound of Tara. For a year afterward, Lugaid was king in Tara, and no grass came out of the ground or leaves on the trees or grain in the corn.[13]

The circular ogham glyph called the *Feige Find*,[23] usually translated as Fionn's Window, is actually a graphic representation of the world tree. The word *feige* means 'roof-tree' or 'ridge-pole'. Its five rings are the five groups of five ogham letters, the five invasions of

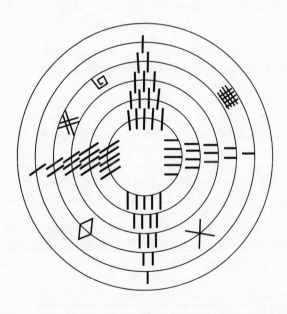

The Feige Find

The Fiege Find is symbolic of a number of fivefold patterns in Irish mythology, and may hold some clues to early Celtic cosmology.

Ireland and her five provinces. In the tale 'Scela Eogain', five rings of
protection were drawn around the infant Cormac. 'When Cormac
was born, the Druid smith, Olc Aiche, put five protective circles
about him, against wounding, against drowning, against fire, against
enchantment, against wolves, that is to say, against every evil.'[24]

The concentric rings may be seen as the circling stars in the
branches of the world-tree, which Taliesin claims for his own. The
Auraicept na n-Eces tells us that 'five words are adjudged to be the
breath of a poet', and it is likely that techniques of breath control
were taught as the poet began to climb the tree. 'Proper to bard
poetry, i.e., its measure to suit the ear, and proper adjustment of
breathing.'[25]

With breath control comes the ability to alter consciousness, to
identify fully with the tree and with the natural world. The ogham is
here compared to a tree. The first set of ogham letters are scores
made to the right of the trunk-line, the second to the left, and so on.
The poet is encouraged to climb the 'tree' of ogham by using the
letters, right hand first, left hand after, all the way up the tree.

Where the poets climb up, the Gods also climb down. The tale
concerning the making of CuChulainn's shield[26] has the deific
craftsman Dubdetha climbing down the ridge-pole through the
smoke hole in a roof, to trace a pattern in the ashes for the craftsman
Mac Endge. Somewhere in the middle of this great world-tree, at a
silent place in the wilderness, Gods and mortals meet.

The preserving shrine of nature holds all of these memories and
stories within it. The Druid studies each of them carefully, piecing
together the ancient wisdom of lichen and stone, listening to the
speech of boar and raven. The poet snatches fragments from the
darkness and, with the spark of *imbas*, builds these keen-edged
shards into song. But how much longer will we have this store of treasure?

In this time, the preserving shrine itself stands in need of preserva-
tion. The memory of the earth is lost, day by day, through the extinc-
tion of species. Poet and letter are not enough. No poem's magic will
recall the salmon when the last one dies. No book will fully describe
the great old growth forest once it has gone. We must be able to see
these things for ourselves, to touch rough bark, hear the moan of the
cougar, taste wild blackberries, and smell the wet scent of cedar in
the air, so that the wilderness within can be complete. We must have
the perfect immovable rock of nature on which to lean if we and our
sibling species are to survive the next century.

NOTES

1. The *Senchus Mor* is a collection of early Irish law texts which include tales and lore which illustrate legal points.
2. Ford, Patrick K., *The Mabonogi and Other Medieval Welsh Tales*, University of California Press, Berkeley, 1977.
3. The Aimirgen quote is from the author's translation of an early Irish poem.
4. The *Auraicept na n-Eces* is a collection of texts from early manuscripts which concern the training of the fili or poet.
5. Cormac Mac Art was a legendary Irish High King who was known for his wisdom and excellent judgments.
6. Meyer, Kuno. *The Instructions of King Cormac Mac Airt*, Royal Irish Academy, Todd Lecture Series, vol XV, Dublin 1909.
7. Fionn Mac Cumhail was the leader of a roving band of warriors called the Fianna. Fionn was famous for his wisdom and generosity. There is a great body of mythology surrounding Fionn and his Fianna. Suibhne Geilt was the King of Dalriada, an early Irish kingdom with territory in Scotland. Suibhne was cursed by a saint and went mad in battle. This madness caused him to live naked in the forest, eating only plants and flying like a bird from tree to tree. He was a famous nature poet.
8. Samhain (also Samain, Samhuinn) is the festival of the dead and the time of the Celtic new year, generally celebrated around November 1st. Beltain (also Beltane, Beltaine) is the festival of the beginning of summer, celebrated around May 1st.
   Imbolc is the festival of the triple Goddess Brighid, the deity of poets, smiths and healers, celebrated around February 2nd.
   Lughnassadh (also Lugnasad, Lughnasad, Lughnasadh) is the harvest festival of the God Lugh, whom the Romans described as 'the Celtic Mercury', celebrated around August 1st.
9. In the tale of Cormac's Cup, king Cormac finds himself in the Otherworld at the palace of Manannan Mac Lir, the sea God, where he encounters the well of wisdom and is gifted with a cup that breaks if three lies are told and repairs itself when three truths are told. It is from this well of wisdom that the five streams of the senses issue.
10. Stokes, Whitley. *The Irish Ordeals*.
11. Airmid is the Irish Goddess of healing herbs. When her father, Dian Cecht the physician, killed her brother Miach the surgeon, 365 herbs grew up from Miach's grave. Airmid arranged them all on her cloak according to their healing properties.
12. CuChulainn was once the young boy Setanta. He was born the son of

the God Lugh. When Setanta was young, he went to the house of the smith, Culann. There he was attacked by the smith's dog. When Setanta killed the dog, Culann was angry that he would have no hound to guard his house. Setanta volunteered to act as Culann's hound until a puppy could be raised to take his place, and so he was given the name CuChulainn or 'hound of Culann'.

13. Dillon, Myles. *Early Irish Literature*, University of Chicago Press, Chicago, 1948.

14. Danu is the primordial mother Goddess who gave her name to the Gods of Ireland, the Tuatha de Danann, which means 'Children of Danu'. She was originally a river Goddess and her name is found as an element in river names all over Europe, such as the Danube, the Donn and the Dnieper.

15. Manannan Mac Lir is the sea God of the Irish Celts. He is a shape-shifter and possesses a cloak of mists, a crane bag containing mysterious secrets, and many other magical objects. Manannan rules Tir na mBan, the Land of Women, and Tir Tairngiri, the Land of Promise in the Otherworld. At the centre of his kingdoms lies the well of wisdom.

16. Oengus Mac in Og is the young son of the Irish father God Daghda and his wife Boann, who is the Goddess of the river Boyne. He is often called the Irish God of love. One night Oengus had a dream in which he saw Caer Ibormeith, and he fell into a deep love-sickness. Oengus searched the world for her, and found her at Samhain in the shape of a swan among one hundred and fifty swans on a lake.

17. Diarmuid was one of the men of the Fianna of Fionn Mac Cumhail and foster son of Oengus Mac ind Og. His half-brother was killed as an infant, but brought back to life as the boar of Ben Bulben. A curse, or geas, was placed on the boar that he would bring Diarmuid to his death. Diarmuid likewise had a geas placed on him, that he should never hunt the boar of Ben Bulben, or he would die.

18. Voudon is an Afro-Caribbean religion. One of its major features is the deep ecstatic trance of the practitioners, who are 'ridden' or possessed by a deity or powerful spirit known as a loa. The one who is ridden is called the 'horse'. Horses, like the Welsh *awenithon*, rarely recall the details of their trances, and they may pass on messages from the spirit world.

19. Geraldus Cambriensis was a medieval Welsh traveller and scholar who collected folklore and observations from his travels in Wales and Ireland.

20. Boann's husband Nechtan guarded the well of wisdom. One day Boann decided that she would get wisdom from the well, and she went to it and circled it three times counterclockwise. The waters of the well rose up

and pursued her down the course of the river Boyne, tearing from her one eye, one arm and one leg before they drowned her. This theme is similar to Odin's giving an eye in exchange for wisdom at Mimir's well in Norse mythology.

21. The Yew of Ross was one of the five ancient sacred trees of Ireland. The poem of the Yew of Ross is found in the *Dindshenchas* or place-name tales, explaining the sacredness of this tree.

22. Stokes, Whitley. *The Prose Tales XVI.*

23. The Feige Find is found in the 14th century manuscript, the Book of Ballymote. It is an arrangement of the ogham letters. This five-ringed pattern is found at a number of early Celtic sites, including the ritual site at Emhain Macha. The pattern may have some ritual significance, and its five rings may be symbolic of a number of fivefold patterns in Irish mythology.

24. O'Daly, Mairin, ed. 'Scela Eogain' in *Cath Maige Mucrama: The Battle of Mag Mucrama*, Irish Texts Society, Vol L, Dublin 1975.

25. Calder, George. *Auraicept na n-Eces: The Scholar's Primer*, John Grant, Edinburgh 1917.

26. Best, R. I. 'Cuchulainn's Shield', Eriu 5, 1911 (Celtic studies journal article).

Erynn Rowan Laurie is a student of the Irish Celts, and has been a priestess of their ancient deities for nearly a decade. A dedicated modem addict, she can often be found online talking about the Celts. She lives with her husband and shares her time with an urban tribe of musicians, poets, writers, gamers, mystics and computer Shamans in the beautiful and mythic landscape of the Puget Sound region. Erynn's published work includes *A Circle of Stones: Journeys and Meditations for Modern Celts*, Eschaton, Chicago 1995. Erynn Rowan Laurie can be contacted by Email at inisglas@seanet.com

@@@@@@@@@@@@@@@@@@@@@@@@@@@@@@@@@@@@@@@

Philip Shallcrass

THE BARDIC TRADITION AND THE SONG OF THE LAND

Sit thou on the heath, O Bard!
and let us hear thy voice.
It is pleasant as the gale of the spring,
that sighs on the hunter's ear,
when he wakens from dreams of joy,
and has heard the music
of the spirits of the hill.

JAMES MACPHERSON (1736–1796)

In Australian Aboriginal religion there exists the concept of Songlines. These are ancient trackways linking together sacred sites scattered across the landscape. Associated with these trackways and holy places are legends of the Gods, Ancestors, and Spirits who have visited them since the Creation, who continue to inhabit them now, and whose presence imbues them with their sacredness. The legends of these spiritual beings are preserved in songs, which, when sung, reawaken the sacred powers resident in the landscape, in the Songlines, and in the holy beings themselves. Knowledge of the sacred songs is thus vital to Aboriginal religion, for the songs reveal the history, nature and powers of the holy ones. Without this knowledge, the rituals appropriate to the sacred places and their indwelling spirits cannot be performed. If the rituals are not performed then the people, and the sacred land itself, will suffer and die. The singing of the Song of the Land becomes, therefore, a sacred act, and a potent ritual in itself.

Pagan Celtic religion also had, and still has for those of us attempting to retrace the ancient ways, its sacred places: its holy springs, wells, lakes and rivers; its sacred woodland groves and hills;

its ancestral burial mounds, prehistoric circles and standing stones; and its ancient trackways linking them together. And it, too, had songs which wrought them all into one great, harmonious whole, binding them with golden chains of enchanted words, rich and strong with meaning for those with ears to hear.

Our Pagan forebears believed that their own holy places, like those of their Australian counterparts, were imbued with indwelling spirits. In later times, these spirit inhabitants became euphemized into the Faery, or Fair Folk, of popular tradition. These were called Sidhe (pronounced Shee) in the Gaelic language of Ireland, and Tylwyth Teg (literally 'the Fair Family,' pronounced Terlooerth Teg) in Wales. However, to the Pagan, these spirits were, and are, the Ancestors, Gods, and other inhabitants of the spiritual realms, in whose honour rituals were performed to ensure the well-being of the land and of all living things.

Like the Australian Aborigines, the Pagan Celts of old Europe had a body of sacred knowledge preserved in prose, poetry, and song which told of the beings connected to holy places, and contained information necessary for the correct rites to be conducted at those places. Among the Celts, this body of knowledge was the especial province of that section of the Druid caste known as Bards. Bards undertook a course of training which spanned between seven and twenty years, during which, theirs being an entirely oral tradition, they were required to memorize the hundreds of myths, historical legends, poems and songs that made up the cultural inheritance of their people.

A trained Bard was expected to be able to recite the legends attached to any standing stone, sacred tree, burial mound, prominent ridge, or other feature of the landscape, whether natural or artificial, which lay within the bounds of the tribal homeland; and of many others which lay beyond. Each time they made such a recital, chanted a poem, or sung one of the old songs, they were, like the Aboriginal singers, recreating the characters and events their words described, restoring them to life in that eternal, mythical present which Aborigines call the Dreamtime. In restoring the spirits of a place to life, they renewed the life of the place itself, thus enabling the Earth to become bountiful, and those who dwelt upon it to thrive and grow strong.

Many modern Bards and Druids are currently working to recover the ancient Song of the Land as a vital part of learning to 'walk the Earth in a sacred manner', as the Lakota Sioux Medicine Man, Black Elk, put it. Given the appalling damage mankind has inflicted on our

planet in recent years, such efforts are seen as essential if we are to
begin to heal the deep scars left on the land by the over-exploitation
of natural resources. Deforestation, the 'greenhouse' effect, depletion of the ozone layer, desertification, pollution of air and water – all
result from a world-view which recognizes, in Oscar Wilde's well-
turned phrase, 'the price of everything, and the value of nothing.'
This attitude sees everything – animal, vegetable and mineral,
including human beings – solely in terms of their economic worth,
and, if it considers the spiritual at all, views it as somehow divorced
from the 'real world' and consequently of no importance. Modern
Druidry seeks to redress the balance in favour of the planet, by
viewing all things as imbued with spirit, and therefore inherently
sacred. From this basic belief stems the love, respect, and spirit of
guardianship for the Earth and all its creatures which are necessary
for the task of healing our ravaged world.

In the quest to restore reverence for the sanctity of the land, one of
the primary functions of the modern Bard is to rediscover and re-
interpret the ways of our ancestors. Several sources can assist in this
quest. Archaeology can provide factual information concerning both
the location and the original use of sacred sites. Many such sites also
have local legends or folk traditions attached to them, which often
provide clues to the nature of the rites performed there. These two
sources can sometimes provide mutual corroboration, as in the case
of the Callanish stone circle in Scotland, where archaeology has
recognized an alignment of stones directed towards sunrise at or near
the spring equinox, while local folklore has it that 'a shining one',
presumably the sun, passes down the stone rows at dawn, heralded
by the cry of a cuckoo, the bird whose call announces the onset of
Spring in Britain.

A third source is the early literature of the Celtic peoples. As stated
earlier, the Celtic Bardic tradition was, for most of its history, a purely
oral one. However, in medieval Ireland and Wales, in the centuries
after the arrival of Christianity, many fragments of the old tradition
were committed to writing by Christian scribes. Thanks to these
monastic scholars, we have a good deal of Pagan lore preserved in a
body of manuscripts dating mainly from the twelfth to the fifteenth
centuries of our Common Era. These provide an invaluable source of
information regarding the Pagan Celtic attitude towards the land.

In medieval Ireland there was a special category of lore called
Dindshenchas, which dealt specifically with legends surrounding
particular places. *Dindshenchas* literally means 'The Ancient Lore of
High Places'. As the name suggests, much of it deals with tales

attached to holy hills, such as Tara, ancient seat of the High Kings of Ireland, and prehistoric burial mounds, such as the great chambered tomb of New Grange. However it also contains legends associated with trees, wells, rivers, standing stones and other sacred places. Two recensions of this lore have survived, one in prose form, the other in verse, both contained in a twelfth century compilation known as the *Book of Leinster.*

The *Book of Leinster* also contains a remarkable mythological text entitled *Lebor Gabala Erinn,* 'the Book of the Taking of Ireland,' which tells of a number of invasions of that country by both Gods and mortals. According to this text, the first human colonists to arrive in Ireland are the Sons of Mil, among whom is the Druid, Amergin. They touch land at Kenmare Bay in Co. Kerry on the first day of May, the old Celtic festival of Beltaine, and Amergin is the first to step ashore. As his right foot touches the soil, he chants the following famous poem, now known as the Song of Amergin:

> *I am the wind which breathes upon the sea,*
> *I am the wave upon the ocean,*
> *I am the murmur of the billows,*
> *I am an ox of seven fights,*
> *I am an eagle upon a rock,*
> *I am a ray of the sun,*
> *I am the fairest of all plants,*
> *I am a wild boar in valour,*
> *I am a salmon in the water,*
> *I am a lake upon a plain,*
> *I am a word of cunning art,*
> *I am the point of a spear in battle,*
> *I am the God who puts fire in the head,*
> *Who brings light to the gathering on the hilltop?*
> *Who announces the ages of the moon?*
> *Who knows the place where the sun has its rest?*
> *Who finds springs of clear water?*
> *Who calls the fish from the ocean's deep?*
> *Who causes them to come to shore?*
> *Who changes the shape of headland and hill?*
> *A Bard whom seafarers call upon to prophesy.*
> *Spears shall be wielded,*
> *I prophesy victory,*
> *And all other good things,*
> *And so ends my song.*

This ancient Druid is clearly identifying himself with those creatures perceived as having power derived from land, sea or sky, and seeking thereby to exercise that power himself, for the benefit of his people, who have come to this unknown land seeking a home. Placing his right foot on the soil physically connects him to the land, enabling him to contact its spirit to aid him in creating the spell. He knows that he cannot hope to subdue the land, or even walk securely upon it, without the active assistance of its indwelling spirits.

At this time, according to myth, Ireland was inhabited by a race of Gods, the Tuatha de Danaan, or 'Clan of the Goddess Danu', whose chief place of power was the hill of Tara. Archaeology has shown this to have been a sacred site from at least 2000 BCE, and perhaps earlier, right through into the early medieval period. On their way to Tara, following the Songlines, the ancient trackways, the Sons of Mil come to three sacred hills; Sliabh Mis in Co. Kerry, Sliabh Felim in Co. Limerick, and Uisnech in Co. Westmeath. At each hill they encounter one of the three Goddesses, Banba, Fodla, and Eriu, who are the wives of the three Gods of the Tuatha; Mac Cuill, 'Son of the Hazel,' Mac Cecht, 'Son of the Plough,' and Mac Greine, Son of the Sun.' On the third hill, Uisnech, a great festival assembly used to be held each year at Beltaine, around a sacred ash tree which grew there. Each Goddess in turn greets Amergin, asking if his folk have come to conquer Ireland, and offering them victory if they will name the island after her. Amergin promises each of them that this will be done, and so it was, for even into the nineteenth century, Irish Bards called the land of Ireland by the names of these three Goddesses. This is one of many pieces of evidence which indicate that our Celtic forebears personified the Spirit of the Land in female form. The inauguration of Celtic kings usually took place on a sacred hill or mound, and involved a ritual marriage to a representative of the Goddess of the sovereignty of the land, for it was by her blessing that the king's reign was made fruitful, and crops and cattle were made bountiful.

Coming at last to the hill of Tara, the Sons of Mil meet with the Tuatha de Danaan, who complain that the invaders should have given them warning of their coming, so that they could prepare for battle. They leave it to Amergin to adjudicate on the matter, with the proviso that he will be put to death if he should show any partiality. Amergin gives the following judgement:

Those whom we found dwelling in this land, have possession of it
    by right,

> *It is therefore our duty to put out to sea past nine green waves,*
> *And if we are then able to effect a landing once again, in spite of*
>   *them,*
> *We may engage them in battle to win the land in which we found*
>   *them living,*
> *And the land wherein they dwelt shall be adjudged ours by right*
>   *of battle,*
> *But though we may desire the land these people have, our duty is*
>   *to show them justice,*
> *And I forbid injustice to those found in this land, however much*
>   *we wish to obtain it.*[1]

After the judgement is delivered, all deem it fair, and the Sons of Mil return to their ships and sail out beyond the ninth wave. They turn back towards the shore, but the Druids of the Tuatha de Danaan raise a great wind which threatens to drive the ships out to sea. Amergin then chants the following invocation to the land of Ireland and its female spirit, powers greater and more ancient than even the Tuatha Gods themselves:

> *I invoke the land of Ireland,*
> *faring on the foam, the fertile,*
> *fertile mountain, the lowland,*
> *lowland wood, the showering,*
> *showering lake, the bountiful,*
> *bountiful bush, the well-spring,*
> *well-spring of the tribe, gathering,*
> *gathering at royal Tara,*
> *Tara, tor of the tribe,*
> *the tribe of the sons of Miled,*
> *Miled of the ship and the galley,*
> *the galley of Ireland,*
> *Eber Dond ('Noble Brown'), very green,*
> *an incantation of choosing,*
> *choosing the beautiful plain,*
> *the beautiful woman, Buagne ('Cow-Heart'),*
> *the great faery woman of Ireland,*
> *[to] Eremon, in the beginning,*
> *the land, the enclosure of Eber.*[2]

This song demonstrates the complementary roles of Bard and Druid. As a Bard, Amergin has access to the spiritual source of poetic inspiration, combined with the ability to express that inspiration in well-formed verse, as well as knowledge of the names of places and of their indwelling spirits. Having used Bardic inspiration and training to create the spell, Amergin then uses Druidic power to connect his words with the powers he seeks to invoke, weaving his spell into the energy patterns of earth, sea, and sky so that the song becomes one with the elements themselves. 'The great faery woman of Ireland' responds to this potent invocation, which she herself has helped to create through her gift of inspiration, and the magical wind created by the Tuatha Druids drops.

The Tuatha, however, have other powerful magicians among their number, including Manannan mac Lir, the God of the Sea, who shakes his cloak creating a wind even more powerful than the first, which churns the seas, causing many of the ships of the Sons of Mil to founder, and the rest to be driven wildly before it. Eventually, the remnant of the fleet comes ashore at the mouth of the sacred liver Boyne, where Amergin utters another spell, this time invoking the aid of Manannan's own element, water.

> Sea full of fish,
> And fertile land,
> Fish-swarming,
> Fish be there,
> Bird under wave,
> Greatest of fish,
> Crab from its hole,
> Fish swarming up,
> Sea full of fish.

At this, the storm finally abates. Note that, against this tempest raised by the God of the Sea, Amergin can only work his spell when he stands firmly on the sacred land whose powers the female Earth spirits have already granted him. With the elements thus not only calmed, but invoked to the aid of the Sons of Mil, they succeed in overthrowing the Tuatha, who withdraw into the Neolithic and Bronze Age burial mounds of Ireland, called Sidhe in the Gaelic language. The Tuatha become the Faery Folk of later tradition, themselves called Sidhe after the mounds in which they dwell. So we see that, by the power of Song, the Druid Amergin can pacify the elements and subdue even the Gods themselves.

Many tales survive in both the literary and oral traditions of Ireland which tell of Bards resorting to prehistoric burial mounds, and undertaking fasts upon them, or being taken into them, in order to obtain gifts of Faery wisdom or poetic inspiration. Similar tales are attached to ancient mounds in Wales, where it is said of certain megalithic chambered tombs that spending a night within them will give either madness or poetic genius, particularly if it is one of the 'Three Spirit Nights' of May Eve, Midsummer's Eve or Hallowe'en. Such widespread tales suggest the possibility that, in the late Neolithic and early Bronze Ages, when these tombs were in use, Bardic initiations may have taken place within them. Traces of a similar rite certainly survived in the Bardic schools of the seventeenth and eighteenth centuries in Ireland, Scotland and Wales, where students were set to lie alone in dark, windowless cells for a day and a night, to fashion a poem on a subject set by their teachers. This process is clearly akin to more recent techniques of sensory deprivation, which have been found to produce powerful visionary and auditory experiences.

The other Celtic lands must once have had their equivalents of the Irish *Dindshenchas*, and scattered fragments of such place lore certainly survive in the medieval literature of Wales. There are, for example, the so-called 'Stanzas of the Graves' supposedly composed by the sixth century Bard, Llywarch the Old, and preserved in the late twelfth century compilation, the *Black Book of Caermarthen*. The Stanzas consist largely of the names of places, and of the people, both historical and legendary, who are supposed to be buried there, but give little or no indication of who they were and what they did. The obvious conclusion is that the Stanzas were intended simply as mnemonic devices, meant to trigger the recollection of the Bard, who would then recite the tale of the buried hero from memory. The following is a fairly typical Stanza;

> *The grave of March, the grave of Gwythyr*
> *The grave of Gwgawn of the Red Blade,*
> *Unknown is the grave of Arthur.*

The Arthur referred to here is, of course, the legendary King of that name, and this verse could be an early allusion to the popular folk tradition that Arthur did not die, but was lain to rest in a hidden cave along with the best of his knights, where they remain asleep to this day, awaiting the hour of Britain's greatest need, when they will emerge to save the nation.

Fortunately, such enigmatic fragments are not all the manuscript sources have to offer in our quest for the ancient wisdom of Britain. There is also the magical collection of medieval legends and folk tales now known as *The Mabinogion*, found largely in the *White Book of*

Rhydderch, a manuscript dating from about 1325. In their present form, the *Mabinogion* tales are probably between eight hundred and a thousand years old, but, like their Irish counterparts, they contain elements which are considerably older, reaching back into the pre-Christian past. These tales, like the Irish *Dindshenchas*, contain many references to specific places. The tale of Branwen, Daughter of Llyr, for example, describes how the severed, but still living, head of Bran the Blessed was carried from Wales to London, where it was buried in the White Hill, where the Tower of London now stands. As long as it remained buried there, facing France, no plague could come to the Island of Britain from across the Channel. This has strong echoes of the old pagan Celtic reverence for the severed head, which our ancestors seem to have viewed as the prime repository of the human spirit, or life essence. Heads, either real or carved in wood or stone, were often placed at the doorways of pagan Celtic shrines and sanctuaries, apparently to provide protection for such sacred enclosures. A curious piece of folklore attached to the Tower of London maintains that if the ravens which are kept there should die, or leave the Tower, Britain will fall to an invader from overseas. Even more curiously, the name of the God Bran, whose head was buried within the Tower precincts, means 'raven' in Welsh.

Another *Mabinogion* tale tells how Pwyll, Lord of Dyfed, goes 'to the top of a mound that was called Gorsedd Arberth', of which it is said 'that whosoever sits upon it cannot go thence without either receiving wounds or blows, or else seeing a wonder.' Pwyll accepts the risk, and sees a magical woman riding 'a pure white horse of large size, with a garment of shining gold around her, coming along the highway that led from the mound...' The woman's name is Rhiannon, which means 'Great Lady', and she is clearly the Goddess, or spirit of sovereignty, associated with this mound, which stands near the royal court of Narberth. Pwyll, of course, marries her. Later in the same tale she is made to enact the role of a horse, carrying visitors to the castle on her back. Her horse associations have led to speculation that she was a horse Goddess. The twelfth century chronicler, Geraldus Cambriensis, tells of a royal inauguration rite that supposedly took place in Ireland, where the candidate for kingship mated with a white mare. A Bronze Age chalk hill figure, the Uffington White Horse, overlooks a flat-topped mound called Dragon Hill, where the patron saint of England, St. George, is supposed to have slain his dragon. According to another version of the tale, he merely subdued the dragon, and was assisted in doing so by a mysterious and beautiful woman; perhaps our Pagan spirit of sovereignty come to the aid of a Christian saint. The dragon is one of the most potent manifestations of the Earth spirit.

In these and many similar tales, including the legend of the Sons of Mil and their encounter with the three Goddesses, we find the consistent twin themes of a sacred mound and a female spirit who inhabits it, and who will, if addressed correctly, grant spiritual and/or temporal power. Celtic literature and folklore both indicate that such power is granted conditionally, and that it will be taken away again if the conditions attached to it are not strictly adhered to. There is a common Celtic folk tale with many variants, in which a man marries a woman of the Faery Folk, who gives him wealth, happiness, and fine children, on condition that she shall not receive three blows from him. He inevitably, albeit accidentally, gives her three blows, at which she disappears, taking with her all that she had previously given. In tales surrounding the High Kingship of Ireland, if the spirit of sovereignty withdraws her favour from the King, the whole land and all its inhabitants suffer; streams and rivers run dry, crops wither, cattle die, women miscarry, and even the sun fails to shine.

The Goddess, or spirit of sovereignty, as well as granting power over the land to the king who espouses her upon her magical mound or holy hilltop, also gives knowledge, wisdom, and inspiration to the Bard who comes to her high place with due reverence. Such Bardic gifts are often represented in the form of a magical drink as in the Welsh tale of Taliesin, who receives three blessed drops from a magic cauldron of inspiration brewed by Ceridwen, 'the Bent White One,' an ancient Pagan Goddess who was referred to by the Christian Bards of medieval Wales as the patroness of their order. The spirit of sovereignty associated with the High Kingship of Ireland was the Goddess Meadhbh, whose very name, meaning 'One Who Intoxicates,' is the same as that of the fermented honey drink, mead. Elsewhere, the Bardic gift of the Goddess is symbolized by a magical branch, often from an apple tree, which commonly bears fruit and blossom simultaneously. In Ireland, Bards carried such branches as tokens of their calling. These were called Branches of Peace, and consisted of a wand or staff hung with bells, which were bronze for a trainee Bard, silver for a graduated Bard, and gold for a chief Bard or Ollamh. As well as tokens of office, these Branches were shaken to call an assembly to silence before a recitation began, or to quell fighting in the meadhall.

How then is the modern Bard to re-establish contact with the spirit of the land, to obtain her precious gift of inspiration, to re-awaken the old pathways of the spirit, and to create anew the magical, healing Song of the Land? Research into literature, folklore, and archaeology can reveal the name by which the spirit of the land was known at a particular place, for our ancestors had many names for her, and these were often connected with specific locations. Ceridwen, for example, is strongly associated with Lake Bala in North Wales, and with a mound called Tomen y Bala, which local folklore maintains was built by the Faery Folk. We saw earlier how the 'Great Lady', Rhiannon, appeared to Pwyll at Gorsedd Arberth. The Goddess Meadhbh was associated with Tara, seat of the Irish High Kings, and we have already come across the three Goddesses, Eriu, Fodla and Banba, each linked to a specific sacred hill. Why is this information important? Well, if you are going to ask for a gift from someone, it helps if you know her name, and where she lives!

Places where Earth spirits have traditionally been contacted include the Sidhe mounds of Ireland; that is, the prehistoric burial mounds which became the home of the Gods, the Tuatha de Danaan; and the Welsh Gorsedd mounds. 'Gorsedd' literally means 'High Seat', and these mounds, like the hill of Tara, were the inauguration sites of Celtic kings, and places of tribal assembly. The term Gorsedd later became attached to the assemblies themselves, and is now particularly applied to gatherings of Bards. Other names associated with sacred mounds include Oenach in Ireland, Twmp or Tomen in Wales, Tor, Toot, Tot, Tote, Moot, Tump, or Mump in various parts of England. Hills which were the site of traditional fairs or seasonal festivals, or which were meeting places for local legislative bodies such as the old English Hundreds, may also have been Pagan sacred sites.

Having located a high holy place, and, perhaps, identified its associated Goddess or spirit, the next step is to visit it. If intending to ask a favour of the spirit of a place, it is fitting to take along some token offering in exchange, perhaps a coin, or some food or drink. At Tara, for example, the Goddess Meadhbh would undoubtedly appreciate a gift of mead, the drink which shares her name.

When making a pilgrimage to a sacred place, it is traditional to circle it three times, sunwise (clockwise), on first arriving. In some cases, it may be possible to perform this threefold circuit whilst climbing the hill in an ascending spiral towards the summit. At the top, seek out a spot which feels comfortable and sit down. Relax for a few moments, taking slow, deep breaths and just absorb the atmosphere of the place. Observe any movement that might occur, whether of clouds, birds, animals, or vegetation stirred by the wind.

If musically inclined, you might like to play something. The spirits of the land respond well to music, even the simple blowing of a horn, beating of a drum, or shaking of a rattle.

When feeling calm and at peace, greet the spirit of the place, using whatever words seem appropriate, which may be prepared in advance, or made up on the spot, based on your knowledge of the place and its spirit. At Gorsedd Arberth, for instance, one might say something like, 'Horse-Mother, pure and white, Great Lady Rhiannon, the beauty of all maidens, and all women I have ever seen, are as naught compared to your beauty. O maiden, for the sake of the one whom thou best love, come unto me.' This speech is derived from the story of Pwyll and Rhiannon as set down in *The Mabinogion*.

Many sacred hills and mounds have no surviving ancient lore attached to them, and here it may be necessary to improvise. You could, for example, simply chant the name of the spirit of the place. If the name is unknown, you could use a more universal chant, such as 'Awen', an old British word meaning 'flowing spirit', used by the Bards of medieval Wales to invoke inspiration. Its Irish Gaelic equivalent is 'Dana', meaning 'spiritual offering or gift, the art of poetry, a poem, or a song.' Such words are traditionally chanted long and low, three or nine times. Then simply wait.

Close your eyes and look within for a vision, or perhaps a voice, to come to you, or open your eyes and look for a sign in the world around you: the sun breaking through clouds, a skylark ascending, a shimmering in the trees, or a pattern in the wind-blown grass. Be completely open. Expect nothing. Observe everything. Sacred sites are meeting places between Heaven and Earth, between the material and the spiritual. Spirit may communicate in many ways, either directly or by manifesting in some material form. Look clearly and you will see. Listen attentively and you will hear.

If, after a time, nothing has happened, do not worry. Maybe this is not the right time for the spirit of this particular place to come to you. There will be other places, and other times. Whether or not you succeed in communicating with her, you should still make your offering to the spirit of the place before departing. You might like to say a few words as you make your offering. Perhaps something like, 'That which came from the Earth, I return to the Earth, with love and reverence. Let all be made whole. So let it be.' But I'm sure you can do better than that... Then retrace your path down the hill.

If you are fortunate, you may be blessed with hearing that part of the great Song of the Land which sings through the holy place you have chosen. If so, memorize as much of it as you can, perhaps by

singing it through, writing it down, or recording it on tape. If some
other vision comes to you, accept it and merge it with the knowledge
you already have, combining them to create a new song for your
chosen hill or mound. And when you have made it to the very best of
your ability, return with it to your holy place and sing or chant it to the
indwelling spirit, offering it as a gift to her, and for the healing of the
land. Then, if you will, pass it on, so that others can add your part of
the Song to those they already know, and between us we can begin to
sing our sacred landscape back to life and health.

And now, to prove that this writer practices at least some of what
he preaches, I give you a part of the Song which came to me. This is a
small part of a work in progress, being made in honour of the ancient
stone circles of Avebury in Wiltshire.

The Banks of Caer Abiri

Caer Abiri, I see your white banks rising
through a haze of ancient mornings
in the falling of the year,
and the present falls away
like the blustered leaves of autumn,
as the scattered seeds are watered
through the season of decay,
and the white-bellied serpent
slides her weary way to earth,
leaving stardust patterns where she passed,
to the subterranean chamber
where she coils to sleep and dream
the lengthening nights away till her re-birth,
when yellow-green and springing shoots
break through the melting snow,
and grey wethers toil among their kin of stone,
sucking icy tentacles of crackling willow-grass,
their breath erupting steamy clouds of white
against the dark and frosted sarsens' sides,
she waits and dreams
and dreams and waits,
for time's long tide to sweep the shores of memory,
and lovers, children, lambs and larks,
old and young, caught up within the flux
of her sweet oceans flow to greet her once again,
with priestly magician, with poet and musician,

> *to take up the chant and rhythmic dance*
> *of seasons come and seasons gone*
> *and seasons yet to be,*
> *as past and future merge within*
> *the banks of Abiri.*

The mighty bank and ditch earthworks surrounding the circles of Caer Abiri are now green-turfed, but, when first constructed, some five thousand years ago, they shone with white chalk. They could thus be seen for miles by pilgrims approaching along the Ridgeway, the prehistoric pilgrim route that links many holy places as it crosses the English countryside, intersecting many other Songlines, Dragon Tracks, Faery Paths, or whatever we wish to call them, each a shimmering strand of gold; a harp-string which, when plucked, sounds out a clear note of the ancient, sacred melody that is the Song of the Land.

NOTES

1. From *Lebor Gabala Erinn*, trans. by Prof. Owen Connellan, vol V, *Transactions of the Ossianic Society*, (no date, but prior to 1910).
2. From *Lebor Gabala Erinn*, trans. by Philip Shallcrass.

Suggested Reading

The Bardic Tradition

Parry, Thomas. *A History of Welsh Literature*, Oxford University Press, 1955. The classic work on Welsh Bardic poetry. The English version includes many fine translations of the poems which preserve the metres and rhyme schemes of the originals.

Miles, Dillwyn. *The Royal National Eisteddfod of Wales*, Christopher Davies, Swansea, 1977. This history of the Welsh Eisteddfod contains a useful appendix setting out all of the main Bardic metres and other poetic devices.

Flower, Robin. *The Irish Tradition*, Oxford University Press, 1947. A history of the Irish Bardic tradition.

Murphy, Gerard. *Early Irish Metrics*, Royal Irish Academy, Dublin, 1961. Scholarly study of the structure of early Irish Bardic poetry.

Matthews, John. *Taliesin: Shamanism and the Bardic Mysteries in Britain and Ireland*, Aquarian Press, London, 1991. There are very few books which deal with the Bardic tradition as a pagan survival. This is perhaps the best available at present.

Shallcrass, Philip. *The Way of the Bard: A Practical Guide to Celtic Bardcraft*, in preparation.

Shallcrass, Philip. *The Bardic Tradition in Britain and Ireland*, in preparation. A history of the Celtic Bardic tradition from its earliest origins to the present day.

Robin Williamson and Bob Stewart are also currently working on a book on the Bardic Tradition, due for publication by Cassell in 1996. Robin is one of our finest modern Bards, and Bob is a leading authority on Celtic folk tradition.

Archaeology and Prehistory

Burl, Aubrey. *Rites of the Gods*, J. M. Dent & Sons, London, 1981. Fascinating attempt to piece together the evidence for religious ritual and belief in Britain from 5000 BCE through to the Claudian invasion of 43 CE.

Cunliffe, Barry. *The Celtic World*, Constable, London, 1992. Excellent general introduction to all aspects of Celtic prehistory, history and culture, benefiting from a good selection of fine illustrations.

Harbison, Peter. *Pre-Christian Ireland: From the First Settlers to the Early Celts*, Thames & Hudson, London, 1988. The title and sub-title say it all.

Hutton, Ronald. *The Pagan Religions of the Ancient British Isles: Their Nature and Legacy*, Basil Blackwell, London, 1991. Brilliant survey of the current state of knowledge regarding British paganism from its Stone Age origins, c.30,000 BCE through to the present.

Raftery, Barry. *Pagan Celtic Ireland*, Thames & Hudson, London, 1994. Good, up-to-date account of the present state of knowledge concerning Irish Iron Age technology, life and beliefs.

Ross, Anne. *Pagan Celtic Britain*, Routledge, London, 1967. A real classic. Nearly thirty years old, but still by far the best single-volume account of pagan Celtic religion in Britain.

Mythology and Folklore

Gantz, Jeffrey (trans.). *Early Irish Myths and Sagas*, Penguin Books, Harmondsworth, 1981. Good modern translations of some of the major Irish myths.

Gantz, Jeffrey (trans.). *The Mabinogion*, Penguin Books, Harmondsworth, 1976. Clear modern translation of this fundamental text of the Welsh/ British Bardic tradition. Eleven tales of medieval (and earlier) myth and magic.

Gregory, Lady (trans.). *Gods and Fighting Men*, Colin Smythe, Gerrards Cross, 1976. First published in 1904. Lady Gregory's telling of the tales of the Tuatha de Danaan Gods, and of the hero, Finn mac Cumhal, and his Dark Age war-band, retain their power to enchant.

Guest, Lady Charlotte (trans.). *The Mabinogion*. First published in 1849 and reprinted many times since, mostly by J. M. Dent & Sons, London, this version of the Mabinogion tales includes the important story of the archetypal Bard, Taliesin, and the Goddess Ceridwen, not included in any of the more modern translations.

Gwynn, Edward (trans.). *The Metrical Dindshenchas*, Dublin, vols. 1–5, 1903–1935.

O hOgain, Dr Daithi. *Myth, Legend & Romance: An Encyclopaedia of the Irish Folk Tradition*, Ryan Publishing, 1990. Well-researched and comprehensive guide, covering both medieval Bardic mythology and more recent folklore.

Kinsella, Thomas (trans.). *The Tain*, Oxford University Press, 1970. Superb translation of the great Irish epic, the Cattle Raid of Cooley, featuring the boy-hero, Cuchulainn, and the Goddess Meadhbh, here transformed into a warrior queen.

Squire, Charles. *Celtic Myth and Legend, Poetry & Romance*, Gresham, London, n.d. First published about eighty years ago, and often reprinted, this remains one of the best introductions to the major surviving mythological tales of Celtdom.

Evans Wentz, W.Y. *The Fairy Faith in Celtic Countries*, Colin Smythe, Gerrards Cross, 1977. First published in 1911, this is the classic study of living Celtic fairy lore.

Philip Shallcrass is joint Chief of the British Druid Order, an Ovate of the Order of Bards, Ovates and Druids, and a Bard of the Gorsedd of Bards of Caer Abiri, which he was instrumental in founding, and for which he composes rituals and produces an irregular newsletter. In addition, he is a Wiccan High Priest and is currently engaged in writing two books on the Bardic tradition, one introductory, the other more comprehensive; he also gives lectures and workshops on many aspects of Druidry and Bardism, as well as performing his own poetry, music and songs. He is also editor and publisher of the magazine, *The Druids' Voice*, and of various books, including *The Druid Directory: A Guide to Modern Druidry and Druid Orders* and *Iolo Morganwg: Bardic Writings*. For further details, write enclosing S.A.E. to Philip Shallcrass (B.D.O.), P.O. Box 29, St Leonards-on-Sea, East Sussex TN37 7YP, England.

II

THE CALL OF
THE DRUID

Nede:	O my sage, what is it that thou undertakest?
Ferchertne:	To go into the mountains of rank; into the communion of sciences, into the lands of the men of knowledge.

The Colloquy of the Two Sages

To be a Druid today means following a path which reverences Nature, and which honours an inheritance of lore and tradition which includes the observation of eight seasonal festivals, and working with gods and goddesses, sacred trees and animals.

In ancient times, Druids were sages, philosophers, judges and advisers to Kings and Queens. Today, when someone calls themselves a Druid, it can mean either that they feel in sympathy with the ideals of the ancient Druids, and celebrate the eight seasonal festivals, or that they are a member of a Druid Order, whose origins may go back to 1717 AD, or which may have been formed more recently.

Some people consider Druidry a religion, others a philosophy, others say it is a Mystery School. However else it is characterized, it is a nature-based spiritual way, that has no sacred texts or dogma, but which has grown up over thousands of years, influencing and being influenced by many historical, religious and cultural movements.

Although at least a millennia separates the eighteenth century Druid Revivalists from the last vestiges of Druid religious practice, as described by the classical writers, and although modern Druid practice differs considerably from both Revival and Classical Druidry, they all share a source of inspiration which exists beyond the temporal and physical.

Isaac Bonewits

THE DRUID REVIVAL
IN MODERN AMERICA

Although some fraternal organizations of Druids, such as The Ancient Order of Druids, have been present in the United States and Canada for over a century, the current Druid revival is rooted primarily in the planting of the Reformed Druids of North America, the 'RDNA', in 1963. Almost all currently existing Neopagan Druid groups can trace themselves back to the RDNA, via my own Druidic organization, *A'r nDrai'ocht Fe'in*: A Druid Fellowship, ADF, and its offshoots, such as the Henge of Keltria, HK. However, before going into this history, we should first review some of the vocabulary used by many modern American Druids, namely the uses of the word 'Pagan' and its three main prefixes – 'Paleo-', 'Meso-' and 'Neo-'.

Paganism, Ancient & Modern

The term 'Pagan' comes from the Latin 'Paganus', which appears to have originally had such meanings as 'country dweller', 'villager', or 'hick'. The early Roman Christians used 'Pagan' to refer to everyone who preferred to worship pre-Christian divinities, whom the Christians had decided were all 'really' demons in disguise. Over the centuries, the word 'Pagan' became an insult, applied to the monotheistic followers of Islam by the Christians (and vice-versa), and by the Protestants and Catholics towards each other, as it gradually gained the connotation of 'a follower of a false religion'. By the twentieth century, the word's primary meaning had become a blend of 'atheist', 'agnostic', 'hedonist', and 'religionless'.

Today there are many of us who proudly call ourselves 'Pagan', but we use the word differently from the ways that most mainstream Westerners do. To us, 'Pagan' is a general term that includes both old and new polytheistic religions, as well as their members. The overwhelming majority of all the human beings who have ever lived have been Pagans, and we believe that there is an enormous wealth of spiritual insight and strength to be gained from following a Pagan path.

'Paleopaganism' refers to the original tribal faiths of Europe, Africa, Asia, the Americas, Oceania and Australia, when they were (and in some cases still are) practised as intact belief systems. Of the so-called 'Great Religions of the World', Hinduism (prior to the influx of Islam into India), Taoism and Shinto, for example, fall into this category.

'Mesopaganism' is the word used for those religions founded as attempts to recreate, revive or continue what their founders thought of as the Paleopagan ways of their ancestors (or predecessors), but which were heavily influenced, either deliberately or involuntarily, by the monotheistic and dualistic world views of Judaism, Christianity and/or Islam. Examples of Mesopagan belief systems include Freemasonry, Rosicrucianism, Spiritualism, Druidism as practised by the Masonic-influenced fraternal movements in Europe and the Celtic Isles, the many Afro-American faiths (such as Voudoun, Santeria, or Macumba), Sikhism, and several sects of Hinduism that have been influenced by Islam and Christianity.

'Neopaganism' refers to those religions created since 1940 or so (though they had literary roots going back to the mid-1800s), that have attempted to blend what their founders perceived as the best aspects of different types of Paleopaganism with modern 'Aquarian Age' ideals, while consciously striving to eliminate as much as possible of the traditional Western monotheism and dualism. The Church of All Worlds, most Wiccan traditions, ADF and Keltria (*see p. 77*), are all Neopagan.

These terms do not delineate clear-cut categories. Historically, there is often a period, whether of decades or centuries, when Paleopaganism is blending into Mesopaganism, or Mesopaganism into Neopaganism. Furthermore, the founders and members of Meso-pagan and Neopagan groups frequently prefer to believe, or at least to seem to, that they are genuinely Paleopagan in beliefs and practices. This 'myth of continuity' is in keeping with the habits of most founders and members of new religions throughout human existence.

Druidism, Ancient & Modern

So how does this vocabulary work in terms of Druidism? We know that the original, Paleopagan, Druids were a social class of intellec-tuals and artists, with counterparts in the other Indo-European cultures, such as the brahmins in India and the flamens in Ancient Italy; however, only the Celtic ones were called 'Druids'. They were of both genders and had several sub-classes, such as Bards, sacrificers, healers, diviners, and judges. They were polytheists, not monotheists, and it is probably true that they did offer human sacrifices from time to time. However, they did not build Stonehenge or the pyramids, did not all have long white beards, did not come from Atlantis, and probably few of them had golden sickles. These Druids functioned primarily as the transmitters of knowledge and culture from one generation to the next, and as performers and supervisors of the ceremonies they believed necessary to keep the forces of chaos at bay. Though deep in their esoteric and exoteric knowledge, they were probably no wiser than the medicine people, Shamans, and Witchdoctors of any other culture.

Most scholars believe that the original Paleopagan Druids were wiped out by the Roman Empire and the Roman Catholic Church, with only scattered remnants of their beliefs and traditions surviving underground among the Bards and brehons (or judges), of the Celtic peoples. There is no sound historical or anthropological evidence for a surviving intact tradition of Druidism – as distinct from scattered folk or family customs – anywhere in the world, with the possible exception of their cousins in the Baltic territories, who may have kept a form of Lithuanian Paleopaganism alive well into the twentieth century.

The fraternal or Mesopagan Druid groups were started in the 1700s, probably well over a thousand years after the last Celtic Druid had died, by well-meaning individuals who were not adverse to 'fibbing' about their individual and group histories. Iolo Morganwg, for example, was an early supporter of (Christian) Unitarianism, and by an odd coincidence, it turns out that the Paleopagan Druids he wrote about were all Unitarians too!

These Mesopagan Druid groups met the needs of many people for a form of Paganism that would not require them to be publicly known as non-Christian. They did this by claiming that Druidism was not a specific religion but rather a philosophy applicable to any faith, and that the Paleopagan Druids had 'really' been, not just monotheists, but 'Pre-Christian Christians', waiting around patiently for Jesus to be born so they could all run out and convert!

One of these Mesopagan Druid groups may have influenced the first of the modern American Druid organizations, the Reformed Druids of North America. Originally founded in 1963 as a protest against coerced religion at Carleton, a small midwestern college, the

RDNA wound up continuing long after the protestors had won. Its polytheology was a sort of Zen Unitarianism, supporting a philosophy of constant questioning and meditation which was applicable to almost any religious quest. In this, as in some of its liturgical language, the RDNA closely resembled the Mesopagan groups. The founder of the RDNA, David Fisher, at one time claimed to have already been a Druid when he arrived at Carleton College.

The RDNA ceremonies invoked the Earth Mother as 'a personification of the material world' or Mother Nature, a Sky God called Be'al (based on a proto-Celtic root 'bel', referring to brightness or fire, as in Belenos, a Celtic Sun God) as 'a personification of the abstract essence of reality', and several Gods and Goddesses from the various Celtic countries. The Buddhist-style meditations and Celtic deity invocations had a powerful effect upon the young people who started the RDNA, (messing around with archetypes can do that), and many of them carried the 'faith' to other colleges when they graduated or transferred from Carleton. However, since the founders were far more concerned with individual philosophical and religious freedom than with the efficient operation of organizational structures, few of the local congregations, or 'groves', seem to have lasted for very long, and no national network was ever successfully created. Nonetheless, new groves still seem to spring up occasionally in the United States and Canada. Carleton College now has as an official part of its library, The International Druid Archives, assembled by recent graduate and RDNA historian Michael Scharding. It includes copies of the just published 'A Reformed Druid Anthology', incorporating my own 'The Druid Chronicles (Evolved)' with much additional material from other RDNA founders and authors. (This is available on the World Wide Web and in electronic format – look for pointers on the <www.adf.org> Home Page and on other Pagan Web Pages).

I was ordained as a Druid priest by Carleton graduate Robert Larson in October 1969. I was actively involved in the RDNA for several years, eventually editing the writings of the founders and adding materials of my own to produce the book mentioned above, 'The Druid Chronicles (Evolved)'. As time went by, I became increasingly convinced that Reformed Druidism should admit to being a Neopagan religion, and I worked to make its liturgy as effective as possible. Not too surprisingly, those early RDNA members who thought of themselves as Christians, Buddhists, and Agnostics, found my missionary zeal appalling.

After several false starts, with the New RDNA, the Schismatic DNA, the Hasidic DNA, to name a few, in 1983 I began 'A Druid

Fellowship', or ADF; a fellowship rooted in the use of modern scholarship, effective liturgical design, and artistic excellence. I wanted to
create a completely new and emphatically Neopagan Druid tradition. Naturally, small group politics being what they are, we have had
a few branchings-out of our own. The largest branch is Keltria, which
'schismed' from ADF a few years ago to focus their energies on
specifically Keltic Druidism (as distinct from ADF's use of Indo-
European sources in addition to Celtic ones), and on the esoteric
aspects of Druidry. For the rest of this chapter, I'll discuss Neopagan
Druidism as practised in ADF. Keltria is similar in most ways, but you
can write to them directly for details (*see the resource list at the back of
this book*).

Neopagan Druid Beliefs

Many of the members of ADF have come to accept most of the
following beliefs. However, it is important to remember that not
everyone would use the term 'belief' in reference to these concepts,
and that every concept mentioned has a wide variety of accepted
interpretations within the organization.

Thou Art God/dess: We believe that divinity is both immanent
(internal) and transcendent (external), with immanence being far
more needful at this crucial phase of human history. Deities can
manifest at any point in space or time they choose, including within
human beings, through the processes known as 'inspiration',
'channelling', and 'possession'.

Goddesses and Gods: We believe that divinity is as likely to manifest in a female form as it is in a male form, and that the word
'Goddess' makes just as much sense as 'God'. Women and men are
spiritual equals, and 'masculine' and 'feminine' attitudes, values, and
roles are of equal importance.

Polytheism: We believe in a multiplicity of Gods and Goddesses,
as well as lesser beings, many of Whom are worthy of respect, love
and worship. We have a wide variety of non-exclusive concepts as to
the nature of these entities. While some of us believe in a 'Supreme
Being', Neopagan Druidism is emphatically polytheistic. We have no
figure of ultimate Evil.

Nature Worship: We believe that it is necessary to have respect and love for Nature as divine in Her own right, and to accept ourselves as part of Nature, rather than Her 'rulers'. Many of us accept what has come to be known as 'the Gaia hypothesis': that the biosphere of our planet is a living being, Who is due all the love and support that we, Her children, can give Her. We consider ecological awareness and activism to be sacred duties.

Cautious Technophilia: We believe in accepting the positive aspects of Western science and technology, but in maintaining an attitude of wariness towards the supposed ethical neutrality of that science and technology. We also consider it important that scientists (like everyone else) pay as much attention to their means as they do to their goals.

Religious Freedom: We believe that monolithic religious organizations, would-be messiahs and super-gurus are a hindrance to spiritual growth. We believe that healthy religions should have a minimum amount of dogma and a maximum amount of eclecticism and flexibility. Neopagan Druidism is an organic religion, and like all other organisms is growing, changing, and producing offshoots.

Positive Ethics: We believe that ethics and morality should be based upon joy, love, self-esteem, mutual respect, the avoidance of actual harm to ourselves and others, and the increase of public benefit. We try to balance people's needs for personal autonomy and growth with the necessity of paying attention to the impact of each individual's actions on the lives and welfare of others.

Religious Toleration: We believe that it is difficult for ordinary humans to commit offences against the Gods and Goddesses, short of major crimes such as ecocide or genocide. Our deities are perfectly capable of defending Their own honour without any need for us to punish people for 'blasphemy' or 'heresy'.

The Good Life: We believe that human beings were meant to lead lives filled with joy, love, pleasure, beauty and humour. Most Neopagans are fond of food, drink, music, sex, and bad puns, and consider all of these (except possibly the puns) to be of spiritual value. However, we do not approve of addictive or compulsive behaviour, and we support people with dysfunctional histories who have entered appropriate recovery programs.

Magic and Mystery: We believe that with proper training, art, discipline and intent, human minds and hearts are fully capable of performing most of the magic and miracles they are ever likely to need. Magical/miraculous acts are done through the use of what most of us perceive as natural, (some say 'divinely granted') psychic talents.

Liturgical Art and Science: We believe that there is an art and a science to creating, preparing and performing worship rituals. Our worship celebrations are continually evolving as we search for the most intellectually satisfying, artistically beautiful, spiritually powerful, and magically effective rites possible.

Connecting to the Cosmos: We believe in the importance of celebrating the solar, lunar and other cycles of our lives. We consciously observe the solstices, equinoxes, and the points in between, as well as the phases of the moon. Such 'rites of intensification' are human universals, as are the various ceremonies known as 'rites of passage' – celebrations of birth, puberty, personal dedication to a given deity or group, marriage, ordination, death and so forth. Together, these various sorts of observations help us to find ourselves in space and time.

Born-Again Paganism: Many of us believe in some sort of afterlife, usually involving rest and recovery in the Otherworld before reincarnating. We have no concept of 'eternal' punishment, refusing to worship deities who could be that cruel.

Hope and Action: We believe that people have the ability to solve their current problems, both personal and public, and to create a better world. Our utopian vision, tempered with common sense, leads us to a strong commitment to personal and global growth, evolution and balance.

Mystic Vision: We believe that people can progress far towards achieving personal growth, evolution and balance through the carefully planned alteration of their 'normal' states of consciousness. We use both ancient and modern methods of concentration, meditation, reprogramming and ecstasy.

Community Responsibility: We believe that human interdependence implies community service. Some of us are active in political, social, ecological and charitable organizations, while others prefer to work for the public good primarily through spiritual means (and many insist on doing both).

Authenticity: We believe that if we are to achieve any of our goals, we must practice what we preach. Neopagan Druidism, like any other religion, should be a way of life, not merely a weekly or monthly social function. So we must always strive to make our lives consistent with our proclaimed beliefs.

Cooperation and Defense: We believe in cooperation and ecumenical activities with those members of other faiths who share all or most of these beliefs. We also believe in resisting efforts by members of dysfunctional religions who seek to persecute us or suppress our human rights.

There is more to Neopagan Druid beliefs than the information given here, of course, and a great deal of variation in how these beliefs are extended to cover other topics. Some of our members are pacifists and others are in the military; some are animal rights activists and vegetarians, others are carnivorous hunters; some are committed to conservative, others to alternative lifestyles. We actively encourage everyone to apply these principles to the practical questions of their daily lives.

Neopagan Druid Ceremony

ADF rituals, including the public worship rites known as 'liturgies', are rooted firmly in what we have been able to reconstruct of the cosmologies of the Paleopagan Indo-Europeans. These were interwoven, complex, and multivalued, though remarkably similar from culture to culture, and were reflected in the social structures and myths of each culture, as the Dumezilian school of comparative mythology has clearly demonstrated. George Dumezil was the scholar who single-handedly rehabilitated the field of comparative religion after decades of it being academically unfashionable. His theories have been substantiated and fleshed out by many respected scholars, as well as by myself and other Neopagan researchers.

One cosmology incorporates the idea of a 'polar' vertical axis reaching from the Celestial Realm above, down through 'Here', or the Midrealm that humans normally live and function in, down to a Chthonic Realm or Underworld below. This vertical axis is often symbolized with a Sacred Fire, a Sacred Well and a Sacred Tree. The Fire represents divinity descending from the Celestial Realm, the Well divinity ascending from the Chthonic Realm, and the Tree represents that which connects all the Worlds and Realms.

Another cosmology is that of the 'Three Worlds' of Land, Waters (sometimes called 'Sea'), and Sky (sometimes called 'Middle Air'). These can be seen as a horizontal axis running through the centre of the vertical one, which is the here and now, with the Worlds being reflected in the Celestial and Chthonic Realms. A polarity of values running through all these is that of 'light' forces and beings (of order/safety, not necessarily of Good) and 'dark' forces and beings (of chaos/danger, not necessarily of Evil) existing in every World and Realm. Yet another polarity is that of 'Here' and 'Outside' (or 'the Otherworld' or 'Faery'), marking a distinction between the physical and the spiritual aspects of reality. All of these cosmological concepts can be seen in Neopagan Druid rituals, with emphases varying, depending upon which particular Indo-European culture a given grove has chosen to focus. (All are allowed, though Irish is the most common.)

The primary deity worshipped by Neopagan Druids is the Earth Mother, also known as Mother Nature or Gaia. She can be thought of as the consciousness of the biosphere, as a personification of the fertility of the Earth, the Mother of all other deities – at least those worshipped by humans on this planet – and so forth. Gaia is the literal and metaphysical ground upon which we stand, the source and mirror of all that lives and dies. She is mentioned prominently near the beginning and end of every Neopagan Druidic ceremony.

ADF liturgy also focuses strongly on a Divine Gatekeeper, deities or other spirits of Bardic inspiration, the 'Three Kindreds' of Deities, Ancestors and Nature Spirits, and even the forces of Chaos – very carefully. Every ADF liturgy has a specific Divine 'guest of honour' or two, to whom the majority of our worship is dedicated. Our offerings consist of songs, chants, dances, ritual dramas, poems and other works of art. These are 'sacrificed' instead of the blood offerings of our Paleopagan predecessors.

The Vision of Neopagan Druidism:

What makes ADF different from other Druidic organizations and other Neopagan traditions? This is how we see it:

In ADF we believe that excellence in scholarship is vitally important. The Goddesses and Gods do not need us to tell lies on their behalf, nor can we understand the ways of our Paleopagan predecessors by indulging in romantic fantasies, no matter how 'politically correct' or emotionally satisfying they might be. So we promote no tall tales of universal matriarchies, of Stonehenge being built by Druid magic, nor of the ancient Druids originally having been Shamanic crystal-masters from Atlantis. We do not whitewash the occasional barbarism of our predecessors, nor exaggerate it. We use real archeology, real history and real comparative mythology – and we are willing to change our opinions when new information becomes available, even if it destroys our pet theories. This approach is rare in the history of Druidic revivals and the Neopagan community.

In ADF we also believe that artistic excellence is important, both in ritual and outside of it. The Gods and Goddesses deserve the very best that we can give them, so we encourage our members to develop their creative skills to the highest levels that each can attain. Our Bards, painters, woodcarvers, needleworkers and liturgists are among the best in the Neopagan community.

In ADF we believe that excellence in clergy training and practice is vital for any healthy, growing religion. To that end, we are attempting to create a professional clergy training programme equal in rigour and superior in results to anything done by the world's other religions. Unlike many alternative religions, we will never have 'instant initiations' into our clergy. Nor do we assume that every member of our religion will have a genuine vocation to the clergy, though it is likely that, for the first couple of decades, a high proportion will. However, we expect that eventually the vast majority of our people will be laity. Nonetheless, everyone is expected to communicate with the Goddesses and Gods in her or his own way – spiritual growth is not a monopoly of the clergy. Every human being needs to learn how to contact the divine fire within, how to talk with trees, and how to unleash the power of magic to save the Earth. If there is such a thing as 'spiritual excellence', we must strive to express that as well.

ADF's study programme is unlike those of any other Druidic organization, in that we assume that the primary purpose of participants
is to undertake leadership roles within the Neopagan Community.
Thus we have a 'university without walls' system of academic and
practical studies, designed to produce professional level clergy,
Bards, judges, healers, ecologists and others. Credit is given for life
experiences and students are expected to be able to demonstrate
their knowledge and skills upon request. While esoteric studies,
including magic and mysticism, are part of the programme, exoteric
studies, including first aid, non-profit management, history, comparative religions, counselling and mainstream science, are emphasized.
It can take several years for a person to work her or his way through
the programme, but we are not in any hurry.

Naturally, we believe that liturgical excellence is rooted in these
other forms of excellence. Sound scholarship (especially historical
and mythological), beautiful art, genuinely competent clergy, and
people who are ready, willing, and able to channel divine energies –
all are crucial to creating the powerful religious and magical ceremonies that we and the Earth so desperately need.

We have two mottos that we have been using so far. The first is
based on the ideas just described: 'Why not excellence?' This
emphasis on excellence as a goal makes us both unique and controversial within the Neopagan community. Although some folks think
that such an emphasis 'isn't democratic', we feel that our concept of
divine immanence implies that everyone has something they are
good at (you just need to contact the deities within you and channel
Their creative power). However, our second motto – 'As fast as a
speeding oak tree!' – serves to remind us all that the achievement of
excellence takes time.

We have already officially declared the first Druidic dogma: the
Doctrine of Archdruidic Fallibility. No one in ADF, not even the
Archdruid, has all the answers. We make no claims of handing down
an 'authentic' unbroken tradition from the past, and have very strong
doubts about any group that does make such claims. Thus we are free
to evolve our systems within the organic structures already created,
adapting them as necessary to suit the needs of coming generations.
We are also free to make many mistakes in the process – a freedom
we've already taken advantage of. Every member of ADF has both the
opportunity and the obligation to contribute her or his time, money,
energy and talents to the adventure.

We believe that Neopaganism is eventually going to become a
mainstream religious movement, with hundreds of thousands (if not

millions) of members, and that this will be a good thing, both for the individuals involved, and for the survival of the Earth Mother. Neopaganism is currently riding the crest of the 'baby boom'. Many people who grew up in the 1960s and 70s are discovering us at about the same time that they are realizing both the desperate state of our planet and the eternal relevance of our youthful ideals. Membership in the Neopagan community is quietly growing at a geometric rate, both through word of mouth and through the many do-it-yourself books now available, giving us an ever greater impact on the mainstream culture as a whole.

All these Neopagans are going to need publically accessible worship, teaching, counselling and healing. Within thirty years we expect to see indoor temples and / or sacred groves throughout North America and Europe, staffed by full-time, paid, professional clergy. These will provide the full range of needed services to the Neopagan community, with no more 'corruption' than that experienced by the Unitarians, the Buddhists, or the Quakers. We anticipate globally televised Samhain rites at Stonehenge, and Beltane ceremonies attended by thousands in every major city. We see Neopagan clergy taking part in international religious conferences as equals with clergy from other faiths. We see our children wearing pentacles, Druid Sigils, and Thor Hammers to school as easily as others now wear crosses, Stars of David, or Hands of Fatima. We see talented and well trained Neopagan clergy leading thousands of people in effective magical and mundane actions to save endangered species, stop polluters, and preserve wilderness. We see our healers saving thousands of lives and our Bards inspiring millions through music and video concerts and dramas. We see Neopaganism as a mass religion, changing social, political, and environmental attitudes around the world and stopping the death-mongers in their tracks.

This vision is very different from that of most current Neopagans, who focus on small groups as their ideal. Those small groups will always be an essential part of the Neopagan religious community, operating both within and apart from larger organizations, just as their equivalents have throughout human history. As we see it, the future of Neopaganism will require a wide variety of different group sizes, structures, and ritual styles. To lose any of the currently existing approaches risks impoverishing our spiritual 'gene pool'. So we are not out to 'replace' other Neopagan traditions, even though we believe that we have something unique and wonderful to share with the world.

Doing that sharing requires 'going public', something that many

Neopagan traditions have been reluctant to do. Granted, it may remain necessary, for another decade or two, for some Neopagans to remain in hiding wherever fundamentalist hate is rampant. Even for those of us in publicly-oriented Neopagan groups, it will take courage and caution for us to safely 'come from the shadows'. Yet, if we follow the lessons learned by the civil rights movements of our generation, we will eventually have full freedom to practise our beliefs. Accepting and encouraging our community's growth, while avoiding missionary fever, will be a vital tool in achieving that task.

We believe that Neopagan Druidism has an important role to play in the future of Neopaganism and the survival of the Earth. Already, other Neopagan traditions are imitating ADF's training programme, our liturgical techniques, and our emphasis on the Arts. If we can attract enough people who are willing to dedicate their time, energy, and money to achieving these goals, the vision can be manifested. We can save the Earth Mother, create a global culture of prosperity and freedom, and usher in a genuine 'New Age'.

Suggested Reading

The following books will get you started on understanding ADF's approach to reconstructing Druidism:

Scott Littleton, C. *The New Comparative Mythology, An Anthropological Assessment of the Theories of Georges Dumezil*, Third Edition, University of California, 1980. This is the best critical introduction to Dumezil's work, with an extensive bibliography of relevant books and articles by Dumezil and others.

Doniger O'Flaherty, Wendy. *Women, Androgynes, and Other Mythical Beasts*, University of Chicago, 1982. O'Flaherty (now known as Doniger) gives an extensive discussion of the sexual politics of the IE myth system using sound research and a clear presentation. She is also the author of: *Shiva, the Erotic Ascetic; The Origins of Evil in Hindu Mythology; Other People's Myths*; and an excellent translation of the *Rig Veda*, among many other books and articles.

Piggott, Stuart. *The Druids*, Thames and Hudson, 1985. The best book on the subject so far, covering the archaeological, classical, and historical evidence concerning the Druids, both Paleopagan and Mesopagan, albeit in a very anti-romantic and anti-religious style.

Adler, Margot. *Drawing Down the Moon*, Beacon Press, 1987. This is the best book that anyone has published about Neopagan movements in America. Note, however, that the discussions of Reformed Druidism do not reflect what is going on in ADF today. There is a nice section on ADF starting at p. 325 in this second edition.

Bonewits, Isaac. *Real Magic*, Samuel Weiser, Inc., 1989. A basic introduction to the theory and practice of magic. Includes an extensive bibliography of other titles that will be helpful.

Freidrich, Paul. *Proto-Indo-European Trees*, University of Chicago, 1970. Primarily a linguistic monograph, this is the only book to cover in detail the various species of trees known to have had names in the PIE language. He includes a great deal of religious and symbolic detail.

Stover, Leon E. and Kraig, Bruce. *Stonehenge, the Indo-European Heritage*, Nelson-Hall, 1978. A harsh but fascinating look at the people associated with the various stages of Stonehenge's construction. The authors belong to the 'hard primitivism' school of IE studies, are hostile to religion and positively rabid about clergy, but the book does an excellent job of straightening out the bewildering array of prehistoric and early IE cultures. The bibliography and research notes are great.

Smith, Brian K. *Reflections on Resemblance, Ritual, and Religion*, Oxford University Press, 1989. A superb introduction to the complex world of Vedic ritual and metaphysics. Much of what puzzles the author will make perfectly good sense to Neopagan ritualists, and will give us some glimpses of what western Druidism must have been like.

Eliade, Mircea. *A History of Religious Ideas*, 3 volumes. Vol 1 – *From the Stone Age to the Eleusinian Mysteries,* University of Chicago Press, 1978, and Vol 2 – *From Gautama Buddha to the Triumph of Christianity*, University of California Press, 1982, are of most value to Neopagans. This is simply the best material on the history of religious ideas available, organized both chronologically and thematically. It includes an enormous amount of information on Paleopaganism and early Christianity.

Rees, Alwyn Brinley. *Celtic Heritage*, Thames & Hudson, 1961. A Dumezilian analysis of Celtic mythology and religion, based primarily on Irish and secondarily on Welsh materials. Gives an excellent overview of basic patterns of belief, and will explain much of the cosmology underlying Celtic mythology and ritual.

Hutton, Ronald. *The Pagan Religions of the Ancient British Isles, Their Nature and Legacy*, Blackwell, 1991. A brilliant review of the history, prehistory and psuedohistory of British Paleopaganism. This is an excellent tour of all 'the things we know that just ain't so', and belongs in every Druid's library.

Lewis, Bernard. *History – Remembered, Recovered, Invented*. Princeton University Press, 1975. A succinct introduction to the ways in which people filter history through their personal and cultural needs, fears and wishes, even when they are trying to be unbiased. An excellent cure for excessive romanticism, scientolatry, and matriarchal fever.

Caesar, Julius, trans. Anne and Peter Wiseman. *The Battle for Gaul*, Chatto & Windus, London, 1980. A modern colloquial translation, filled with dozens of explanatory maps, photographs and drawings.

Carr-Gomm, Philip. *Elements of the Druid Tradition*, Element Books, 1991. A brief introduction to the facts and fancies of Mesopagan Druidism, by the current Chosen Chief of the Order of Bards, Ovates and Druids. Overtly romantic, yet honest about absent historical evidence. Includes excellent guided meditations and good ideas about bridging the gaps between Meso- and Neopagan Druids. Also recommended is Carr-Gomm's *The Druid Way*, the story of a vision quest/pilgrimage through the landscape of southern England, Element Books, 1993.

Some 300 or so additional recommended books can be found in the back of *The ADF Study Manual*.

We do **not** recommend any non-fiction by Robert Graves (on Celtic topics), D.J. Conway, Douglas Monroe, Lewis Spence, H.P. Blavatsky, Edward Williams (aka Iolo Morganwg), or any works by others based on their writings, nor those of Merlin Stone, Barbara Walker, or other revisionist ideologues. Much of what is available in print about the ancient Druids is hogwash, so read carefully and beware of univerified assumptions, nationalistic biases, monotheistic reinterpretations, or claims of intact underground family traditions of Druidism. When in doubt, consult your nearest tree …

Isaac Bonewits has been a Druid priest for over 25 years, and a Wiccan priest for 15 years. He is one of North America's best-known authorities on Neopaganism, Druidism, Witchcraft and the Occult. He holds the only accredited (B.A.) degree ever given in Magic, (U.C. Berkeley), and is the author of the classic introductory textbook, *Real Magic*, as well as the infamous FRP game magic system, *Authentic Thaumaturgy*. He is the founder and Archdruid Emeritus of *A'r nDrai'ocht Fe'in*: A Druid Fellowship ('ADF'), the largest and best known Neopagan Druid movement in North America, and co-leads a Gardnerian coven with his wife, Deborah Lipp. He is also a singer and songwriter of Pagan songs, some of which have appeared on two albums: 'Be Pagan Once Again!' and 'Avalon Is Rising!', with a third, 'We Are One Family!', to be released in Winter 1995/6. He was an early fighter for Aquarian civil rights, having written the *Aquarian Manifesto* and started the seminal Aquarian Anti-Defamation League in 1974. On January 1, 1996 he resigned his position as Archdruid of ADF and is currently finishing books on Neopagan polytheology and liturgical design, as well as his own histories of Druidism and Witchcraft.

He can be contacted through P.O. Box 1021, Nyack, NY, USA 10960-1021, as well as through IBonewits@aol.com and via other online services. He is especially interested in hearing from European and South American Druid organizations.

@@

Steve Wilson

THE IRISH BARDIC TRADITION

For the greater part, the modern Druidic revival has depended on Welsh, or Brythonic, material and associated lore for its written sources. It is strange that the Gaelic tradition, best represented in Ireland, has been so far rather neglected. It is true that this tradition lacks some of the features that make the Welsh material so attractive; there is little mention of King Arthur and none whatsoever of the Grail; but what initially seems to be missing is more than made up for in other ways, and it is a great mistake to consider the Irish tradition as merely the same as the Welsh but in a different language.

The differences between Gaelic and Brythonic Druidry pre-date the legends of Arthur by many centuries. There is ample evidence to show that the Brythons, who are the ancestors of the Cornish, Welsh and Bretons, and the Gaels, ancestors of the Irish, the Manx and most of the Scots, were separate cultures before either arrived in the British Isles. The Brythons appear to have arrived from the east, and a supposedly Germanic tribe called the Cimbri retained their Celtic name, which is analogous to 'Cymru', long after their kin colonized Britain. The Gaels appear to have arrived from the south. Above all, the Gaelic peoples were never part of the Roman Empire. While British and Gallic Druids were sought out by emperors and philosophers, the Gaelic Druids remained beyond the influence of Rome, beyond Hadrian's Wall, beyond the Irish Sea. Only when the Empire began to disintegrate did Gaels invade any other part of Britain, establishing colonies in North Wales. It is this small-scale colonizing that has obscured an important fact: that the Ogham script so beloved of modern Druids is uniquely Gaelic; the Ogham stones found in Wales are all in this tongue.

Furthermore, when the Anglo-Saxon peoples settled in what was to become England, their long struggle with the Brythonic peoples, which, even today, is far from over, did not really affect the Gaels for an entire millennium. True, England and Scotland would war occasionally but, until less than four centuries ago, the Gaelic language was never put under the same pressure as Welsh and Cornish. The same is true of its Druidic tradition.

In Wales, as in the rest of these islands, Christianity demanded the removal of anything Druidic, but the Kings and Princes refused to give up their Bards. It was an essential part of Celtic royal life to have a trained singer in court who could praise his master, his master's ancestors and his master's land holdings. The English, however, constantly attempted to suppress Bardism, and later the entire language. The result has been that Brythonic Bardism has had to concentrate on keeping the language alive and the poetry pure. With the Gaels it has been a very different story.

The most well known description of the 'grades' of Druidry comes from Caesar, who speaks of Bards, Vates (often known today as Ovates) and Druids proper. In Wales, it seems that only the Bardic grade survived. In Gaeldom the response to Christianity, free from Anglo-Saxon pressure, was less clear cut. The Irish certainly had their three grades; the Bard, the Faidh (Vates) and Draoidh (Druid, now pronounced dree). However, just under a millennium ago a new grade appeared, that of the filidh ((pronounced feel-ye). This group took over from the Bards as the custodians of Ireland's lore while the Faidh and Draoidh apparently disappeared. So who were they? To answer this, a little of their history and training methods must be examined.

In spite of its remoteness from the rest of the western world, throughout the dark ages Ireland was the main centre of learning in the Roman Catholic world. Knowledge of the Greek language died out in Rome before it did in Ireland, and scholars from all over the west would come to Ireland to learn. They would, if they passed their exams, add the word 'Scotus' to their name to boast of the quality of their education; Scotus meant a member of the tribe of Scota, the Irish clan that colonized much of northern Britain before the Romans arrived, and who gave their name to Scotland. This legacy remains in the shape of the letters of the Irish alphabet, which is clearly of Greek rather than Roman design.

Eventually, Irish learning seems to have declined, yet this coincided with the rise of the Filidh. It is no mere speculation to suggest that the Druids retained their knowledge at the universities, and then passed it to the Filidh as pressure for orthodoxy increased. Certainly, the Bards seem to have gladly passed their mantle on to the newcomers, and the Filidh amply fulfilled the Bardic role. It is in their training that we see that there was something more involved.

We know from Julius Caesar's 'Gallic Wars' that the full training programme, from apprentice Bard up to fully qualified Druid, took about twenty years. Caesar says little more, but it certainly seems a long time, which makes it even more surprising when we find out that training as a Filidh took the same period. This was not a full-time course, as it were, running only throughout the winter, but it takes only a small leap of imagination to guess that this was the way all Druids were originally trained. Even more revealing is the method of training. Filidhs were housed in windowless bothies, or turf cottages, throughout daylight, only emerging at sunset. Obviously, this rather unhealthy lifestyle seems totally unnecessary simply to have become an accomplished poet. What we can see here is something even older than the Druidic tradition: the underworld initiation of the Shaman. This process, found in one culture after another, takes the form of a journey from life, through death and then to rebirth. In Druidism, or in Filidhic training at the very least, this was taken to extremes. What is more, the twenty symbolic deaths and rerbirths coincided with the same process in the natural world, beginning as the last leaves fell and finishing as the first buds re-appeared.

We can hazard a further guess as to the process undergone, since some of the training schedule for the Filidh survives, and includes '20 Oghams' to be memorized each year. Some interpret this to mean 20 scripts, for besides the straight-line Ogham script used on monuments, the mediaeval *Book of Ballymote* lists many more. However, an Ogham also meant a list, again of twenty. The first of these is the twenty-letter Irish alphabet, memorized by naming each letter after a tree. The survival of the names of these trees indicates that this Ogham, generally known as the Celtic Tree Alphabet, was the foremost. Even the most exoteric of modern Irish dictionaries gives each letter a name; that of its relevant tree. Indeed, the Irish for 'letter' means 'tree', and although the modern alphabet contains 25 letters, we can deduce from the original 20 the nature of the training. The 20 death-and-rebirth semesters were necessary for absolute completeness, and while Druidism has always been associated with the number 3, 20 is equally important.

So what exactly were the 400 Oghams, apart from the Tree and the less well-known Bird Oghams? In simple terms, they were lists rather like those we use to teach children the alphabet: 'A is for Apple, B is for Bird' and so forth. But why so many? The answer lies in the importance of language to the Filidh.

During the period in question, the Old Irish language was evolving into the Mediaeval Gaelic in which the Filidhic poetry was composed. This is a highly formalized language, understood from the South West of Ireland to the North East of Scotland. It contains, like the earlier Gaelic tongue, traces of an extremely peculiar grammar, one which has been compared to that of the mysterious Basque peoples of southern France, Andorra and northern Spain. Unlike English, it has a completely regular system of spelling, and retains a peculiar pronunciation where every English consonant becomes three: 'long, short and breathed'. Even in Sanskrit, which is also an Indo-European language formalized by the wise, there are only two forms. This allows for much flexibility in poetry, something distinctly lacking from the actual rules of Filidhic verse, as we shall see.

The Filidh, and, it is reasonable to surmise, the ancient Druids as well, saw a divine origin in speech and writing, and believed that there was an intrinsic connection between things according to their names. Such a system is found in most esoteric schools, and is referred to as the doctrine of correspondences. Examples are the Hebrew Cabala, Laya Yoga and the Runic system. What is unusual about the Gaelic system is that it relies upon the first letter of a name or word. This must mean they assumed a divine origin not only to things, but also to the names of things. So the learning by rote of 400 lists of names was not for poetic reasons, it was to establish the magical links between different parts of creation. As such, this demonstrates that the Filidh was learning not only the art of the Bard, but also that of the Faidh, the magicians and healers.

If this seems mere superstition, remember that the practical tasks of Druidry had been in place long before the various Celtic languages split, and as such the naming of herbs, bushes, and birds would have been influenced by what the Druids knew. So if a herb and a tree had similar properties, it was simple enough to give the herb a name with the same initial letter as the tree. After all, most common herbs in English have several names, especially those with healing powers.

There was even more that the Filidh had to learn. Astonishingly, they had to memorize both the geography of the whole of Ireland and the family tree of the rulers of each clan, as well as being conversant with the 'Ulster Cycle' of myths, and later the tales of Finn MacCool. There was a practical purpose here, since each knowledge would be useful in composing court poetry for a particular king, but this does not seem to be how it was used for the most part. There were, after all, only so many courts and so many court poets. But the task of the Druidic grade was always that of law, and fell into two main connected categories, sovereignty and land. The Druids determined royal successions and mediated in land disputes. Suggestions in the *Book of Invasions*, a collection containing perhaps the earliest Celtic lore surviving today, indicate that division of the land was of paramount importance to the Gaels.

Thus the training of the Filidh incorporated both the Bardic, Faidhic and Draoidhic practices, all under the guise of poetry. So how can the modern Druid use this system and set about reviving it?

The first and most important thing to note is that the Filidh tradition never actually died out. When Cromwell invaded Ireland, the chief Filidhs fled to France, where they remained for only 30 years before returning. They used this time to commit much of their art to writing, and this, perhaps, contributed to their decline. Printing has made memorizing less necessary, and the modern Gaelic Druid can learn a great deal without having to repeat by rote for years on end. A second factor in this decline was the fragmentation of Gaeldom. Mediaeval Gaelic gave way to Early Modern Irish, and the Manx and Scots varieties began their drift away both from Irish and from each other. Soon a situation arose where the classical poetry was only understood by scholars. What is more, Filidhic poetry was chanted rather than sung, and by the eighteenth century, Ireland, like the rest of Europe, preferred stressed verse. There was no longer an audience for the complex poetry of the Filidh.

But the tradition had merely changed. The Aisling, the vision of sovereignty, continued in the writings about Caitlin Ni Houlihan, the symbolic figure representing poor, colonized Ireland. This love of song has continued to the point where Irish music dominates much of the world music industry in its American form, Country and Western, which is almost entirely Irish in origin. Dance, too, has gained, since the step-dancing accompanying Irish song also mutated in the USA into what we now call tap dancing. For that matter, in recent years Ireland has come to almost monopolize the dreaded, and often dreadful, Eurovision Song Contest.

But perhaps the final blow to the Filidhic tradition came when all but the six remaining colonized counties gained independence. Early independence fighters had little or no care for the Irish Gaelic language. Indeed, it is often forgotten that many early leaders were from the Protestant tradition, which despised Gaeldom (although

their ancestors had spoken the same tongue some 200 years earlier).
As such, language was much less of a factor in the Irish struggle than
in the Welsh. Even so, and perhaps worse in some ways, when independence came, modern Irish became a compulsory subject in Irish
schools. This should have ensured its survival, but generations of
Irish children instead came to detest having to learn their mother
tongue, seeing it as an antiquated hindrance in the modern world.
Compare this situation with that of the Welsh tongue, where the heat
of the battle against compulsory English-only schools has resulted in
an increasing number of speakers cherishing what was almost stolen
from them, as sadly has happened in Cornwall (except amongst
worthy nationalist revivalists).

Unfortunately, too many Irish people see Gaelic as part of the past;
irrelevant in the future and annoying in the present. The English-
speakers resent the fact that half of Irish broadcasting is in a
language only one-tenth of the people now understand. It is to be
hoped that some way is found to re-stimulate interest in this tongue.
Perhaps a revival of Filidhism would help, but this would suffer from
the other factor of 'semi-independence' for Ireland, due to the almost
cast-iron link between the Republic and the Catholic Church. Even
in modern Ireland it is not unknown for some rabble-rousing priest to
encourage the destruction of ancient Pagan monuments. The past of
Ireland is in very shaky hands.

But the path of the Filidh can and is being revived. The methods of
the past have been modified and adapted, but the rich spiritual life
gleaned from this ancient system is rewarding indeed, and this is how
it is being done.

The most prominent feature of both Celtic and Nordic poetry is
the existence of strict rules of composition. In the Filidhic tradition
these are extreme, and have been adapted for English versions.
There are many forms of this poetry, but all feature the following
aspects: a fixed number of lines in each verse; a fixed number, or
range of numbers of syllables in each line: rhymes at the end of
particular lines; internal rhymes within lines, between lines or both;
and alliterations within lines, between lines or both. This makes for a
very difficult task.

To understand why such exacting forms were developed, we can
turn to the other side of the world. Spiritual practice is not designed
to be easy, but to test and extend the abilities of the aspirant. This is
taken to extremes in Japan. Heavily influenced by Zen Buddhism,
the most famous poetic expression of this land is the Haiku. On the
surface this seems a simple verse of three lines containing, five,

seven, and again five syllables. However, it is the task of the poet to encapsulate an experience of supreme personal importance into this brief lyric. Japanese, unlike Chinese, is a polysyllabic language such as our own, so this is a very tough assignment. But it is the very toughness of the work that makes it worthwhile: the poet is forced to explore every avenue of thought, every expression available within the language, to succeed. And so it is with the Filidh. It is also noticeable that in both Japan and Ireland the basic subject is nature. The would-be Filidh must first express the beauty and spiritual content of experiencing the natural world in a particular place and time before going on to compose heroic or elegiac verse.

This was made even more difficult by what at first seems an extraordinary restriction. The student Filidh was encouraged to explore his surroundings during the warm months where there was no tuition. It is unlikely that such a student would be exempt from the agricultural duties of the rest of the people, although he was exempt from military service, so this exploration must have been a spare-time activity. Since he, like his tutor before him, would be expected to know much topography and geography, it would be natural to suppose that he sat in groves, or on hills or mountains, beside streams or waterfalls, composing verses about the place. In fact, this was strictly forbidden. Only in the darkness of winter, long removed from the beauties of spring and summer, would he be set verses to compose. His tutor would know his pupil's area from his own training and so be able to check the factual details, as well as set composition tasks that should be within the pupil's grasp.

I am not suggesting that no student ever cheated, memorizing features in advance, perhaps in the various poetic styles, so as to be ready for anything. Nor do I doubt that the tutors set surprise tasks, such as poems on a particularly unusual or inaccessible view. The point is that there seems to be another reason for this prohibition – the concept of incubation. It is as though the experience was meant to be denied, so that it could ferment in the subconscious, to be brought out again around the hearth when warm days were only a memory. Perhaps this is one of the reasons, though I can think of many more, that Irish song is often at its best, if saddest, when addressing what was long ago and far away.

In modern, anglicized Filidhism a similar approach is used, although in our training we use the cycles of day and month, rather than years. We explore our personal places of natural beauty, be it an ancient wood or a single tree in a road choked with traffic; we drink in and absorb the experience, and then avoid the same place until, one night, we begin the task.

So too do we explore the history of our surroundings. Place, and the correct ordering of things, was as essential to both Celt and Saxon as it is to the businessmen of Hong Kong, who employ 'Feng Shui' experts before building the most modern of office blocks. We learn our relationship, not only to ancient sites and features, but to their modern equivalent. It is all very well knowing that a spring rises near by, but where does the water you use to make your morning coffee actually come from?

This is no trivial point. The love of nature, history, geography, healing and justice, all essential to the Druid, cannot be confined to a study of the past. The Court Filidh had the power to force his employer to stand down by the use of satire, and there are many injustices in our world to which the modern Filidh can direct his or her words. Roads, water, heat, light; all are as essential now as ever, yet the control of them has too often fallen into the hands of people that the Celts of old would have despised. Roads are built through ancient sites and nature reserves, car fumes choke our children, our water is polluted and the modern source of much of our light and heat is a dangerous substance that will threaten us for literally thousands of years. Discovering just who controls the essentials of our lives can bring other surprises. Remembering that the question of sovereignty has always been of prime importance to the Druid, you may be shocked to discover just how many officials from public or even private utilities are legally empowered to force entry into your home.

Consequently, the modern Filidh must master the arts of irony, satire and parody, as well as those of scorn, polemic and invective. Without doubt his most effective poetic weapon is a contrast between the land as it was then and how it is now. But there are many other sources. And while it is good training for the Filidh to practice modern forms of the ancient poetic systems, for public recital modern, stressed verse and catchy tunes are far more important than correctness of form. And these can be of great use in defending our land.

This is not mere romanticism. The Filidh today cannot rely on Oghams to remember the properties of the natural world – not in English anyway – but a study of the principles of ecology is essential. Through modern sciences, we, the heirs to the Faidhic art of old, can understand exactly how our immediate environment, and the part we play in it, affects the rest of nature. This will lead to new concepts of justice, and new principles upon which laws, good laws, should be based.

All these issues bring together the wisdom of the past, and the needs of the present. We can see how the natural world *is*, and, through our Faidhic study, incubate the experience while applying Druidic principles of justice to see how the world *should be*. And, as spiritual values are lost in the rush for material wealth, the Bard can inspire others, using the knowledge of the Faidh and the wisdom of the Druid to begin righting the many wrongs being done to our planet. Where and how is up to the individual Filidh. Kings no longer want our services, nor do their successors deserve them. But just as the Bards of Wales and Filidhs of Ireland took their art into the 'hedges', teaching the people in secret, away from the government schools, so we too can educate outside the system.

The modern Filidh sees many carrying out this task who are unaware of this heritage. The protest-singer who accompanies the ecologist to the demonstration, where concerned citizens denounce the road-building and the relentless depletion of the planet's resources, defending the past and future from the blindness of the present; all are following part of the Filidhic tradition. And when today's warriors, without violence, hamper the destruction of our heritage, new songs and poems arise from those who are most inspired. The task of the modern Filidh, then, is to continue the Bardic tradition, not to do something that is not being done. It is just to use methods steeped in ancient tradition, in a way that is as inspiring as a Bard can make it, as true as a Faidh can determine, and as just as a Druid can determine. This is the primary task of the Filidh today.

Suggested Reading

Graves, Robert, *The White Goddess*, Faber, 1947, reprinted regularly.
   Justly criticized by many Druids for historical inaccuracy, this is essentially a book about poetry, and is an individualistic, creative and inspired work rather than the Pagan textbook it is usually consulted for. Its conclusions demonstrate how the poet can reach a personal vision (*Aisling*) of deity through the work of poesy, and should not be taken as objectively true. For all its flaws, without this book the entire modern Pagan movement, especially Druidry, would be very different.

Yeats, W.B, *A Vision,* 1929, many editions. Again, an inspired work, and again it should not be taken as objectively true. In point of fact, three quarters of this material was actually obtained from his wife's mediumship.

de Blaian, Aodh, *Gaelic Literature Surveyed,* Talbot, 1929, reprinted. Despite its dry title, this is the book that could have aided Druidry considerably when it was published, but everyone was reading Yeats' *Vision* at the time and it was missed. Contains all the rules of Irish Bardic poetry.

Aburrow, Yvonne, *The Enchanted Forest,* Capall Bann, 1994. An excellent work on tree lore.

Thorsson, Edred, *The Book of Ogham,* Llewelly, 1995. Better known for his work on Runes, Thorsson develops an entire system of thought based upon Ogham structure which should not be dismissed.

Recommended Poetry

The Poetry of Charles Williams. Too Christian for my own liking, Williams nevertheless shows how complex metre and mysticism can be welded together. His *Taliesin through Logres* demonstrates this at its best. He also wrote some great fiction.

The Poetry of Robert Graves. Recognized as Britain's greatest romantic poet of this century, Graves went to extreme lengths to wring each word from his deliberately tortured emotions. He also wrote some great fiction.

The Poetry of Aleister Crowley. For how not to do it: for all of his genius, Crowley was an appalling poet and as a mystic demonstrates what happens when form triumphs over content. Indiscipline in poetry, he inadvertently proves, is not in disobeying poetic rules, but in doing little else but obeying them. His inspired works, which are not truly poems, show what could have been. He also wrote some fiction.

The Poetry of Ross Nichols. An accomplished prose writer, essayist, editor, and water colourist, Ross Nichols was editor of *The Occult Observer,* author of *The Book of Druidry* (Aquarian, 1990) and Chosen Chief of *The Order of Bards Ovates & Druids.* Jay Ramsay, who has selected and introduced a new collection of his poetry entitled *Prophet Priest & King* (Oak Tree Press, 1996), considers him as one of the 'Apocalypse poets' of the 1940s, because of his preoccupations with myth, redemption, and rebirth. The Grove of the Four Elements of the Druid Clan of Dana was founded in honour of Ross Nichols and his poetry is well worth reading.

Steve Wilson has been involved in Paganism since the 1970s, and is currently an Ollabh (Chief Bard) in the Druid Clan of Dana, a daughter group of the Fellowship of Isis. He has made numerous radio and TV appearances as media officer for *The Council of British Druid Orders*, and has written *Robin Hood, Spirit of the Forest* (Neptune Press, 1993) and *Chaos Ritual* (Neptune Press, 1994). He edits *Aisling*, the Clan magazine, and organizes a course based on the Irish tradition known as the 'Filidhs of Oisin'. This course is assessed and is free of charge as long as stamps or IRCs are sent. For details on *Aisling* or the course write to PO Box 196, London WC1A 2DY. It is especially recommended to poets, authors and musicians, as well as other artists. The material in this chapter forms the core of a forth-coming book on Druidry.

Dr Michel Raoult

THE DRUID REVIVAL IN BRITTANY, FRANCE AND EUROPE

Although documents about Druids are quite rare, that does not mean they do not exist and that it was simply enough for Caesar to occupy Gaul to make the Druids and the whole of Celtic society surrounding them disappear as if by magic. Although the Druids and their traditions were undoubtedly sitting ducks – first for the occupying Roman armies, then for the militant Christian church which systematically allied itself with the various victorious invaders – they have never totally disappeared from the European continent.

The Importance of the Celtic area in ancient Europe

Practically the whole of Europe was of Indo-European origin and was in the majority Celtic. In effect, the Celtic domain stretched from the Baltic to the Mediterranean, from the Caucasus to Ireland and Spain. According to tradition, the famous Greek philosopher Pythagoras was welcomed into an Order of Druids at Marseille in 529 BC. We ought to remember that the Galatians, who founded Galatea, which later became Constantinople, were Celts who came from the Toulouse region of Gaul under the name of the Tectosage tribe; the very same tribe which established the Celtic realm of Ancyre, which eventually became Ankara, in Asia Minor. Indeed the Galatians were mentioned in an Epistle of Saul-Paul, the Christian missionary of the apostolic period, which would have been at a time before their conversion to Christianity and later to Islam. There were then, in this part of the world, Celts of the Druidic religion.

Afterwards, the term 'Celt' was only used to refer to the inhabitants of the various Gauls, and then further reduced to the far ends of

Occidental Europe, Ireland, Scotland, the Isle of Man, Wales, Cornwall, Armorican Brittany (the ancient name for the West part of Gaul), and Spanish Galicia. But the whole of ancient Europe and beyond was once populated by Celts and, despite the different invasions, the core of the European populations remained Celtic in origin.

Christianity Conquers the Empire

According to certain traditions, Christianity entered Gaul as early as the apostolic period with the first landing of Christian disciples near Marseille, among them Joseph of Arimathea and Mary Magdalene, who is said to have found shelter in a cave known as Sainte-Beaume where she is still worshipped today. Here, according to legend, was a Druid centre that eventually became a famous place of pilgrimage, visited even by the kings of France, as well as being an obligatory stop for the journeymen of the trade guilds since the dawn of time. Joseph of Arimathea, however, continued his voyage towards the Casseterides Islands, arriving in Great Britain and finally at Glastonbury, known as the ancient Celtic Avalon.

The Clash of Religions

The clash of religions mainly took place in Ireland with Saint Patrick, and it is likely that a certain number of Druids, who had been converted more or less superficially, joined the Celtic monasteries whilst others, faithful upholders of the ancient Druidic religion, went underground. One not very well-known group adopted a position halfway between these two tendencies and continued to exist autonomously under the name of the Culdeans or Culdees.

Druid-Monks or Monk-Druids?

It is certainly thanks to the initiates, who had become scribes in the monasteries, that the oral traditions of the Celts were transcribed on to manuscripts, which reached us with the inevitable alterations made necessary by the new Christian religion. Due to these manuscripts, however, many of our traditions were preserved. The influx of Celtic monks from the renowned Celtic monastic centres of Ireland, Scotland and Wales – one only has to think of personalities such as the Celtic monk Columba, (famous for saying, 'Jesus, my druid … ') and Colomban, (who expanded Celtic monasticism in Europe) – influenced the new Occidental Christian church to such an extent that it ended up adopting a certain number of Celtic traditions. Despite the various councils of the Church held in Gaul which officially condemned 'inconvenient' Druidic practices, the Celtic Christian missionaries somehow managed to assimilate and Christianize these traditional practices. Thus various Druidic traditions have filtered down to us – ritual processions following itineraries or labyrinths which were probably based on local telluric, or ley-line currents, such as tromenies (processions that turned around hills); tours of the parish; the pilgrimage to St-James-of-Compostella; Rogations (processions all around the parish territory, with clergy and parishioners); agrarian festivals of sowing and harvesting of the fruits of the earth, especially wheat and apples; festivals of horned animals or horses; even festivals of certain Celtic divinities such as Lugh, Cernunnos, and Dana, which were literally rehashed as festivals of St Michael, St Cornelius, and St Ann. Solstices and equinoxes were soon Christianized. Thus the Christian liturgical calendar was inevitably influenced by the Celtic festivals of the Druidic calendar that was already established, although these nevertheless varied slightly according to whether the Celtic tribes used either the lunar or the luni-solar calendar.

How the Festivals are named

An example is the festival of Samonios, the Irish Samhain, the meeting of the living and the dead, which is celebrated at the first new moon after the autumn equinox, either at the end of October or the beginning of November. This was adopted by the Church as the festival of all saints and became the Catholic 'All Saints Day' on November 1st, together with 'All Souls Day' on November 2nd.

Goddesses become Virgins

The same phenomenon occurred with Brigantia, the Irish Imbolc, the festival of the Goddess Brigit, which is celebrated at the end of January/beginning of February. This is also associated with Gallic divinities such as Epona or Belisama, the Druidic festival specifically dedicated to women, which was taken up by the Christians as the Purification of the Virgin Mary, and the Presentation of Jesus at the Temple on February 2nd, which is Candlemas.

Beltan, Beltane, or Beltaine, the festival and fire of the God Belenos, at the end of April/beginning of May was replaced by the festival of the apostles Philip and James-the-Younger on May 1st.

This was framed by that of Mark the Evangelist on April 25th, and of St-John the Apostle, on May 6th – which duplicates the festival of the same apostle on December 26th – and by the celebration of the apparition of Saint Michael on Mount Gargan (in 492 CE in Italy) on May 8th.

The Great Queen of the Celts becomes the Grandmother of Jesus

Lughnasad, the festival of the God Lugh the Luminous, which occurred around August 1st, became the festival of St Peter 'the Prince of the Apostles'. The brilliance associated with the festival of Lugh was echoed in the celebration of the Transfiguration of Christ on August 6th, which is flanked by important Christian festivals: the festival of the apostle James-the-Elder of Compostella in Galicia on July 25th and, on July 26th, the festival of St Ann, the official 'Great Mother of the Breton people' and patron of Brittany, as well as of Quebec, Montreal and Ottawa (undoubtedly because of the great number of people of Breton origin in Canada). Indeed, this St Ann, who was supposedly the Virgin Mary's mother and therefore Jesus' grandmother, but whose name does not appear in the New Testament, seems to be a substitute for the Goddess Dana, the High Queen of the Dana people, the Tuatha de Danaan of Celtic mythology.

Druid History Through Early Mediaeval Times to the Renaissance

The migrations of Celtic populations from the British Isles to the European continent in the sixth and eighth centuries contributed, despite barbarian invasions of all kinds, to a substantial Celtic revival in Europe. The Celtic Christian clergymen, generally called Scotts (which include the Culdeans as well as the Bretons, the Welsh and the Irish) either preceded or accompanied the migrants, and still communicated pre-Christian Celtic traditions which clashed with the Christian beliefs of Roman Latin influence.

The people that certain chroniclers labelled Saracens, referring to their invasions in the seventh century, were not necessarily all Muslims. They could also be Viking invaders who were still Pagan, as well as indigenous Celts who were militating in favour of a return to Druidic Paganism.

The Bards at the courts of the Irish and Welsh kings were the only members of the ancient Druidic sacerdotal class to be tolerated by the new Christianized society, which was in the full throes of change. They did not miss any chance to recall or transmit, albeit in a coded way, what is called 'the Matter of Britain' (Britain including both Greater Britain and Lesser Britain, or Brittany). This material served as the base for the compilation of the various versions of the 'Breton novels' of the Round Table cycle to the members of their brotherhood or fellow trouvères (a form of Bard, or minstrel) initiated into the princely courts and European castles. The Breton novels do not speak openly about Druids. However, the presence of characters such as Merlin the Magician – true initiate, pontiff, vehicle of the Druids' tradition and 'bridge', or continuity, between pre-history and the Age of Aquarius – is significant enough to convey the message. Indeed, the model of chivalry, as represented by the Round Table and inspired by Celtic tradition, re-enlivened even the warrior class, and women were once again respected, thanks to the diffusion in the West of a true cult of the Lady.

And the producing class should not be forgotten: the trade guilds modelled their organizations on the cathedral builders who put into practice the secrets of the trade they had inherited from the builders of megaliths, with the discreet support of the clandestine Druids, who left signs of their participation for those who know how to read the stones.

Certain dates are marked over this time. It is said that a grove of Druids known as Cor Emrys was established in the City of Oxford before 1066 CE. This name, Cor Emrys, or City of Ambrosia, is rich in innuendo, and evokes at the same time: the Pleiades constellation, the earth's magnetism, the circle of giants of Ambrius Hill – the megalithic astronomic calendar of Stonehenge – the traditions of Atlantis and Hyperborea, and characters such as those in the Round Table cycle of Breton novels.

In 1136 CE Geoffrey of Monmouth, the Canon of Oxford, published his *History of the Kings of Britain* thus making the keys to western tradition available to enlightened scholars. In about 1155, the Norman poet Wace followed in his footsteps by popularizing the legend of the Knights of the Round Table, which fired the Celtic imagination and which would literally enchant all of the Middle Ages. Tradition has it that in 1245, a grove of Druids known as the Mount-Haemus Grove was founded in Oxford. This name was a reference to the ancient centre of initiation of the Balkans, which symbolized, for the Greeks, the direction of the magnetic pole; choosing it indicated an adherence to the tradition of the Hyperboreans who, in ancient times, would make pilgrimages to this mount.

The first known writer of the Renaissance to have written about Druids is Annius di Viterbo, in 1498. His work was popularized in 1510 by John White of Basingstoke, who also used the writings of Geoffrey of Monmouth. From that time, there has been an almost uninterrupted stream of authors who invariably publish their own opinions on Druids, rather than the real content of the tradition. However Rabelais (c. 1494–1553) appeared on the scene, with the exciting but coded adventures of *Gargantua and Pantagruel*, in which one finds the characters of Celtic mythology and Arthurian legend. Despite everything, the tradition was preserved and carried forward.

Reappearance of Druids of a first kind – the lineage of hyperborean tradition with John Toland in 1717

At last, during the autumnal equinox of 1716, the Enlightenment heard the call of John Toland, the Irish philosopher raised in Scotland, who sounded on London's Primrose Hill the call, 'facing the Sun, the Eye of all Light'. This call was launched for the benefit of all accessible Druids, for a public gathering at The Apple Tree Tavern in London, a year and a day hence, according to the Celtic tradition. Thus we suddenly discover that there were still Druids and even organized groves.

John Toland's call to the Druids was made possible by a certain ambient British liberalism, and we must presume that it carried well, since the gathering did indeed take place on September 22nd 1717 at The Apple Tree Tavern, Charles Street, Covent Garden, London. Not only were the representatives of the groves from London, York, Oxford, Wales, Cornwall, The Isle of Man, Anglesey, Scotland and Ireland present, but also a delegation from the European continent represented by Pierre des Maiseaux from Nantes in Brittany, which proves that an organization of Druids also still existed on the continent.

This assembly decided to create a kind of confederation of ancient circles and groves of Druids or Bards under the Celtic name of An Druidh Uileach Braithreachas (A.D.U.B.), The Druid Circle of the Universal Bond. Although written accounts of this meeting only appear much later, it is to this meeting that the Ancient Druid Order traces its origin. This was the first group of the contemporary Druidic renaissance in Great Britain, which has remained active ever since.

1st Type: DRUIDS
Hyperborean Tradition

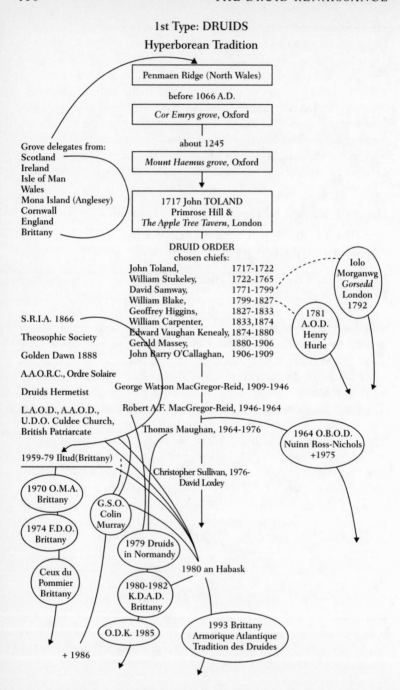

Penmaen Ridge (North Wales)

before 1066 A.D.

Cor Emrys grove, Oxford

about 1245

Mount Haemus grove, Oxford

1717 John TOLAND
Primrose Hill &
The Apple Tree Tavern, London

Grove delegates from:
Scotland
Ireland
Isle of Man
Wales
Mona Island (Anglesey)
Cornwall
England
Brittany

DRUID ORDER
chosen chiefs:

John Toland,	1717-1722
William Stukeley,	1722-1765
David Samway,	1771-1799
William Blake,	1799-1827
Geoffrey Higgins,	1827-1833
William Carpenter,	1833,1874
Edward Vaughan Kenealy,	1874-1880
Gerald Massey,	1880-1906
John Barry O'Callaghan,	1906-1909

Iolo
Morganwg
Gorsedd
London
1792

1781
A.O.D.
Henry
Hurle

S.R.I.A. 1866

Theosophic Society

Golden Dawn 1888

A.A.O.R.C., Ordre Solaire

Druids Hermetist

L.A.O.D., A.A.O.D.,
U.D.O. Culdee Church,
British Patriarcate

George Watson MacGregor-Reid, 1909-1946

Robert A.F. MacGregor-Reid, 1946-1964

Thomas Maughan, 1964-1976

1964 O.B.O.D.
Nuinn Ross-Nichols
+1975

1959-79 Iltud(Brittany)

Christopher Sullivan, 1976-
David Loxley

1970 O.M.A.
Brittany

G.S.O.
Colin
Murray

1974 F.D.O.
Brittany

1979 Druids
in Normandy

Ceux du
Pommier
Brittany

1980 an Habask

1980-1982
K.D.A.D.
Brittany

O.D.K. 1985

1993 Brittany
Armorique Atlantique
Tradition des Druides

+ 1986

@@@

This group of Druids defined itself as philosophical and without allegiance to any Christian denomination, promoting instead a return to the very roots of the traditional religion of the Celts. Despite the presence of a representative of the continental Druids at the gathering at The Apple Tree Tavern, it seems that there was no public reappearance of Druidic groups in continental Europe at that time. One can only assume that the circumstances were not yet favourable. However, it must be said that ten years later the work of the Benedictine Monk Jacques Martin entitled *The Religion of the Gauls,* drawn from the purest sources of antiquity, was published in Paris in 1727.

Celtomania explodes

The *Commentatio De Druidis Occidentalum Populorum Philosophis,* published in 1744 in Ulm by Jean Frickius, contained a very important fifteen page bibliography, showing that between 1514 and 1744 there were at least 261 authors who wrote about Druids; in other words more than one per year, which shows just how constantly the subject remained a focus of interest, at least for the scholarly.

What is peculiar about the Druidic resurgence of 1717 with John Toland is that it nearly coincided with the creation of the Grand Masonic Lodge of England on June 24th 1717 in London. This lodge merged four speculative Masonic lodges of London together, one of which used to hold its meetings at the Apple Tree Tavern! It seems as if at that moment in time, the history of initiatory societies took a decisive turn. However, there was an important choice to be made which was taken differently by the two organizations.

Christians or Pagans?

On the one hand, Freemasonry decided to confirm its attachment to the Judeo-Christian tradition and established itself in accordance with the civil and religious authorities already in place. Conversely, the An Druidh Ulieach Braithreachas, if only because of its Celtic name, appeared to be an original and anti-establishment group going against the mainstream, turning instead towards the ancient tradition of the Druids, and promoting a return to the natural roots of the Celtic civilization and of the Druidic religion. Calling one of its founding groves after Mount Haemus was also highly indicative of its adherence to the esoteric lineage of the ancient Hyperborean tradition.

Since 1717, tradition states that the Ancient Druid Order has not ceased its activities, although there are no contemporary documents which can prove its existence prior to the early part of this century. However, this order has been able to generate other groups of the same lineage, the most significant of which split away in 1964 to become the Order of Bards, Ovates and Druids (O.B.O.D.) led by Ross Nichols.

Appearance of Druids of a second kind – the mutualistic lineage with Henry Hurle in 1781

The Druidic resurgence of 1717 does not seem to have been followed unanimously. In 1781, a carpenter, Henry Hurle, created a new association known as the Ancient Order of Druids (A.O.D.) at the King's Arms Tavern in Poland Street, London. This new neo-Druidic branch came to enjoy a considerable expansion throughout the world because, on the philosophical level, it established itself in the Judeo-Christian sphere by placing the Bible upon the altar of its closed temples. Unlike Freemasonry, which was then still very much reserved for a certain élite coming from the establishment, the Ancient Order of Druids opened its doors to the working class and the lower middle class. Without wanting to upset the status quo, the Ancient Order (and more particularly its break-away groups which included The United Ancient Order of Druids, The Order of Druids, The Sheffield Equalized Order and the Manchester Order of Druids) started a highly effective chain of solidarity, by creating a whole social system of mutual insurance, far ahead in time of the National Health Service. This social system was committed to visiting sick people at home or in hospital; widows and orphans; and even offered the possibility of loans for buying private houses. Many of these evolved later into various types of property and family insurance, including life insurance, and culminating, with the progress of technology, in motor insurance! This mutualistic branch of neo-Druidism spread to all the territories of the British Empire, to English-speaking countries and beyond.

Some internal differences resulted in the creation of yet another group in 1834, the United Ancient Order of Druids. Then in 1913 the International Grand Lodge of Druidism created a federation of these two groups, and other mutualistic Druid orders. In the end, these events proved extremely beneficial for the international

2nd Type: THE MUTUALIST DRUIDS

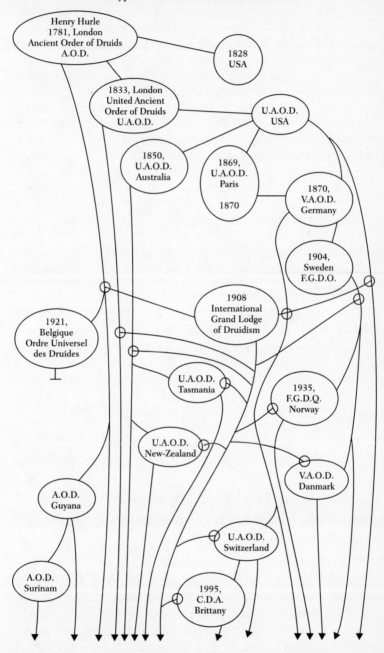

expansion of this very dynamic branch of contemporary Druidism.

In fact, the spread of these neo-Druidic groups across territories and populations which had probably long lost sight of their possible ancient Celtic origins, did not necessarily favour the Druidic aspect of the activities. The emphasis was essentially on fraternal mutual aid. However, homage should be paid to the courage and self-sacrifice of the thousands of people who, after all, carried a small flame of the ancient thought of the Druids, and who were particularly concerned with social problems. It is only fair that respect should be given to this original aspect of contemporary Druidism.

It was within the framework of this branch of mutualistic Druids that the movement was propagated from Great Britain to the Americas. One day, Nicolas Dimmer, an American Druid of German origin, came back to Europe from the United States and decided to stop over in France where he founded the European continent's first U.A.O.D. lodge, the 'Perseverance' Lodge of Paris, in 1869.

Unfortunately, this first introduction of neo-Druidism to 19th century France was brought to a premature end by the declaration of war between France and Germany in 1870. Brother Dimmer went on to spread the United Ancient Order of Druids from Germany to Northern Europe, Sweden, Norway, Denmark, and Switzerland. The very same branch of neo-Druidism also spread of its own accord throughout the British Empire and soon lodges, impressive by the number of their members, were established in Australia, Tasmania and New Zealand. One can only approve of the present contacts established between the I.G.I.D. and the U.A.O.D., and by French or Breton Druidic groups for whom it was unquestionably a matter of making up for the lost opportunity of 1869. There could now be an excellent opportunity for the upholders of mutualistic Druidism to reconnect with their Celtic roots.

Appearance of Druids of a third kind – the lineage of Bardic tradition with Iolo Morganwg in 1792

A third branch of neo-Druidism was to see the light of day, once again in London – the true initiatory centre of neo-Druidism. This time, the story centres around Edward Williams, known as Iolo Morganwg, a Welsh Londoner and a humble mason by profession who had such a good knowledge of the family traditions of Glamorgan that he started to make a compilation for the Gwyneddigion Society, an association of the Welsh community in London.

After the Apple, the Rose

On the 21st June 1792, once again on Primrose Hill, the site chosen in 1717 by John Toland, Iolo Morganwg held the first assembly of Welsh Druids in modern times. The ceremony was successfully repeated in Wales but on a wider scale. Iolo Morganwg's intuition propelled him to associate the Gorsedd – his reconstitution of Druidic ceremonies – with the traditional competitions of Bards, known as Eisteddfodau, which had always remained very popular in Wales. The Gorsedd became a kind of organizer and official jury of the Eisteddfod, and thereafter the Gorsedd enjoyed great success at all Eisteddfodau, becoming much more Bardic than authentically Druidic in character. However, during the early days of this Welsh Bardic revival, certain personalities such as Evan Davies (1801–1888) – Myfyr Morganwg by his Bardic name – and Dr William Price of Llantrisant, attempted to restore the Druidic cult of pre-Christian antiquity, but without much co-ordination. In spite of their efforts, the Gorsedd soon became a sort of haven for Protestant preachers with Welsh affinities, who were no doubt missing the traditionally Celtic outdoor speech competitions. Unfortunately, with this development, the philosophical and esoteric aspects of Druidism became neglected.

However, it seems that some political refugees from France, where the bloody civil war of the revolution – the 'Terror' – was raging, came to know of these three different reappearances of Druidism in London. The Breton writer Francois-René Chateaubriand was a refugee in London at that time. In 1809, he published *Les Martyrs* which contains the famous episode in which the female Druid Veleda revolts against the Romans. (William Stukeley, recalling this event, named Augusta, Princess of Wales, 'Veleda, Archdruidess of Kew'. The princess was apparently the patroness of his Druid Order.) Others from Brittany who became interested in the Druid revival were Jean Francois Marie Le Gonidec, a refugee in Wales, who published the Celtic-Breton Grammar; the Breton Hersart de la Villemarque, who was initiated along with two other Bretons at the Welsh Eisteddfod at Abergavenny in 1838; and the French writer and politician Alphonse de Lamartine, who was to have participated in the same ceremony but could not go. However, he had his friend Louis de Jaquelot recite a poem that he had specially written for the occasion. We have no evidence of Lamartine wanting to create an assembly of Druids or Bards in France, whereas in 1855 La Villemarque established the first Bardic group called *Breuriez*

3rd Type: DRUIDS
Welsh Bardic Tradition

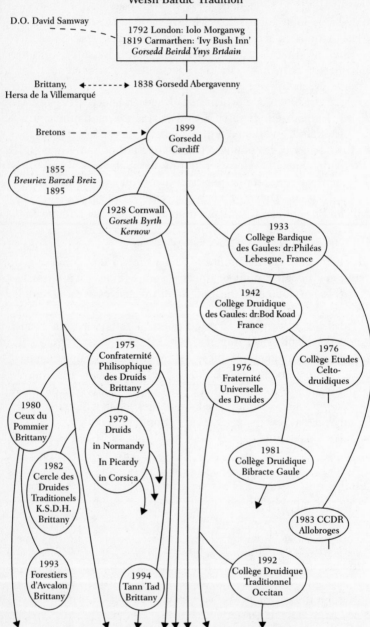

D.O. David Samway

> 1792 London: Iolo Morganwg
> 1819 Carmarthen: 'Ivy Bush Inn'
> *Gorsedd Beirdd Ynys Brtdain*

Brittany,
Hersa de la Villemarqué — → 1838 Gorsedd Abergavenny

Bretons — — → 1899
Gorsedd
Cardiff

1855
Breuriez Barzed Breiz
1895

1928 Cornwall
*Gorseth Byrth
Kernow*

1933
Collège Bardique
des Gaules: dr:Philéas
Lebesgue, France

1942
Collège Druidique
des Gaules: dr:Bod Koad
France

1976
Collège Etudes
Celto-
druidiques

1975
Confraternité
Philisophique
des Druids
Brittany

1976
Fraternité
Universelle
des Druides

1980
Ceux du
Pommier
Brittany

1979
Druids
in Normandy
In Picardy
in Corsica

1981
Collège Druidique
Bibracte Gaule

1982
Cercle des
Druides
Traditionels
K.S.D.H.
Brittany

1983 CCDR
Allobroges

1993
Forestiers
d'Avcalon
Brittany

1994
Tann Tad
Brittany

1992
Collège Druidique
Traditionnel
Occitan

Barzed Breiz, The Fraternity of the Bards of Brittany. This fraternity was essentially intended for writers of the Breton language, but died with its creator in 1895. Then in 1862, the French 'Parnassian' poet Lecomte de Lisle published his *Poemes Barbares,* a collection in which the capture of Mona (Anglesey) by the Romans is evoked.

Through the regionalist Breton Association, links between the Bretons and the Welsh were revived in 1898, and the following year about twenty Bretons were initiated by the Welsh Gorsedd. Finally, a constituent assembly was called on the 1st September 1900 at the tavern of 'La Veuve Le Falc'her' in Guingamp in Brittany. This Breton Gorsedd, an offshoot of the Welsh one, was instantly acknowledged by its 'parent-Gorsedd' as the 'Gorsedd of the Bards of the Breton peninsula', implying a certain degree of dependence on, and a recognition of, the pre-eminence and supreme authority of the Welsh Archdruid.

The Gorsedd has some offspring

A Bardic Gorsedd was founded for Cornwall on the 21st September 1928. This Gorsedd was unusual in that it only gathered Bards together under the authority of a Grand Bard. In 1933, the Bardic College of Gaul came into being under the aegis of the Welsh Gorsedd with the patronage of the Breton Gorsedd. It was founded for Gaul, that is to say essentially for France, with the astonishing peasant poet Phileas Lebesgue as Grand Druid. However, after the demise of its founder in 1958, this group became dormant.

If the mutualistic groups of Henry Hurle spread throughout the world without being particularly concerned about whether or not its members were of Celtic origin, then the groups linked to the Welsh Gorsedd did protect themselves from the intrusion of non-Celts, or even non-celtophiles, according to the Caerlyon Bay Agreement of 1971, since their ideology was essentially based upon the promotion of Celtic languages.

However, it must be acknowledged that the groups of the Gorsedd still carry out outstanding work for Celtic culture. Although their expansion has been limited to only three so-called Celtic countries, their membership throughout the world is very large because of Celtic émigrés, especially throughout the Commonwealth. Even some Irish and Scottish people are active members of the Welsh Gorsedd.

Nevertheless, the Druids of this third strand of Welsh Bardic lineage gave rise, without their consent, to groups de facto separated as a result of the terms of the Caerlyon Bay Agreement of 1971. Thus, the Druidic College of Gaul (created in 1942 by Paul Bouchet, who was also known as the Druid Bod Koad) which claimed to be from the line of Phileas Lebesgue, was not recognized by the Welsh Gorsedd when contacts were re-established between Great Britain and the continent after the Second World War. Nonetheless this College continued to develop, without hesitating to visit occasionally the Breton Gorsedd when it was on bad terms with the Welsh Gorsedd, as well as the Druid Order of London, which was also not recognized by the Welsh Gorsedd.

The Druidic College of Gaul also suffered a split when the son of the Grand Druid founded his own College of Celto-Druidic Studies in 1976. A certain number of members broke away from the College of Gaul and set up a Universal Fraternity of Druids. This fraternity is particular in that it has been led by a female Druid since 1979. The first Grand Druidess died in 1991 and was replaced by another female Druid.

Other colleges claimed to descend from the line of the College of Gaul, including the Druidic College of Bibracte, and the Celto-Druidic College of the Allobroges.

The Breton Gorsedd also underwent schisms. In 1975, some members of the Breton Gorsedd split on philosophical grounds to form a Philosophical Brotherhood of Druids under the leadership of Druid Coarer Kalondan. This new Grand Druid took advantage of his own emancipation to encourage the creation, from 1979 onwards, of new Druidic groups in France such as the Druids of the Celts of Normandy, the Traditional Druidic College of Corsica and the Traditional Druidic College of Occitan, which strives today for the creation of an Institute of Advanced Celtic Studies in the South of France.

Reappearance of Druids of a fourth kind – lineages from clan tradition

Here, we deal with those groups which appear every now and again and sometimes disappear just as quickly. These belong to the oral tradition, technically known as acroamatic, that is to say transmitted by word of mouth and received with great attention. This usually takes place within the ambit of the same family or, more precisely, of the same clan, which is where the term clan tradition comes from. Usually the teaching is spread out and lasts for years. Secrets can be passed into the memory of children who will only remember them much later on, in adult life. At a key moment in life, a trigger or an emotional shock might occur which causes the teaching to resurface at a conscious level. There can also be a transmission to adults with secret rites and precise instructions regarding the future transmission of this information. Some of these lineages are also the source of the traditions of Witches, wizards, healers, midwives and village bonesetters who often uphold fragments of the Druidic tradition.

All is possible in such a subtle field. The downside is that it is not easy to control charlatans. All the same, for those who know where to look, there are unmistakable signs from all sides. A real initiate will not be abused by a fake. But to cite one group or another is not the same as presenting a certificate of authenticity. The groups mentioned here are part of those who claim to come from the clan tradition themselves. Although they are part of the contemporary Druidic scene, we must remember to allow room for doubt.

For instance the Great Oak is meant to be a survival of Druidic tradition in Gaul (France) which lasted until 1943. It was reactivated in 1960 by Druid Mic Goban (who died in 1993), claiming to go back to the age-old tradition and the mysterious Order of Gawre.

Clan Traditions surface in Brittany, Auvergne and Picardy

In 1936, a manifesto of the new Celtic journal Kad was published in Brittany which announced the formation of a *Breuriez Spered Adnevezi*, a 'Fraternity of Regenerating Belief', inviting the Bretons to renounce the authority of the (French) State and of the Christian Church simultaneously in order to encourage a return to Celtic roots. One of the founders claimed his Druidry from the Clanic Tradition of his Breton Clan Ar Gow. Some of them also had known connections with the Freemasonry of the Grand Lodge of France without, it seems, having received any particular mission. The Second World War did not put a stop to the efforts of this group who published outstanding studies on the tradition of Druids in the journal 'Nemeton', edited by Morvan Marchal, Druid Artonovios, and the designer, in 1923, of the modern Breton flag.

After the war, the group continued its activities under the name of *Kredenn Geltiek*, 'Celtic Belief'. This was the first group to claim its adherence to the neo-Pagan Druidism which would prove so controversial. Shortly before the death of Drwiz Meur Gudaer, the Grand

Sacerdotal Druid Raffig Tullou, alias Newen Lewarc'h, in 1990, the *Kredenn Geltiek* had already witnessed the growth of an unofficial offshoot called *Comardiia Druvidiacta Aremorica* or 'The Druidic Brotherhood of Armorica'. Yet the *Kredenn Geltiek* carries on, using several titles such as *Goursez Tud Don* 'Assembly of the Tuatha-de-Danan' or even 'The Assembly of the Dana Clan', or *Heureudevriez Tud an Derv* (Ancient Brotherhood of the Oak People).

In Britanny, the Druid Goff ar Steredennou is the only Druid still living to claim to be of an Armorican clan tradition which existed prior to the arrival of Bretons on the Armorican peninsula. He was responsible for the creation in 1950 of the Great Oak Forest Celtic College of Broceliande; since then he has also been involved in the creation of other groups and has founded the Kengerzhwriezh Drwizel an Dreist-Hanternoz, the Druidic Guild of Hyperborea, more often called Oaled Drwized Kornog (literally, the Hearth of the Druids of the West) in 1982.

In 1978 the Druidic Order of Avernia, claiming to come from early antiquity and the Druidic sacerdotal tradition, reappeared in the Auvergne region in the centre of Gaul. This order which certainly brings to mind the intangible aspects of the Druidic and Celtic Communities mentioned below, published in 1994 an excellent practical handbook of about two hundred pages for the education of its postulants.

The tradition of the Ch'dru (meaning Druids in the Picard language) which had been maintained in the Picardy region was re-activated in 1979.

Mysterious Celtic and Druidic Communities appeared in France in 1980 with their administrative centre for Gaul in Reims (traditional city for the coronation of the kings of France). These communities proclaimed themselves to be of age-old tradition and of the Druidic religion, existing clandestinely since 317 AD. Despite a seemingly sophisticated structure, a vast ostensible knowledge and an impressive number of followers, this went back underground as quickly as it had surfaced. No one can tell whether their claims were reality or myth.

Some British and American groups also claim to be from the age-old clan tradition. For certain groups it is difficult to distinguish clearly between Druidism and Wicca of the Celtic tradition. These two manifestations of the tradition sometimes appear to be nearly identical; for instance, the American Church of Y Tylwyth Teg, the Church of the Magic Fairy People, originating from traditional Welsh Wicca. Also, the Fainne of Avalon appeared in the Ardennes region in the north of France in 1992 under the leadership of an Irish woman from the Banshee (the women of the Sidhe, meaning of the next world) clan tradition.

Even more recently, a new Druidic group has appeared in Ireland in 1993 – The Order of Druids of Ireland (O.D.I.) led by Michael Mile McGrath. Although Ireland is the land of Druids par excellence, so miraculously spared as it was by the legions of Rome, the presence of Catholicism has until recently proved an inhibition to those interested in Druidry. The few Irish people who dared to take an interest in modern Druidism and to call themselves Druids usually had to join secretly the Gorsedd of neighbouring Wales. But now, as well as the O.D.I., the Druidic Clan of Dana has been established in the Republic. This originated from the remarkable work carried out for the renewal of ancient religions in Ireland, by the Honourable Olivia Robertson, since 1976. This leads us to contemporary Druids of a fifth kind.

Appearance of Druids of a fifth kind – Druids of spontaneous generation

The expression 'Druids of spontaneous generation' is not at all derogatory. Various groups even proclaim it. It simply means that these groups constituted themselves by free will. They might have put forward the 'privilege of necessity' by declaration after a year and a day, according to the bardic tradition of Brittany. However, in the context of modern communication and except for cases involving persecution, nowadays it is increasingly possible to contact one or even several groups without the need for this sort of self-proclamation. I will highlight the most significant examples.

An avant-garde church

In 1885, Henri Lizeray, whose possible links with the three different lines of Druidic renewal are not known, founded a Druidic and National Church in Paris, which did not enjoy the success he anticipated. This group is notable for using the term church to designate a group of Druidic expression, since the term church is only usually used for Christian designations, although, as etymologically this term means 'assembly', any assembly ought to be able to use it. Yet due to the strong connotation of the word, this is not usually done. In the case of Henri Lizeray, provocation rather than a possible indication of Christian affiliation probably motivated this choice.

5th Type: DRUIDS
Druids of spontaneous generation

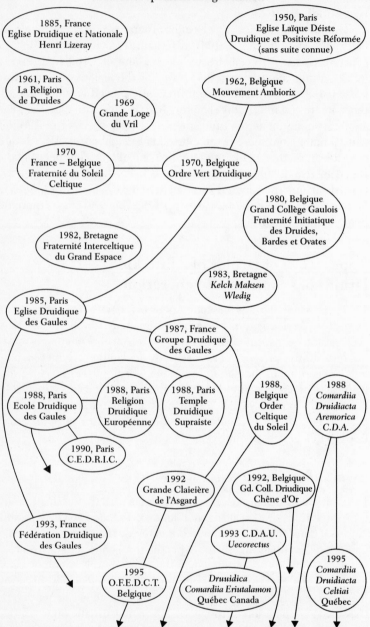

Many other groups created since the 1960s, which only had short-lived existences, are of a very different nature. For example, the Green Druidic Order of Ronan ab Lugh was founded in Belgium during the 1960s and was a springboard for the Druidic Church of Gaul (D.C.G.) of Pierre de la Crau in Paris, which since then has constantly and courageously generated many publications of Pagan influence. In 1993, the group became the Druidic Federation of Gaul, with Pierre de la Crau for his part continuing with his publications. In 1987, a branch of the D.C.G. became the Druidic Group of Gaul, a group with Pagan affiliations, actively based in the east and central France.

In 1988, the mysterious Celtic Order of the Sun was founded in Belgium. It too claims Pagan affinities and seeks to reconstitute a tripartite Celtic society with its sacerdotal, warrior and producing classes. To this end it advocates a confederation of Gaul. Then, in 1992, a very interesting, dynamic Order appeared in Belgium, the Grand Collège du Chene d'Or (G.C.C.O.), proclaiming themselves to be of spontaneous generation (5th type), and claiming to have received their initiation from the Collège Druidique de Bibracte en Gaule (France, 3rd type). This group circulates an accessible instruction through very well presented monographs.

In Brittany, the Comardiia Druvidiacta Aremorica split in 1993, with the original branch continuing to exist under the slightly changed title of *Comardiia Druvidiacta Armorica Uecorectus*, 'The Armorican Druidic Brotherhood of the Sacred Law'. These Gallic names prove a certain adherence to NeoPaganism. However, if these affinities with Paganism are clear in these two groups, they are more questionable for the traditional lines, since their creation only goes back to 1989 and its sacerdotal character is purely self-proclaimed. Nevertheless, interestingly the *Comardiia Druvidiacta Armorica* is currently becoming closer to the groups from Henry Hurle's mutualistic lineage on the continent. The Comardiia also has real fraternal links with the neo-Druidic groups in Canada they initiated.

It is interesting to note the blossoming of Druidic groups in America, especially from the 1960s onwards and in the circles of Celtic origin (Welsh, Irish, and Scottish). This movement attracted the attention of Tadhg MacCrossan, a young American of Irish origin, who in 1991 published *The Secret Cauldron* (Llewellyn Publications, U.S.A.), an extremely interesting summary made possible by his broad knowledge of the Irish clan tradition and his links with various Druidic groups in Brittany and Gaul. Its impact reached Canada where the interest of the Quebecois of French origin was so aroused that they in turn made contact with the Druids of Europe.

Druids of a sixth kind

To complete this overview of the various Druidic branches, one might add that we are presently witnessing the emergence of Druids of a sixth kind: Druids of multiple lineage.

This phenomenon began with individuals having double, triple or more adherences to groups of various lineages, in which they would be initiated each time. This practice was copied by others. Not very well thought of, and even forbidden by some leaders of Druidic groups, it is presently becoming widespread, especially among the young initiates. They, by undergoing successive initiations, are gathering together various lineages. This is happening to the extent that, nowadays, new groups appear which simultaneously uphold Druidic lineages of different origins. One might wonder how this development could be controlled. The truth is there is no umbrella structure to control all the different groups, no body to certify and guarantee the authenticity of the Druids and groups of Druids expressing themselves publicly. But, in any event, would this really be desirable or necessary?

It is not always the lineage that matters ...

Soon, there will probably no longer be grounds for challenging any Druid because of their lineage, since all Druids will have the possibility of belonging to all known lineages. From then on, the status of Druid will have to be based on something other than supremacy of lineage. Indeed, one does not become a Druid to collect lineages, no matter how prestigious they may be! A Druid should, above all, be concerned with putting their knowledge into practice, for their own spiritual fulfilment and for the service of others.

And for those who wish to further their interest: experience has taught me how difficult it is to know of all the Druidic groups existing in the world today. Far from having mentioned all the known Druidic groups, I realize that there are some which I do not even know of. For instance, some research could be carried out into the Druidic groups in existence in South-Western (the Galicians and other Iberian-Celts), Southern, Central and Eastern Europe, not forgetting Mount Haemus or even Turkey, where our Galatian cousins founded the city of Galatea-Istanbul and established the ancient Celtic Kingdom of Ancyre-Ankara.

Thus, researchers and students in Druidology or simple Druidophiles still have a great deal on their plate! There is a Breton phrase which means, in essence, Good luck! Literally translated it means 'The seed is coming through!' Traditionally, in Breton villages this phrase, *Egi an Ed!*, would be chanted in the villages at the time of the Winter Solstice, signalling the beginning of the growth of the wheat seeds.

So – Egi an ed!

Suggested Reading

The only comprehensive study of modern Druid movements is at present my own book, *Les Druides: Les Societes Initiatiques Celtiques Contemporaines*, Monaco: Editions du Rocher, 1992, third edition, revised.

For a briefer guide to modern Druid groups in English, see Philip Shallcrass, *A Druid Directory*, privately published by The British Druid Order, PO Box 29, St. Leonards-on-Sea, E. Sussex TN37 7UP, England.

French-speaking readers should find the following books of interest:
Carr-Gomm, Philip. *Initiation a la Tradition Druidique*, Editions Du Rocher 1995.
Blanchet, Regis (ed.) *Le Druidisme Antique et Contemporain*, Editions du Prieure 1993.
Ambelain, Robert. *Les Traditions Celtiques*, Editions Dangles 1977.
Rabanne, Paco. *La Force des Celtes – L'Heritage Druidique, Entretiens avec Philip Carr-Gomm*, Editions Michel Lafon 1996
Reznikov, Raimonde. *Les Celtes et le Druidisme*, Editions Dangles 1994.
Markale, Jean. *Le Druidisme*, Payot 1985.

Michel Raoult is Chosen Chief of the Breton Druid group, Kredenn Geltick – Goursez Tud Donn. In 1958 he was a disciple in the Gorsedd of Brittany, and became a Bard in 1960. Since that time, he has joined a number of Breton and French Druid groups, and was welcomed into all three grades of the Universal Druid Order in England in 1980 by Desmond Bourke and Colin Murray. In that same year he received his doctorate in Masonology from the University of Upper Brittany. His thesis had been on contemporary Celtic initiatic societies, and this was adapted and published by Editions du Rocher in 1983 as *Les Druides; les Societes Initiatiques Celtiques Contemporaines*. He has known personally many of the key figures in the Druid Renaissance, including Robert MacGregor Reid, Thomas Maughan, Ross Nichols, Ithel Colquhoun, and Colin and Liz Murray. He is now the representative of Breton and Gaulish (French) Druid groups in the Council of British Druid Orders, and is a member of the Pagan Federation.

III

THE RE-ENCHANTMENT

Sea
Makes the Ugly
Beautiful:
Again

Waves
Take me,
Make me
Whole:
Again.

TRACY

In the past, the Ovates were the specialist healers within Druidry. They knew the healing properties of herbs, and almost certainly practised a type of folk medicine, which continued to exist widely in Britain and Europe up until the middle of the last century, and could still be found as late as the 1930s in some villages. Many Druids today are interested in herbalism and holistic healing methods. On another level, following the Druid way can be seen as a healing activity in itself – helping us to get back in touch with Nature, with the rhythm of the seasons, and with that part of our Self which is nourished by ritual and poetry, pilgrimage to sacred sites and communion with the Otherworld.

Frank MacEwen Owen

NEMETON: HEALING THE COMMON WOUND AND THE RE-ENCHANTMENT OF EVERYDAY LIFE

The word nemeton is a very ancient Celtic term which translates from the old Irish words *Nemed* and *Fidnemed*, to mean a shrine or a woodland sanctuary. Although forms of the word also have roots in Latin and Greek (*nemus* and *temenos*), the meaning is consistent throughout. Its direct translation usually means a sacred grove of trees, considered a holy site for meditation and ceremony by the various manifestations of Druidry throughout the British Isles, Gaul (present day France), and even Germany.

Beyond the realm of etymology, however, there is an essence and feeling connected to the word. A nemeton is a sacred place, a holy site which nourishes and replenishes the soul, offering both refuge and renewal through communion with nature and the divine.

In the ancient Celtic world of my Scottish and Irish ancestors, there was a deep and abiding awareness of the divine, at a great many holy wells and groves of trees that were used for ritual. A day did not pass without a conscious and active participation in the dynamism of the landscape. Prayer, meditation, offering votives, paying homage and aligning oneself to a place through chanting and intoning; leaving holy gifts in the form of food, ale, and sometimes even objects of gold; these were everyday occurrences. These actions represent the contemplative and earth-centred practices of a neglected – but still available – Celtic spiritual tradition.

Yet one does not have to be Celtic or begin formally practising the Druidic tradition to benefit from the essence of the nemeton or the reverence one can cultivate from an encounter with such a place. Each and every one of us, regardless of ethnic and religious background, has this possibility available as a gateway or portal to experience. It is universal, and represents an interfaith potential present within us and within every passing moment.

Taken out of literal context, nemeton suddenly becomes much more than just a place; it is an experience of attentiveness, present-centredness, and overall communion with our life and the world in a fully engaged manner. In this way, any encounter has the possibility of being an abundant and fertile 'nemeton experience' and sacred awareness is no longer limited to just a particular holy place. Life itself is the nemeton, the sacred site that we commune with and which can nourish our soul. Slowly we come to the realization that, at every moment, our life is a pilgrimage to a holy place at which we are arriving.

Where I have served as a witness to this, in a very potent form, is in the psychotherapeutic relationship. Eighty per cent of psychology seems to be based on a model of generalization and homogenization, as if all human beings could possibly be squeezed into one category or another of a labelling system. In my current training and work, however, I have discovered that through suspending the arrogance that is the paradigm of most of psychology, and completely opening myself to the soul of the person I am working with, counselling and psychotherapy suddenly become an experience of communion and worship.

Akin to the sacred wells and oak groves at which my Druidic forebears worshipped, the client becomes like a shrine that I find myself approaching with great awe and respect, paying homage to them through the offerings of time, awareness, and attention. Energy is exchanged, in some cases healing occurs, and a sense of having been blessed by the presence of the soul of the person presents itself to me as a tangible experience. Even in those instances when the work is difficult, the prayerful state of the nemeton is present as an undercurrent.

As someone working in both the field of Ecopsychology and in the resurgence of Celtic spirituality, I have had the opportunity to encounter many different people of all ethnic and religious backgrounds. The nemeton experience of soulful connection has presented itself with people on airplanes, with Baptist ministers in hospitals, with Jews and Native Americans seeking to heal cultural wounds and reconnect with their spiritual heritage, and with adolescents struggling for a sense of the rites of passage in a society that has forgotten the numinosity of ritual. Whether in informal chats, or in the more formal individual consultations and group work I sometimes engage in, a common theme presents itself over and over again, sometimes with subtlety and at other times with great catharsis and emotional upheaval.

The Common Wound

I have come to refer to this theme as The Common Wound. Its symptoms are alienation, loneliness; a deep level of pain at being somehow dispossessed, disenfranchised in spirit, or displaced from a sense of 'home' or 'place'. Sandra Ingerman, modelling her work on ancient shamanic understanding of the person, has called this 'soul loss'.

While the symptoms are wide and varied, the cause is rather one-pointed. The collective sting of The Common Wound comes from a thirst for one's individual life and the world at large to become resacralized, and reimbued with meaning. The healing of this wound is the most prominent task facing psychology for the next century, and it is only through a psychology that returns to its original meaning of 'a study of the soul', that this will be accomplished.

With its openness to the wisdom of the world's spiritual traditions, mythologies, and religions, transpersonal psychology is the embryo of this coming evolution of consciousness. Perhaps the single most important factor in transpersonal psychology is that it does not seek to cover over the wound, but rather to enter into it, viewing even crises and states of mental disintegration as a gradual and temporary process leading to spiritual awakening. The wounds we suffer then become Holy Wounds of an initiatory nature. This idea resounds over and over, from Stanislav Grof's concept of spiritual emergency, Joseph Chilton Pearce's work with the concept of metanoia (death of the old self to the new), and even in more ancient expressions, such as St. John of the Cross (The Dark Night of the Soul), C.G. Jung (The Night-Sea Voyage), and for my Irish Celtic ancestors, The Immram. This period is a trial by fire, an initiation, a burning off of the extraneous by the energy of the wound we enter.

I have heard it stated before, that the healing of a wound must come from the blood of the wound itself. This is no less true of The Common Wound we all face. In the Arthurian traditions of ancient Wales and Britain, this is spoken of through the Matter of Logres[1] (the Matter of Britain and the myth of the Holy Grail). The once abundant and fertile earth becomes a Wasteland when the king sustains the Holy Wound. This is poignant, for it shows us that the wounding of the land and the wounding of our soul is a simultaneous process.

In this ancient story, the only way in which the Wasteland can be re-enchanted is through obtaining the Holy Grail (a feminine symbol whose prototype is the more ancient Celtic symbol of the Cauldron of Inspiration and Cauldron of Rebirth). We see in the various versions of this myth that the only way to come by the Grail is by asking the proper question, which in the story falls to the Knight Percival.

Just as in the model of 'going into the blood of the wound itself', the only question that wins the Grail, heals the wounds of the ancient king, and re-enchants the Wasteland is: 'What ails thee?' Almost as if through magic or alchemy, by simply acknowledging the wound and asking: 'What ails thee?' or 'What ails me?' the energy in the psyche that is tied up in the wound itself is released for the healing process.

Perhaps then, this is our task as contemporary peoples living in a world of disintegrating community, increased inner turmoil on the collective level, and the rapid transformation of the abundant earth into a Wasteland. We must ask ourselves and each other the sacred question: 'What ails thee?' and go to the blood itself of The Common Wound. Here we find a sacred place of potential healing of the soul and renewal of our individual and collective life energy. It is here we find the nemeton.

NOTES

1 The Matter of Logres, from my particular place on the Druid circle, refers to the larger spiritual history of Britain. Modern people have a tendency to think that we are the culmination of history, that everything has come before us and this is it. However, as soon as we enter into the concept of the Matter of Logres we realize that there is a complete other dimension that we must relate to: the future. The Matter of Logres takes into account all that has happened, but also what will happen. Nations come and go, leaders come and go. With the Matter of Logres we find all of the various stories about Arth Vawr's return (King Arthur), the return of Merlin, or the return of Owen Glyndower in Wales (who is believed to be Merlin by some Welsh people). The essential spirit of the Matter of Logres has to do with the divine spirit within the land throughout Britain and the returning of this power within the land into fullness. The return of Druid teachings in such abundance, the return of the Goddess despite the overtly industrialized and wounded state of the world, and the resurgence and blooming of the ancient British archetypes, gods and goddesses is part of the Matter of Logres. In effect, it is difficult to understand this concept because it isn't a stagnant reality; it is a living process that is unfolding, much like the unfolding of modern Druidry.

Frank MacEwen Owen, B.A. Jungian Psychology/Native American Studies M.A. Candidate, Transpersonal Counselling Psychology, The Naropa Institute. Of Scottish-Irish and Welsh ancestry, MacEwen is a Transpersonal counselling intern whose focus is Ecopsychology, reviving the eclipsed earth wisdom of Celtic tradition, and assisting people to establish a numinous connection with the sacred earth and their creativity. He co-founded the Native American Studies program at The Naropa Institute in Boulder, Colorado, and spent twelve years studying with Native American healers among the Crow, Seneca, Cherokee, and Ojibway, eventually reconnecting with his own Celtic lineage and ancestors in a traditional Sun Dance ceremony with the Lakota.

MacEwen leads groups throughout the U.S., utilizing the Nemeton Process, an ecopsychological approach, which works with the energies of the ancestors, the totems, and the wounds of earth and person. He is currently working on his first book.

To sponsor **Frank MacEwen Owen** for workshops or to find out about his work, write to: Sacred Grove Center/The Nemeton Project, c/o Frank MacEwen Owen, 2301 Pearl Street, Box 74, Boulder, Colorado 80302, United States, or Email at: theoakseer@aol.com (for workshops dealing with Ecopsychology, The Nemeton Process, or Druid/Celtic spirituality). MacEwen's wife, Angelique Espinoza, is a practitioner of Goddess-centred ritual and offers workshops in ritual and celebrating the Wheel of the Year.

Christine Worthington

THE SEARCH FOR
THE MABON

From joy springs all creation
By it, it is sustained
Towards joy it proceeds
And to joy it returns

Mundaka Upanishad

*I stood and looked at the earth, the trees, the grasses and flowers,
the rocks and mosses. I saw the joyous rush of water with its
sparkling spray of light in the sunshine, and the hawk which
soared in the clear blue sky high above me, and the glorious
shining sun. I looked at the earth and sun and knew that in the
beauty of all nature I witnessed the joy of their union, that sacred
union, without which, life on this planet, our home, would not
exist. And in that moment I knew myself also to be a child of that
joyous union, that each one of us, all of life, lives within the
blessing of that sacred joy.*

I lay back on the earth and the sun warmed my body, but the understanding I had gained warmed my heart. That understanding, that
knowledge of life, is there for the touching: that deep and sacred
knowledge that we see written in the earth, left by our ancestors in
stones and mounds, barrows and gateways. It speaks to us in every
rainbow when sun and rain, fire and water, shine together in a brilliant spectrum of colour across the heavens. We feel it as our fingers
touch the icy cold water of a mountain stream, when we breathe in
the soft musty air of damp woodland, when we listen to the song of
the wind in the leaves of the trees, or as our bare feet walk along

the soft sand warmed by the summer sun. The sacred and the sensual are united in the joy of being alive.

However we hear it, whatever form it takes, when the call comes we cannot ignore it. It comes from deep within our soul – a longing to find something, we know not what. Something we instinctively know will be healing, will make us whole. Within the spiritual traditions of these lands, we find the stories of the Cauldron and the Grail. These stories span both the older indigenous Celtic and Druidic beliefs and the more recent Christian religion. They belong to neither one nor the other, but speak with the voice of the land, the Spirit of the land. These holy vessels impart wisdom, inspiration and healing to all those who seek the truth.

But sometimes we seek without knowing what it is we are looking for, and, like Percival during his search for the Grail, we don't even know what questions to ask. We start with a need to know, a need to be of service, in whatever way we can. There is a need to connect again with something much deeper, something that unites the very depths of our soul with the heart of the land we live upon; something that echoes in the stars of the deep dark night. The journey we begin as we answer the call is long, and filled with all that we have been and all that we will become. Each journey is unique, but the paths have been travelled many times and in many cultures.

The stories of the Old Ones, the stories rooted deep within the land and the people of those lands, speak with wisdom to the seeker after truth …

My own journey had taken me to Scotland – a place whose heathered moors and mountain streams speak to my soul, a place where the spirits of the wind soar on eagles' wings in the high and wild places. I had responded to a call that was so strong within me I could not ignore it, and for three days I had been staying at *Samye Ling*, the Buddhist retreat centre at Eskdalemuir. Having acted on such an urgent call, and the strange awareness that I was looking for an unknown something, the past three days had been decidedly uneventful. I had no idea of what I was looking for, or why, as a Druidess, I should find myself staying in a Buddhist centre. I began to feel despondent and confused. That night I had slept badly, but awoke to the most beautiful sunny morning. I decided to stop looking and simply take advantage of the glorious weather and the beautiful landscape all around me.

After breakfast I decided to set off in whatever direction the spirit took me. The sun was hot, the wind blew and the sky above was vast and clear. After walking for an hour or so, I made my way through a field of marshy grass to the edge of a steep-sided, fast-flowing stream. The path down to the water looked dangerous and led over rocks that were wet and slippery, and for a moment I hesitated. But the pull of this place was too strong, and I clambered down to a small ledge of stone within a bowl of rocks, and sat in the sunshine. A little way upstream the water flowed deep and free, filling a pool with great stillness. But as the stream narrowed, the water below me forced its way between the rock face of the far bank and a massive rock that rose up from the river bed. The water boiled and turned in its cauldron of stone – dark peaty water, swirling and foaming, trying to find the small channel that would set it free to continue its journey.

I lay against the stone at my back and allowed myself to let go. The roar of the water was strangely helpful in stilling my mind, and very soon I drifted into that deep state where tangled thoughts no longer trouble one and a greater clarity emerges. For a while I rested within that deep inner stillness until, like a sword rising from the lake, an awareness arose sharp and clear. It brought me suddenly back to my physical surroundings and I knew myself to be in a place that I had seen in meditation the week before I arrived in Scotland.

My whole being tingled with excitement as my mind searched for the missing pieces and tried to fit them together. Yesterday, I had gone with Hannah, whom I had met at the centre, in search of Merlin's Wood, an ancient piece of woodland filled with old beech trees. Like any gateway to the mysteries of life, it had hidden itself well – simply by being too obvious. Early on in our search we had walked straight past it; its entrance was masked only by a thin covering of bramble and holly, but those spiky guardians had been enough to deter us. I'm sure Merlin chuckled to himself as we foolishly walked for hours in every other direction possible. But in some inner way I had felt its presence, and so I allowed the spirit of the wood to guide me to it. We made our way cautiously past its guardians and found ourselves surrounded by beautiful old beech trees. The earth was carpeted with soft green moss that shimmered as the sunlight filtered through the leaves of the trees. We spent some time in silence resting against those strong old trees. The clouds had hurried across the sky and the wind had brought rain, but the old beech tree sheltered me. I did not know whether the spirit of Merlin dwelt in the wood, for I had no sense of him, but the next day, as I sat by the cauldron of rock and remembered my meditation of the previous week, I had a strong impression that he did.

For in that meditation I was met by Merlin. Together we rushed along a path until we came to a rocky area. I climbed down into what appeared to be a large bowl of rock. A small waterfall filled the bowl with clear water, and within the water swam a salmon. As Merlin sat beside the pool, I slipped into the water, to be met by the salmon. He seemed very old and very wise, and I knew that I had something to learn from him. Together we swam down to the bottom of the pool and there in the dark depths was a small pile of hazelnuts. Without stopping to think, I asked the salmon if I could have some of the nuts, and then was astounded by the presumptuousness of my question; in the Druid tradition the salmon is known as the Oldest Animal, and draws its wisdom from the hazel nuts which grow by the side of the sacred pool. In the Mabinogion story of Culwch and Olwen it is the only animal which knows where the Mabon can be found. Within my meditation, the salmon answered me by saying, 'yes, all you had to do was ask.' I took three nuts, two of which seemed in some way to be joined together. I swam up to the top of the pool and thanked the salmon, having a strong impression of his great age and kindness. I then thanked Merlin and my meditation was ended.

So the Spirit of Merlin had been in the beech wood yesterday, and today He had guided me to this, the physical place of my meditation. Here was the same bowl of rock, the same pool of water. I sat in the sunlight and offered a blessing to the Elements and the Spirit of the Earth.

With the blessing of the Great Bear of the starry heavens and the deep and fruitful earth, I thank the powers of the North.

A tree was growing out of the rock face high up to my left, a small insignificant looking tree, but my attention was drawn to it. I looked away, but once more it drew me back and I could not seem to focus on anything else. Many lovely trees grew around the edge of this great cauldron of rock, including rowan, birch and oak, but for some strange reason this small tree held me within its grasp. 'Hazel', I suddenly thought, but then realized that I wasn't too sure what a hazel tree looked like. 'Hazel', my mind persisted, and suddenly I knew absolutely that it was. But I needed some proof – this could be simply fanciful, triggered by my memory of the meditation. I stared at the tree in the vain hope that I would remember what a hazel tree looked like. Amongst the leaves I saw tiny pale shapes shining in the sunlight. It was difficult to believe that what I saw were nuts. I had to get nearer to the tree, but the climb up the rock face was too dangerous. Then suddenly I knew that if this was indeed a hazel tree, the nuts that I needed to find would already be in the water. I climbed down to the water's edge, trying to hold back my excitement – and there, lying below the tree in a shallow pool at the water's edge, were two tiny hazelnuts. 'There must be a third,' I thought, as – dizzy with apprehension – I searched for it. But then I looked more closely at the two I had found, and discovered that, in fact, one of these hazelnuts was two joined together – just as I had been given in my meditation. Tears filled my eyes as I understood that I had been given something very precious. I thanked the tree for its gift and Merlin for being with me, and to the salmon I offered my blessings.

In the name of the Salmon of Wisdom who dwells within the sacred waters of the pool I thank the powers of the West.

For some time I stood by the water, filled with such a joy of life. I felt truly blessed and honoured by all that I had been given. I stood and looked at the earth, the trees, the grasses and flowers, the rocks and mosses. I saw the joyous rush of water with its sparkling spray of light in the sunshine, and the hawk which soared in the clear blue sky high above me, and the glorious shining sun. I looked at the earth and sun and knew that in the beauty of all nature I witnessed the joy of their union, that sacred union without which life on this planet, our home, would not exist. And in that moment I knew myself also to be a child of that joyous union and that each one of us, all of life, lives within the blessing of that sacred joy.

When I walked through the gateway that led to Merlin's Wood, I had entered another realm of understanding. Here the Old Ones dwelt. I knew that their wisdom and their knowledge was alive once more within the world. And in those wild and silent places, where humankind lives in harmony with the spirit of the land, the Old Ones can still be heard, and their stories have much to teach us in our own time.

As I walked back from that magical place, I looked up to the sky and saw a hawk circling high above me. Suddenly, as if with the vision of the hawk, I began to understand what I was searching for – all at once it was clear I was searching for the Mabon, the lost Child of Light. Mabon, the Divine Youth, and Modron, the Mother: their stories are interwoven into the fabric of our Druidic heritage.

In 1992, on Iona, the Isle of the Druids, I had become Modron of the Order of Bards, Ovates and Druids. It had been a long and eventful journey that had led me to Iona in the spring of that year, and I had been long troubled by the weight of what I knew must be.

Some years before, I had come to a point in my life when all that I held safe and comfortable was falling apart – my job, my health, my marriage. At that time, it was so easy to plunge deep into an unknown part of myself, as if retreating from an unsafe world. But, unwittingly, I plunged into that deep well of the Self that has a strength so centred in the truth of things, that whilst everything in one's known world falls apart, the core of one's being touches something that is long-forgotten but as old as time.

In that moment, I had experienced the Divinity of the Feminine – the Goddess. The presence of Her was profound, and I was left with the understanding that I had work to do, that in some way I must help.

Thinking back to that time, it would be a romantic notion to think that from that point on my life changed totally – that I could speak with wisdom, could see clearly my path in life, could begin a vocation of healing. The truth was that I was just 'me': wife, mother of two children, with a job to do, a home to run, and an awful lot to learn. The difference was that I began to see my role of mothering in a new light, and began to honour the role of mother in a sacred sense. I stopped trying to add something to my life in order to make it worth-while, and instead truly began to see the Life that I had. My new understanding was part of my healing and part of the long journey I believe we are all taking back to wholeness. There was a newly awakened sense within me that fired my search for meaning, for truth.

That search led me to Druidry – a spiritual path that was rooted deep within the lands of my Ancestors. It spoke to me of the sacredness of all life, holding within its teachings the magic and wonder of the Bardic stories. It was resonant with the spirit of the Celts. My journey through its teachings has been difficult, wondrous, demanding, empowering and much, much more.

And then, one evening, as I worked within the Grove of the Ovates beneath a star-filled sky, I felt Her presence once more. Just as before, She came without words, but the sense of Her Being was almost overwhelming, and I came to understand that She needed a more visible place within Druidry. I told no one of my experience; as powerful as it had been, I felt that it would be challenging the traditional and established roles within Druidic Orders to suggest that the Feminine was in some way to be represented in the Order. For many months I struggled with what I knew I must do, but could not bring myself to speak of it. Yet each time I tried to ignore it, Her presence touched me, gently but firmly. She would not be ignored.

Finally, someone I had met only once before came to tell me of all that I had been trying to ignore. In meditation, he had been told of the work that I was to do. But still I couldn't speak of it. What if I was wrong? What if my ego had become deluded or inflated? The panic I felt kept me awake at nights. But in that still centre of my being, I knew it to be true – I was to work with the role of the feminine within Druidry. The role was that of Modron. However, before I could accept that role fully, something else was to happen that changed my life forever. My daughter Lucie died. It happened three weeks after her seventeenth birthday. Three weeks after she died I became Modron of the Order of Bards Ovates and Druids. Some months later I was to read a book by Caitlìn Matthews in which she speaks of the Modron's loss and the necessity to relinquish her child to a higher destiny. I don't profess to fully understand the meaning of all that happened, but sometimes we touch upon a place where the inner and the outer worlds meet, where deep and mythological experience speaks clearly in our lives.

The Goddess expresses the feminine principle of life – in ourselves, in Druidry, and in the world around us. She exists, in all her aspects, in each one of us, whether we are male or female. She is maiden, mother, wise woman and crone, giver and taker of life, inspirer and healer. She is the Cauldron, the Grail and the Land itself. And for too long we have lived upon this earth, separated from the wisdom that comes from being in touch with the part of ourselves that speaks with the voice of the Great Mother; that deep inner knowing that honours the physical world as a sacred part of our existence. This is the knowing that, in Roger Housden's words, 'proceeds not from thought but from a larger intelligence that knows where it is going in the same way a river does.' (*Soul and Sensuality*, Rider, 1993). We have separated mind and body, spirit and matter, masculine and feminine. We have even elevated mind, spirit and the masculine, to a superior position in our understanding, leaving body, matter and the feminine to bear the brunt of our greed, our frustration and our pain.

As the great wheel turns and we fast approach the twenty-first century, humankind lives with the menacing results of that separation. Our history tells of the long and painful journey that we have taken together as a result of our denial of the divinity of the feminine and our focus on an all-powerful God. The consequences of this have brought us to a point where, through the paranoid denial of the Divine Feminine, we have the weaponry, the technology and the power to destroy ourselves and all life on earth. The catalogue of our destruction of life, the sustaining web of existence, is evident throughout the world and, like children calling out in the darkness, we call to She who gave us life. We call out with the pain of our wounding, the pain of the split between our earthly and our spiritual lives – we long to be healed, to be whole.

Within the stories of Modron and Mabon we find the understanding of the union of opposites and the fruit of that union. We see the image of wholeness and balance; she exists only in relationship to him and he to her, they are independent yet interdependent. As the Great Mother, she carries him within her womb, and at the time of the Winter Solstice, known in the Druid tradition as Alban Arthuan, the Light of Arthur, she gives birth to her Child of Light.

But on that day in Scotland I had come to know that what I searched for was the meaning of the Mabon. As I followed the lane back to the retreat centre and supper, the hawk circled high above, always a little in front of me. As I reached the end of the lane, he swooped down, and for just a few moments perched on a telegraph pole very near to where I stood. I sent my thanks to him as he soared once more and was lost to my sight beyond the trees. I felt filled with light and joy and wonder.

> *With the blessing of the Hawk of Dawn soaring in the clear pure air, I thank the powers of the East.*

In the teachings of the Druid tradition, the Mabon is known as the Great Prisoner, the Great Son who has been lost for eons, taken from his mother while still a babe, and imprisoned – to become the goal of many a spiritual quest. The story of Mabon and Modron can be found in a number of the old tales. One of these tells of an exalted prisoner who spent three nights in Caer Oeth and Anoeth. That particular prisoner was Arthur, but the legends of these lands tell of others, such as Pryderi, son of Rhiannon, who was stolen at birth and his mother unjustly accused of eating her own child. Years later, he was returned, and the time of her penance was over. Like Mabon, Pryderi was the Wondrous Youth who was lost and then found. Like Modron, Rhiannon's re-finding of her child brings an end to her grieving.

That evening I looked at a map of the area. I had a sense of something very close that I should look for, and there, not five miles from where I was staying, was Castle O'er – just too similar to Caer Oeth to be dismissed.

The next day, Hannah and I set off to find the ancient site of Castle O'er. In the brilliant August sunshine we set off to drive through the valley of the Esk. Along the road we stopped to watch an old man making hay-ricks by the river. He had made six ricks so far – just the old man and his pitch fork slowly working in the summer sun. The hay looked brown and spoiled, but no doubt it would still be nourishing, made in the old way with love and attention. An old shaggy goat was tethered to a nearby fence. It was sporting a red rosette that looked as old as itself. It must have been a very handsome creature in its time, but like the brown hay it would eat and the old man working the hay, it now looked weather-beaten and mellowed.

We continued on our journey to a point just before the rivers of the Black and the White Esk meet, turned off the road and left the car by the edge of the forest track. After a mile or so, I felt the need to walk amongst the trees – commercial pine planted in regimented rows to be used, after their short life, to satisfy the needs of a consumer age. Somehow I felt a sadness for those trees – they would be planted, grow to maturity and die, their only apparent value a commercial one. As I entered the dark stillness, I felt the quality of the place; it touched me deeply and I opened up to it in welcome. Amongst those tall majestic beings was something we very rarely find in our lives: absolute stillness and silence. Nothing grew beneath the dense dark canopy that separated the earth from the sun. The roots drew their nourishment from the rich earth, whilst high above me, the new growth reached out toward the sunlight. The small branches that I tried to use for support broke away in my hand, brittle and dead. Just one small patch of earth glowed, with an ethereal light, as the sun broke through a small space between the high branches, and where it touched the ground, soft green moss carpeted the earth. As we stood amongst the silent trees, I had a sudden vision of the old temples of Egypt, with their vast columns of stone reaching up into the darkness. It felt so similar, that I was struck by the impression that, in planting such enormous tracts of regimented forest, man has created vast temples of silence, as if in some unconscious way we are trying to redress the balance of our noise-polluted planet. Great pockets of still silence now cover Europe, and suddenly I felt, not sadness for their short and commercial life, but a need to honour them for what they are: tall majestic beings silently redressing the balance of our folly. I thanked the Spirits of the trees and we continued on our way.

Soon the trees had parted and in front of us, stretching into the distance, was a smooth-grassed, rolling hill that climbed up to the horizon. Upon this hill stood a monument built by the owner of the land in memory of his dead son: yes, the spirit of the Mabon dwells within this land. I looked at the circular building with its conical roof and felt a bond with this unknown father who had lost his child; and

I thought of the oak tree, that with the people of our village, my family had planted in memory of our own child. We turned away from the hill and on to an overgrown trackway, a wide green path that ran between two plantations of trees. It soon became clear that it was impossible to negotiate this stretch of the journey. Young trees had fallen into the marshy ground and over the years had been covered by long grass and reeds, making it hazardous to walk through. Castle O'er must have been beyond the ridge, not 300 yards from where we stood, just out of reach. We were too close now to turn back, so we decided to skirt the edge of the trackway amongst the dense woodland. Soon the land began to rise and the dark tangle of branches gave way to bracken as we climbed beyond the water level, over the last rise. And there was Castle O'er spread out before us – its ancient stone walls fallen and grassed over.

Two circles, like banks and ditches, were clearly visible, marking the once mighty walls of the castle. We stopped between the two stones, which stood as sentinels at the entrance to this ancient fort, and acknowledged the presence of those who dwelt there. I walked around the outer ditch following the path of the sun. To the south-western side the land dropped away steeply into the valley below. The view was magnificent. This must have been a formidable stronghold. One could see for miles in every direction; any invading tribes would have been seen long before they came anywhere near the hill-top fortress. The land in the valley below would have supported the animals and grown crops. Life must have been hard in that wild place, that eagles' nest of a home. And, like the eagle, my spirit soared to be in that high remote spot somewhere between land and sky.

I walked between the ruined walls to the centre, and sat on the short cropped grass. For a while, the resident sheep complained bitterly at my intrusion, and then they wandered off to leave me to my thoughts. I began to feel the strong presence of those whose home this had once been, those wild warriors who had once fought and loved and lived here. I sat within their circle, a place so powerfully filled with their presence and, across this thing we call time, the Ancestors spoke. They welcomed me with the hospitality and eagerness of the Celts. Strong people, alive and vibrant, their spirits spoke across the years. And like a traveller who has just arrived at a remote farmstead, I was welcomed by a people hungry for news from a world beyond their own. I told them, with great sadness, how we had lost touch with something so precious that we were in danger of destroying ourselves and all life on earth; how through our thoughtless greed we are turning this beautiful planet into a sad and polluted place that will no longer be able to sustain and nurture the peoples of the earth.

The Old Ones listened in silence; warriors used to challenge and hardship, cruelty and death. But this was beyond their under-standing. How could the children of their children in the generations beyond their time have so lost the sacredness of life that they would put their own children's lives in danger? Once again I spoke of that which we had lost. What was it that had damaged us so much that we had turned away from that which makes us whole? There, in the welcoming place of the Ancestors I asked for their help. And in that high place, deep within the past, as if we were sitting around their hearth-fire, sheltering from the turbulence of life, their stories came flowing to me strongly across the ages:

'Long ago in ages past, an Ancestress, a great Matriarch of the people, carried within her womb the golden child of light, he who was the fruit of the sacred union of the earth and the sun. He who represented for the people not just the creation of the harvest, be it in grain or fruitful livestock, or the continuation of the people of the land, but also the sacred and spiritual union of man and woman: the honouring and acceptance in true understanding of the divine nature of humanity. With the birth of the Mabon on the shortest day of the year, there would be witnessed the joy of creation in the return of the Child of Light; the midwinter sun born from the nurturing and fertile womb of darkness. Each child born into the tribe would take the people closer to the unity which is the Great Spirit, the divine mascu-line and the divine feminine joined, whole within a tiny form of light. Each child was a gift to the world, a gift to be honoured and nurtured, allowing his or her own sacred nature to blossom. The child repre-sented the sacred link between the people, the earth and the spirit which flowed through all life. There was no separation, no wound. Humankind instinctively recognised the mutual interdependence of all life in the great web of being. Their very survival depended upon it.

'But our journey together, as we learn and grow, has been a long and painful one and instinctual behaviour and our intuitive under-standing of the oneness of all life are only part of humanity's full potential. And as the great wheel turned, another facet of ourselves began to emerge and change things for all times.

'At the time of Lughnasadh, the time of the harvest when the Great Mother's belly was swollen and ripe with the fruit of her womb, she was set upon, raped and beaten. They tried to take from her the precious thing which she carried. Through ignorance and greed they sought to own that which envy and fear blinded them from knowing was truly theirs already. And in the fading autumn light, as the sun sank deep into the waters of the west, the child of the sacred union of earth and sun drowned in the waters of the womb. The child had died and the mother's grief filled the earth. With the death of her unborn child she hid her sacred self, her divine nature, and wept. In that one act, the sacredness of the union between man and woman, spirit and matter was torn apart, the wound deep and painful.

'The sun rose again on the people and their crops grew, they loved and produced children, they filled their bellies with the fruit of the earth, but they no longer saw the sacredness of all this. The Great Mother mourned the death of her divine child through the ages, her grief consumed her and though the God of Light, her consort, begged her to open fully to their sacred union again so that once more they could bring forth the healing child of light, her pain was such that in their union she was with him in all but her divine nature. The sacred spirit of her being had been defiled and abused and her child viciously taken from her.

'The people of the lands continued to live and work and feed from the earth, but because of their lack of awareness of the sacredness of life, their behaviour changed and her consort, in his need for full and sacred union with her, became resentful and withdrawn. He blamed other men for his pain, and fought and competed with them for land and the fruits of the land, desperately searching for that which he had lost. His pain flowed down into all men and in their turn they too fought and competed, seeing only division and that which they needed to own. In their need for a deeper union with the Goddess they asked from women that which women could no longer give. For, through the pain of the great Ancestress, women had lost the aware- ness of their sacred natures, the knowledge of their inherent divinity buried deep within the wound. Both men and women felt the pain of the gulf between them, felt the longing for true union, but the cause of the wounding had been lost beyond memory. They were truly sepa- rate, their divine natures longing for the union that would once more bring forth the divine child of that union, the Mabon'.

I sat in shocked silence. Just as the Old Ones had listened to my story, I had listened to theirs. Across the ages we sat in silence, feeling numbed by the impotence and barrenness that was touching us. 'But how do we heal this?' I pleaded with them. 'You will know', they said, 'the answer is very close.' I was aware that it was becoming difficult to hold the link and so I thanked them for the great gift of their story. I told them that as our Ancestors, we honoured them in our place and time for their help, and their spirits were cherished in our hearts for their part in our healing. And then I saw them for what they were; our family, our tribe back through the ages. They care and feel a need to help us. We must listen to the stories of our Ancestors – our heritage is rich with the wisdom woven in their words. I thanked all those who had guided me to this place, and returned to see the sun dipping low to touch the lands of the west, and rolling clouds that spoke of rain. Rejoining Hannah, we thanked the guardians of Castle O'er and walked back through the bracken-covered land-scape, and into the darkness of the forest. We walked in silence for much of the way and it was Hannah who turned when we heard a noise behind us. She caught her breath and I turned to see a red deer leaping out of the rough area of felled trees across the track and into the dark forest. So those great dark temples of silence do contain life, and in the form of deer. Oh! How magical life is.

> With the blessing of the Great Stag and the inner fire of the sun, I thank the powers of the South.

I thought about the enormous task of healing that we face in this world. But each of us is not alone; our companions span time and space, gender, nation, religion and age. The barriers of class and education are meaningless divisions in the pure light of truth. Consider how much we give when we simply smile at another human being with genuine warmth in our hearts. We must learn to communicate as though there were no barriers, just knowing that through our pain we are all longing for the same thing, to be loved and to love in freedom – to know the wholeness of being human.

> I come to this place as a child of future generations. My gift is the gentle flame of hope that each new life brings into this world. I, and those who follow me, ask that those of you who gave us life protect this sacred flame. You who are the earthly guardians of wisdom unite together in peace and harmony to protect this planet, our home. This I ask for the children of the world.

> The Mabon's Prayer

Much has happened since the time I spent in Scotland with those who shared my journey. *Samye Ling* gave me a place of retreat from which to explore my own heritage and the wisdom of the teachings of this land. People such as Hannah and others who live and work there, gave me the gifts of their time, their companionship and their support, and I wish them well on their own journey.

But what of the meaning of all that I have spoken of? Do we somehow try and recreate what some may think of as a lost and golden age, misguidedly trying to retrace our path back to a time when humankind had taken only a few simple steps along the way which, eventually, will lead to us being fully awake upon this earth? Or do we turn once more to those spiritual traditions which honour the divinity of the masculine and feminine as equal, and their union as the dynamic, flowing dance of life? One of Druidry's great strengths, is its ability to reflect the needs of the times we live in, and to help us to find answers to those needs. Like a great tree planted firmly in the earth, it has its roots deep within our heritage, drawing nourishment and wisdom from the past and those who went before us, so that together we can work towards the vision of a peaceful and joyous world.

As the great wheel turns and we move into the Age of Aquarius, the Spirits of Time and Place speak once more with the voice of the Great Mother. Many of us are beginning to hear her voice, and what touches us most profoundly is that it sounds so familiar. Her voice comes from deep within our own soul, she is so much a part of ourselves that we wonder how we could ever have denied her. She speaks to us through the cycles of our own bodies, through the cycle of the seasons, through the land we live upon, through the rivers and oceans of the world. But deep within the mysteries of our Druidic tradition she speaks to us from the fire that burns within the centre of the earth, the sacred fire that warmed the cauldron from which the Awen flowed, the Divine Inspiration that was the gift of the Goddess. And, as if to reinforce her voice, the spirit of Aquarius speaks to us of equality, balance and relationship. The Old Ones knew that the whole universe exists in a state of relationship between the masculine and feminine principles. In varying degrees, where one exists so does the other. The dynamic relationship between the two is the very essence of our existence in the physical world. And in Druidry we honour the sacredness of that relationship in all life, not only that of the Great Mother and her Divine Child, but also the sacred union between man and woman, spirit and matter, intellect and intuition. The creative dance of opposites, light and dark, summer and winter, life and death; all are honoured as they interact and transform – always changing and being changed by the relationship.

The stories of Mabon and Modron speak to us in a specific way that can have meaning for each one of us. For we are all born of the dark womb of the Great Mother, and within each one of us burns the gentle flame of hope.

*In honour of the Great Mother who gave us Life and of her son the
Child of Light, may we work together to provide a future strong
and secure in the roots of our heritage, allowing the future generations to grow, reaching out towards one another, beyond boundaries of race, religion, class or gender, and into the Light of Truth.*

The Modron's Prayer

As I finally left Scotland, I made one last effort to find the Mabon.
Making a short detour, I hoped to find Clochmabenstane, the Mabon
stone, a prehistoric stone just one and a half miles from Gretna.
There was no clear information as to where it stood, and as the
weather had changed for the worse, I considered driving straight
home, but as I neared Gretna the sky began to clear, the rain stopped
and the sun began to shine. I knew that I couldn't go home without
completing my search. After driving through the village, I followed a
road that eventually took me to a dead end by the mouth of the river.
I got out of the car and looked around, but there was no stone. A car
was parked nearby and a man and a young boy were changing muddy
shoes before driving home. I asked the man about the stone, and his
face lit up. After trying to explain the best way through the waterlogged fields, he insisted that they take me to it. A magnificent bull
kept a wary eye on us as we picked our way across the muddy ground.
The bull appeared to be quite content to stay amongst his female
companions, but I was relieved to scramble under the fence on the
far side of the field. As we walked, my guide told me that he had a
memory of there being two stones, but for many years now he had
only seen one and possibly he had been mistaken.

We climbed the small rise beyond the fence, and there in front of
me was Clochmabenstane, a large egg-shaped stone that legend says
once sheltered Robert the Bruce. This was it, the Mabon stone, and
if I had expected any great revelation, none came. My companion
was trying to understand his memory of a second stone that he said
was much smaller and had lain by the side of the other. He spoke of
field boundaries being moved and wandered off to search the area.
Suddenly, he called to me from the hedges that bounded the field; I
rushed over while he excitedly pointed to something that he was
standing on. There, in hawthorns some twenty feet away, was a
smaller stone. From its side protruded a strong metal bar and a length
of heavy chain. It had been dragged away many years ago from the
sheltering side of its companion. Images of Modron and Mabon

flooded my thoughts. Here was the Mabon stone, bound by chains and hidden amongst the hawthorns. Here was The Great Prisoner, taken from his Mother when a few days old; their stories reflected here in those two great stones.

The knowledge we seek is written in star and stone. Our Ancestors knew this; it is time for us once more to listen to their wisdom.

Christine Worthington is a Druidess and Modron of the Order of Bards, Ovates and Druids. Having concentrated on building a home and raising a family, she trained in hypnotherapy, psychotherapy, reflexology and polarity therapy. She has a strong interest in alchemy and its transformative power, and believes that within the spiritual teachings that Druidry embodies lies a transformative process which leads to healing and wholeness, both on a personal and a planetary level. Much of her work is dedicated to reaffirming the presence of the Wisdom of the Divine Feminine within the Druid tradition and she has run workshops for women both in Britain and Holland.

Louise Larkins Bradford

THE HERBS OF
THE DRUIDS

In ancient Ireland, in the days of the mythological Tuatha De Danann, there once sprouted a crop of magical herbs. 365 stalks of grass – each a cure for any illness of the 365 nerves in a man's body – sprang up on the grave of the healer, Miach, son of Diancecht, physician of the gods. Miach's sister, Airmid, spread out her mantle and separated the herbs according to their properties. But Diancecht, who had killed his son in a fit of jealousy over his healing skills, came and confused the herbs so no one henceforth would know the proper cures unless the Holy Spirit taught them.

When the gods withdrew, the knowledge of herbal lore did not vanish entirely, but passed into the hands of the wise men, the Druids. Their secrets, too, are largely lost since all their teaching was oral. Nevertheless, we can glean some information from various outside sources.

The best and oldest written account is found in the *Natural History* of Pliny the Elder, who reported on the herbs of the Druids of Gaul during the first century. Later, a few mediaeval manuscripts contain what may be vestiges of Druidic practice in Britain and Ireland. The most notable is a Welsh herbal said to have been written in the thirteenth century, and possibly containing material dating from the sixth century. This herbal was published in the nineteenth century under the title, *The Physicians of Myddvai*, (*see Bibliography*) and contains what seem to be vestiges of the old belief in the supernatural origins of herbs. The book begins with a folktale about the first Myddvai physician, Rhiwallon, and how he learned all about herbal lore from his mother, a Lady-of-the-Lake who emerges from time to time to instruct him at a place called Mountain Gate. The book also gives Welsh mythological names, including Taliesin, Olwen and Bronwen, to several herbs.

From Pliny we hear of only four plants. One is verbena, a name the

Romans gave both to altar plants in general and specifically to the herb vervain. Another is selago, an evergreen club moss which later herbalists guessed was probably heath cypress. A third plant, samolus, also lacks certain identification, but has been referred to as brook-weed, pasque-flower, water pimpernel and marshwort. The fourth is the mistletoe.

Pliny's descriptions contain a considerable number of details about when and how the Druids harvested and prepared the herbs, as well as about their use. Rituals accompanied the gathering of all four. Important considerations included the colour of clothing to be worn, and the materials to be used for receiving the newly picked herb; the time of the day, month or year; sacrifices, offerings and prayers; the tools either required or prohibited; and the manner in which the plant was handled.

Vervain, the Druids told Pliny, was to be gathered at the time when Sirius, the Dog-star, was rising – midsummer – at an hour when neither sun nor moon could see what was happening. Honey and honeycombs were to be offered to the Earth as compensation for the loss of such a treasure. The harvester was required to draw a circle with an iron implement, then pull out the plant with his left hand and raise it in the air. Then the leaves, stem and root were to be separated and dried in the shade.

The Druids thought highly of vervain and claimed that it could cure all diseases without exception. All one had to do – for anything from banishing a fever to making all wishes come true – was simply to rub it on. For snake bites, however, the herb crushed in wine was recommended. They also believed, as did others in the Mediterranean world, that guests at a party would become 'merrier' if you sprinkled the dining couches with an infusion of the herb. Pliny also mentioned that the people of Gaul used the plant for telling fortunes and prophesying, although it is not clear if he was referring specifically to the Druids.

The mediaeval Welsh herbalists hinted that some pagan rite of gathering 'vendigaid' (the Welsh name for vervain) persisted, since they specified that the herb should be gathered 'in the name of God and not in the name of the devil, as some say.' They did not specify a time of year beyond 'when in seed,' although mention of the association of this herb with Alban Hervin, the summer solstice, appears in the nineteenth century introduction. The herb could either be roasted and powdered, then mixed in bread dough, or boiled in ale, mead or milk. Considered efficacious for running sores and scrophula, it also served as a general tonic.

The Druids also highly esteemed the club moss selago. If the gathering ritual was performed properly, it was believed the herb had the power to prevent all accidents and misfortunes, while its 'fume' would alleviate all eye problems. The person assigned to gather the moss first had to don white clothing and wash their feet, leaving them bare. Before setting out they were to offer a sacrifice of bread and wine to the gods. No knife or iron tool could be used and they could touch the plant only with their right hand, while with the left they held out a portion of their garment to conceal their actions – as if they were trying to steal it secretly. They then wrapped it in a new linen napkin.

Samolus was given only to swine and oxen, in the hope that it would ward off all their diseases. Nevertheless, it, too, was collected in a reverent manner. Only someone who had been fasting was allowed to touch it, and they were forbidden to look at it, or place it anywhere except the watering trough. The herb was then crushed for the animals to drink.

The king of Druidic herbs was, of course, the mistletoe. Not ordinary mistletoe, though, found almost anytime on various trees such as apple, pear or hawthorn, but only that which adorned a Valonia oak. Since it appeared only rarely on this evergreen tree – itself considered sacred – such a plant was considered a gift from heaven, and a sign that God had singled out that special tree. When an oak-mistletoe was discovered, its plucking had to be postponed until the right time came – when the crescent moon reached its sixth day. There was no mention of any special time of year, such as the winter solstice.

The harvesting of this mistletoe involved considerable ceremony. It began with preparations for a banquet and for the ritual sacrifice of two white bulls. After a great cry was uttered – a salutation to 'that which heals all things' – a priest robed in white vestments climbed the tree and cut down the plant with a golden sickle. It was not allowed to fall to the ground, but was caught in a white cloak. What happened to it after that, no one knows. As the bulls were slaughtered, the priests prayed to God that his gift would be a boon to the recipients.

However, in spite of this elaborate ceremony and the hail to the All-heal, the only medicinal claims the sages made for mistletoe were that it would make any barren animal fertile, and could serve as an antidote for all poisons.

The Welsh leeches, perhaps repeating Pliny's words, called

mistletoe 'Oll Iach' – All-Heal – as well as 'Yr Uchelfar'. In one section of the Myddvai herbal, they said the plant could strengthen the body more than any other. The addition of a berry infusion and roasted powdered leaves and sprigs of mistletoe to any drink was prescribed for all kinds of diseases of the nerves, joints, back, head or brain, stomach, heart, lungs and kidneys; for epilepsy, paralysis, and all weakness of joints, sight, hearing or senses, as well as for 'fruitfulness and the begetting of children.'

The best time for gathering it, they said, was in the depths of winter from St. Andrews' day to Candlemas, when the berries ripen. But the green herb could be gathered any time from the feast of St. James to the Calends of November. A reference to its association with Alban Arthuan, the winter solstice, appears only in the nineteenth century introduction.

The Mystery of the Mistletoe

Ever since Pliny wrote his account, people have been puzzled by the mystery of the mistletoe. Why did the Druids specify no other use for it than promoting animal fertility and counteracting poisons, while apparently hailing it as the ultimate healer? Why did the great Greek physician, Dioscorides, author of the most highly esteemed European herbal until the sixteenth century, recommend 'viscum' (mistletoe) for little more than the treatment of swellings and malignant suppurations? Why was it not mentioned as a sacred herb in Anglo-Saxon herbals, or even listed in two mediaeval Irish pharmacological tracts? Why did even the Myddvai leeches – the only ones who called mistletoe 'All-Heal' – include it in no specific recipe except one for epilepsy?

Modern botanists have searched in vain for its miracle-drug potential. And while anthroposophical physicians believe a mistletoe-based preparation may be effective in the treatment of cancer, most herbalists recommend it mainly for cases of epilepsy and other nervous diseases. In fact, the berries, which are poisonous, can cause convulsions. Even Pliny provided several antidotes for mistletoe poisoning!

On the other hand, Pliny mentioned in 38 entries another plant specifically given the Latin term for all-heal: *panaces*. As he said, the name alone – that of Asclepion's daughter Panacea – promised a cure for every disease. He identified four varieties of this 'panaces': giant fennel, wild origanum, chironium – probably elecampane – and centaurion – centaury. (Today the herb entitled panax is ginseng.)

And then the Druids also told Pliny that vervain could cure all diseases without exception.

Perhaps the answer lies outside the field of botany. What if the druidic salutation was not, in fact, to the mistletoe? Pliny's phrase, 'omnia sanantem appellantes suo vocabulo', which follows a section on both moon and mistletoe, has been often translated as 'They called the mistletoe by a name which means "all-healing" in their language.' But Cambridge scholar H. Rackham suggested by his 1945 translation that the Druids' native word for 'healing all things' belonged not to the plant but to the moon. Might there be even another alternative: that it referred to both?

In ancient India, where many links with Celtic tradition can be found, due to their common Indo-European roots, there was a lunar-linked sacred beverage which may shed some light on the mystery. This drink was called Soma. The name had several simultaneous meanings: a sacramental drink; the plant from which it was extracted; the drink as a divine nectar stored in the moon; and the moon itself – both a grail endlessly emptied and refilled, and a god. Over a hundred hymns of the Rig Veda, one of the oldest Hindu sacred texts, praised the plant as a god; all of the related collection of chants, the Sama Veda, was dedicated to it.

In its earthly form, the Soma drink was produced by crushing the 'king of plants' – Asclepius acida – then mixing its milky juice with clarified butter and letting it ferment. When ready, it was offered as a sacrifice and consumed by priests. The sacramental liquor symbol-ized the liquid essence of life itself, manifest in many forms: sap, semen, milk, rain, the semen or urine of the cosmic horse, the seed of Shiva's linga permeating the universe. Yoga masters taught that Moon-Soma ruled the mind, and that by meditative practise men could learn to distill the vital essence in their own bodies in a way that would provide the soul with everlasting life.

In ancient Iran, the oldest known rituals required the sacrificial immolation and consumption of a yellow elixir made from the 'haoma' plant, which was perhaps the same as Soma. Bull-sacrifice formed part of the ceremony, and partaking of the bull's flesh symbol-ized achieving immortality for the body, while drinking haoma guar-anteed it for the soul.

As we know from Caesar and other ancient writers, the Druids also believed that the soul survives the death of the body. When they cut down the golden-hued mistletoe with a golden crescent-shaped tool, did they then prepare a potion that symbolized the cure for death? Was the elixir a liquor of lunar light? Was it the same drink that Diancecht's brother, Goibniu, prepared for the gods: the Ale of Immortality?

Suggested Reading

Daniélou, Alain. *The Myths and Gods of India*, Inner Traditions International, 1991.

Grieves, Mrs. M. *A Modern Herbal*, Dover Publications, 1982.

Hopman, Ellen Evert. *A Druid's Herbal for the Sacred Earth Year*, Destiny Books, 1995.

Pliny the Elder. *Natural History*, Loeb Classical Library. Vol. IV trans. H. Rackham; Vol. VII trans. W.H.S. Jones, Harvard University Press, 1986 and 1980.

Rohde, Eleanor. *The Old English Herbals*, Dover Publications, 1971.

Stokes, Whitley. *The Second Battle of Moytura*, Revue Celtique XII, 552–130, 1891.

Trans. Goodver, John 1655, ed. Gunther, Robert. *The Greek Herbal of Dioscorides*, Oxford University Press, 1934.

Trans. Pughe, John, ed. Williams, Rev. John, *The Physicians of Myddvai*, published for the Welsh Manuscript Society, Llandovery, D.J. Roderic-Longman Company, 1861.

Zaehner, R.C., *The Dawn and Twilight of Zoroastrianism*, G.P. Putnam's Sons, 1961.

Louise Larkins Bradford is a musician and occasional freelance writer who has studied mythology and ancient religions independently for over 25 years. Long an investigator of various traditional healing practises, including herbalism, she became interested in Druidic herbs during the five years spent working with the material of the OBOD correspondence course. Her home is in Philadelphia, where she lives near a large oak.

IV

DRUID CEREMONY

Ritual is poetry in the world of acts

Nuinn

Druids love ritual. In the three-year training programme of *The Order of Bards Ovates and Druids*, thirty-six rituals are given – including tree-planting ceremonies, initiations, and seasonal rituals.

The cornerstone of Druid practice is the observation of a cycle of eight seasonal rituals, with one of them – the Summer Solstice – actually being made up of three ceremonies, at midnight, dawn and noon. Every six weeks or so, someone following the Druid way will celebrate a seasonal ceremony, either by themselves or in a group (often called a 'Grove'). The origin of the form and content of these ceremonies is hard to trace prior to the time of the Druid Revival in the eighteenth century. In the twentieth century they were enriched and developed, probably the most by George Watson MacGregor-Reid (the Summer Solstice and Equinox ceremonies) and by Ross Nichols (the Winter Solstice and fire festivals, except the Samhain ceremony used by OBOD which can be traced to Britanny). Many groups are writing new ceremonies, or adapting old ones, tuning in to the Spirit of the Times, and recognizing that each age must express Druidry in its own way, while still honouring its heritage.

Whether old or new, the rituals of the eightfold cycle connect us to a system of ritual observance which is both elegant and profound, as will be seen from the articles that follow.

Chris Turner

THE SACRED CALENDAR

The Celtic inhabitants of Britain in the period which ended with the coming of the Romans in the first century AD, marked their year by eight regularly-spaced festivals. The correct timing and observance of these would have been under the jurisdiction of the Druids, in their capacity as lore-keepers. From such evidence that survives the Roman invasion and the subsequent Christianization of the islands, it can be inferred that these eight festivals are, in fact, two separate series of four which alternate throughout the year.

The first four festivals we shall look at are the Sun Feasts. These belong to the set of observable celestial phenomena that ultimately underpin all calendars. The marking of particular days by observing the rising and setting of the Sun and stars has always been absolutely predictable. These settings absorb the slight backwards drift of one day in every four years caused by the true length of the year being 365 days plus an extra quarter day. Nowadays, we correct this drift with our Leap Year system. Some calendars which are based on the cycles of the moon still ultimately observe the Sun's rising as a check of accuracy.

An excellent example of a star-rise calendar is that used to set the ancient Egyptian year. This started on the day that the star Sirius was observed to rise, July 17th by our calendar. The Egyptian year contained three seasons only, there being no appreciable Winter in Egypt, and was a flat 360 days made up of 12 months of 30 days each. The Egyptians then tacked on 'extra' days to bring the tally up to 365, when Sirius was once again observed to rise and a new year begin. The start of the year was set afresh each time and never varied more than a day's length for century after century.

As far north as Britain, the weather and visibility just isn't good enough for observations of an Egyptian standard. We do, however, see a Sun that is a much more precise timekeeper than that which shines over Africa. The further away one is from the Equator, the further north and south one sees the Sun rise and set in its annual swing from midsummer to midwinter, and the plotting of the points on the horizon where these events take place is all the more accurate. The events of midsummer and midwinter, 21st June and 21st December respectively, represent allegorically the concept of vitality followed by death and rebirth. These are highly symbolic concepts and the means of observing these festivals, in both an astronomical and religious sense, are evident in many of our prehistoric monuments.

The time of the Equinoxes, 21st March and 21st September, is the time of the greatest daily movement in the Sun's rising and setting points and therefore the easiest and most precise to fix. The Equinoxes have other notable special properties which makes them worthy of careful observation and recording. On these two days only are day and night the same length, twelve hours each exactly, hence the name equi-nox – equal night. If observed over a flat horizon, such as water, only on these days is the point of sunrise exactly opposite the point of sunset, all three points (including the observer in the middle) making a straight line. This line, from sunrise to sunset, also points exactly East and West. Most importantly, these observations, for these two days only, hold true for every place on the surface of the Earth: Europe or Africa, America or Asia.

Midwinter, Vernal, or Spring Equinox, Midsummer and the Autumnal Equinox are the four great Sun festivals which have been marked and honoured by most of humanity since the earliest times. Some, like the peoples of the far North, placed greatest emphasis on the Sun's rebirth at Midwinter. Others, such as the Persians and Romans, living in more temperate lands to the South, noted the coincidence of Spring with the many mystical aspects of the Equinox and counted the rebirth of their years from the 21st March.

Over the wide sweep of time, the celebration of seasonal festivals came to serve two distinct purposes. One was to foster the spiritual consciousness of the people and guide them in their journey through life towards the Higher Goal. The other was to assist and regulate the necessary mechanics of survival – hunting, planting and reaping in proper season. In the cradle of civilization, the Mediterranean Basin and the Middle East, these two aspects coincided well. But in the broad band across central Europe, including the British Isles, that was home to the ancient Celts, the coincidence of the seasons with the Sun feasts was not such a good match. It became necessary to define a new set of Feasts to regulate the Pastoral year.

In Britain, the Vernal Equinox on the 21st March is, with the best will in the world, a long way from the balmy flower-filled Spring day that you expect to find in the southern lands. In warmer climes, this is the point at which crop-planting should be finished and celebrations held to mark the successful completion of the second great task of the pastoral year, the first being the preparation of the soil from Midwinter onwards.

Here in the North, however, any seeds sown in the open before the Vernal Equinox are at severe risk from lack of sunlight, and frosts and snow that run on to the end of April. You may as well throw half of them away. In our harsher British climate, the sowing season has to be postponed for six weeks or thereabouts to guarantee any reasonable chance of success. Thus it starts at the Equinox and must be completed by the time of a new Feast that falls roughly midway between the Sun Feasts of Spring Equinox and Midsummer. Originally marked by great celebrations in which giant bonfires figured prominently, this festival is still celebrated in a rather muted form (and recently has sadly fallen prey to party politicking). We know it as May Day.

As our British winters are long, so our summers are short. We plant late and harvest early. The ancient Celts, under the guidance of their Druids, had to sow their seeds six weeks later than the Solar calendar suggested and reached the high point of their harvest six weeks early. Rather than celebrating the bounty of Nature at the Autumn Equinox in September, it became more appropriate to hold the Northern celebrations seven weeks earlier at the beginning of August, now known as Lammastide, the Feast of Loaves, because of the freshly harvested grain.

This movement of feasts created a fourth Season, the season of lying fallow. This is the time when the year is dying, when leaves fall, nothing grows, no fodder is to be found for the beasts, no seed sprouts, and crops that have not ripened rot on the vine. The start of this season was marked by a Feast that closed the year and falls roughly midway between the Solar markers of the September Equinox and Midwinter. Now known as Hallowe'en, the bonfires that always marked this Feast have an atavistic echo in the celebrations of Guy Fawkes Night.

The ice, snow and bitter frosts of the deep Northern winter made it impossible to prepare the ground for planting with rudimentary implements in December and January. So the time marked for preparing the soil to receive the seeds of the new planting was postponed from Midwinter to the beginning of February, the Feast of Candles.

The principal effect of this rearrangement of the seasonal markers was to separate the dual aspects of the original Feasts: the Spiritual aspect from the Pastoral. The Solar Feasts remain; whatever the plants and animals are doing, the Sun will always rise at just this point on Midsummer's Day and always set exactly due West on the Equinoxes. As this is evidently part of the Great Plan manifest, the nature of the four Solar Feasts becomes predominantly spiritual and esoteric. On the other hand, the four markers of the pastoral year are critical for the survival of the community from year to year. They are essentially practical, but nonetheless contain a strong element of

The Solar Feasts
Celestial and Spiritual

The Fire Feasts
Pastoral and Corporeal

awe and wonder at how the mysteries of life, death and rebirth are writ large in the cycle of the seasons. The spiritual nature of these festivals is much more personal and introspective.

It is notable that at least three of the pastoral festivals have a fire focus. May Day and Hallowe'en feature bonfires and Candlemas emphasizes the less considered aspect of fire: light. Lammas may also represent the 'tamed' fire of the hearth that bakes the loaves. In our modern electrical society, we forget that until recent years fire was struck as much for light as for heat. This highlights the distinction between the two sets of Feasts. The Solar Feasts now take the nature of celestial fire/light, representing the spiritual planes, while the pastoral festivals or, as I shall now call them, Fire Feasts, in their use of burning wood and candles, relate to corporeal fire and represent the material universe and all creatures that dwell in it.

The four pastoral markers of the ancient Druidic Year are still known to us in corruptions of their late Irish names: Samain, Imbolc, Beltane and Lugnasad. Even after successive waves of invaders and proselytizers, the ancient and sacred Calendar of Britain was established too deeply to be entirely overlaid by the Romans, Saxons or Christians. Admittedly, Samain could not be celebrated except under the guise of All Hallows, nor Imbolc except as Candlemas, but the pegs of the Sacred Calendar remained. Of the four-and-four Great Feasts, the names of the other four, much older, Sun Feasts of Midsummer, Midwinter and the Equinoxes, have not survived.

We now see a calendar of eight feasts, four of the Spirit and four of the Material World, alternating throughout the year like the interlocking teeth of two cogwheels (*see page 169*).

The cycle of the Druidic Year appears quite straightforward. It is generally agreed that the end-of-harvest feast of Samain marked the turning of the year. In this context, 'harvest' does not mean the gathering of corn and first fruits which happens around August, but when the Earth is exhausted at the turning of November and has nothing more to offer: neither bounty for man nor fodder for beast. The next Celtic feast is not Midwinter but Imbolc. Midwinter is a much more ancient feast which, then as now, belongs to the ethos of Albion, the mystical personification of Britain, and seems to resonate with the rocks and very fabric of these Islands rather than the culture of the current dominant race.

Date	Solar Feasts Celestial	Fire Feasts Pastoral	Celtic Name
February 1st		Candlemas	Imbolc
March 21st	Vernal Equinox		—
May 1st		May Day	Beltane
June 21st	Midsummer's Day		—
August 1st		Lammastide	Lugnasad
September 21st	Autumn Equinox		—
November 1st		All Hallows	Samain
December 21st	Midwinter's Day		—

I refer to the Solar feasts of Midwinter, Midsummer and the Equinoxes as 'older' festivals and I feel this opinion needs a word of explanation. Prehistoric dating is notoriously difficult. There is, by definition, no written record and much of the evidence is negative. In most cases there has to be a large element of personal interpretation. My own opinion is based on the fact that where solar alignments can be implied from the ancient pre-Celtic megalithic monuments, these are usually centred on Midwinter, Midsummer and the Equinoxes. The Celtic feasts do not coincide with any notable solar phenomena and it seems to me that in order for these feasts to keep their true position year after year, they must be set by being related to observations at the solar quarter-days. It follows that the solar calendar of Midwinter, Midsummer and the Equinoxes must have been established first in order for the feasts of the later Celtic peoples to have been set in relation to it.

After the dying of the year at Samain, Imbolc is the purifying flame of the nadir of the year through which the Mother is reborn as the Virgin. Set at the beginning of February, it later became known to the Christians as Candlemas. This is followed in the Celtic year by the lusty Mayfire of Beltane, quickening the seed in the womb of the Earth that burgeons with the bounty celebrated at Lugnasad the Fruitful, the Motherfeast of August which fades, as all things fade, into November's Samain, the Death-in-life of the Northern Winter.

An obvious cycle? Well, obvious to any culture that measures its year by one of the three usual methods: firstly, the time it takes for the Sun, or a specific fixed star, to get back to where it started from; secondly, as many moon cycles (plus or minus the odd one now and then) to achieve the same effect or thirdly, the visible and demonstrable completion of the cycle of the seasons. It may appear that the Druidic Year follows the third but, as with so many things associated with the strange and bewildering Celts, appearances are deceptive.

It appears that the ancient Druidic approach to the construction of a calendar was somewhat unorthodox, the Druids measuring time in a cyclic rather than linear system. This may simply have been dismissed by the later Church and State as irrelevant. It seems that aspects of the Celtic calendar and other lore were not identified and, not being identified, were not suppressed. Thus it transpires that so much survives across the centuries more or less intact and the traditions, myths and ancient wisdom can be retrieved and reconstructed from fragments and clues passed on unrecognized through the ages.

Perhaps the single most notable facet of the ancient Celts' view of the cosmos is their concern with triplicity. Tricephalic stone heads, triple Goddesses and their Triadic sayings are examples that spring readily to mind. Uniquely, the Celts appear to have reconciled this triadic viewpoint with a four-season year in a system which is astonishingly simple in concept, but which operates on a level of breathtaking elegance. In the Irish *Book of Rights* there is a description of the Lugnasad Fair at Tara that makes two remarks regarding the passage of time. Firstly, that the Fair lasted seven days. I shall return to this later. Secondly, that the Fair was not an annual event, but was held every three years. This is unusual, but not unique: the four-year cycle of the Olympiads is a similar case. Lugnasad, however, does not stand alone, but is part of the larger four-feast cycle.

So how does this four-part annual system reconcile with a three-year repetition format? The synthesis becomes dazzlingly clear if the Celts in fact only celebrated every third Feast throughout the cycle. This can be seen more clearly in the following table:

Feasts in brackets are marked but NOT celebrated.

	November 1	February 1	May 1	August 1
CYCLE I				
Year 1	SAMAIN	(Imbolc)	(Beltane)	LUGNASAD
Year 2	(Samain)	(Imbolc)	BELTANE	(Lugnasad)
Year 3	(Samain)	IMBOLC	(Beltane)	(Lugnasad)

Thus Year One starts with Samain, which is celebrated. The next two feasts, Imbolc and Beltane are skipped over and the next celebrated Feast is Lugnasad, the last in Year One. The first in Year Two is Samain which this time is skipped over as is the next, Imbolc. Beltane is the only Feast to be celebrated in Year Two as Lugnasad is skipped together with Samain, Year Three. The Feast of Imbolc in Year Three is celebrated, Beltane and Lugnasad skipped, and this brings us to the celebration of Samain, Year Four, which starts the whole three-year cycle again:

	November 1	February 1	May 1	August 1
CYCLE II				
Year 4	SAMAIN	(Imbolc)	(Beltane)	LUGNASAD
Year 5	(Samain)	(Imbolc)	BELTANE	(Lugnasad)
Year 6	(Samain)	IMBOLC	(Beltane)	(Lugnasad)
CYCLE III				
Year 7	SAMAIN	(Imbolc)	(Beltane)	LUGNASAD
Year 8	(Samain)	(Imbolc)	BELTANE	(Lugnasad)
Year 9	(Samain)	IMBOLC	(Beltane)	(Lugnasad)

And so on. As described at Tara, Lugnasad, like all the feasts, is celebrated once every three solar years. The order in which the feasts are celebrated reverses so instead of Samain, Imbolc, Beltane and Lugnasad, they run (year number in brackets): Samain (one), Lugnasad (one), Beltane (two), Imbolc (three) and so on.

This calendar now takes on a dual aspect. First, the pastoral calendar of the seasons which the people must follow and relate to, in order to survive. Second, an esoteric Year Round of three solar years when every third feast has been celebrated once and the cycle renewed.

That every third feast should be celebrated is in itself a format that would have appealed to a people obsessed with threes, but the underlying significances run much deeper. The equating of the solar year with the male principle and the lunar cycle with the female principle is predominant throughout the Western Tradition. The Celts seem to be unusual in being able to grasp the fact that these two principles are not necessarily antithetic. Together they can, in fact, represent the concept of the Implicit behind the Explicit. Through the example of the time period and the higher harmonics of the cycle of pregnancy, the old Calendar of Britain seems to show a simulacrum of the psychic progress of the Soul through its phases of development/enlightenment on its long journey back to union with the Creator.

As male and female represent the explicit principles of virility and fertility, so there is the implicit expectation of the harmonious fusion of the two. Through the cycle of the resulting pregnancy comes the synthesis of the masculine and feminine principles in a new cycle that transcends them both. Although they are regarded as opposites, man and woman are, as Pythagoras stated, 'compatible opposites'. So too with our Self and our Higher Self. We have no business being at war with ourSelves. We are not two alien beings, but two incomplete aspects of the greater One, yearning for union on the Way Home. The custom of one of a couple referring to their partner as 'my better half' is perhaps not so trivial as it seems.

The term of pregnancy, from conception to birth, is equal in length to the time between any three quarter-year feasts. A period of four pregnancies is equal to one Druidic Year Round of three solar years. A child conceived on the Feast of Samain will be born on the third feast following; that is Lugnasad. Similarly, a pregnancy starting at Lugnasad will come to term on the next Beltane. The Beltane child will be born at Imbolc, and the Imbolc pregnancy will arrive at Samain three years from where we started, so completing a new Year Round which is neither male nor female in character, but an intimate and harmonious inter-relationship of the two. The three solar years of the Cycle are masculine in character, the four Fire feasts are essentially feminine, being largely concerned with planting and harvest: they come together as three parts Sky to four parts Earth. This in itself is a paradigm for the reconciliation of Spirit and Matter, Circle and Square, Female and Male.

We can look at the idea of four pregnancies in three years a little

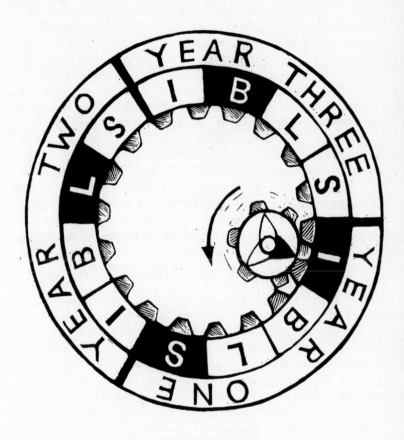

The Year Round
key: I = Imbolc, S = Samain, L = Lugnasad, B = Beltane
The outer wheel represents the Year Round of three Solar Years each with its
four Fire Feasts. The inner wheel represents the period of three Fire Feasts,
marking every third Feast (in black) to give four Feasts in every complete cycle.

closer. Gray's *Encyclopaedia of Biological Sciences* gives the average length of human gestation as 273 days from ovulation to birth. The actual period from Imbolc to Samain (taken as February 1 to November 1) is also exactly 273 days. So is the period from Samain to Lugnasad (November 1 to August 1) and Lugnasad to Beltane (August 1 to May 1). The period from Beltane to Imbolc (May 1 to February 1) is, however, 276 days. This is necessary to complete the three full Solar years of 365 days each of the old Year Round and bring the next Year Round to its true starting point. As we shall see, this also sets the mechanism for another, higher level of cycles.

This period of 273 days is exactly 39 weeks long. Each of the first three cycles above, starting Imbolc, Samain and Lugnasad, must also be exactly 39 weeks long and must, therefore, all start on the same day of the week. The fourth cycle also starts on the same day but finishes on the third day following, setting a new day to run through the next Year Round of three solar years. It would seem that a run of four Feasts all starting on the same day of the week, for example a Tuesday, may have a distinct character from a run of four Feasts starting on a Friday. I will therefore refer to the start day of any set of four Feasts as the Keynote Day.

While the pastoral year starts at Samain, the Year Round starts at Imbolc, when the Keynote Day changes. Each Year Round has a different aspect, taken from the Keynote Day: the day of the week that dominates that particular cycle. The aspects run in order: Tuesday, Friday, Monday, Thursday, Sunday, Wednesday, and Saturday, making a Grand Cycle of seven Year Rounds, each of three solar years. This takes a full 28 celebrated feasts, each nine months from the last, and is complete in 21 years.

This will show more clearly on the following table:

	November 1	February 1	May 1	August 1

YEAR ROUND I   **KEYNOTE DAY: TUESDAY**

Year 1		IMBOLC/TUES	(Beltane)	(Lugnasad)
Year 2	SAMAIN/TUES	(Imbolc)	(Beltane)	LUGNASAD/TUES
Year 3	(Samain)	(Imbolc)	BELTANE/TUES	(Lugnasad)
Year 4	(Samain)			

YEAR ROUND II   **KEYNOTE DAY: FRIDAY**

Year 4		IMBOLC/FRI	(Beltane)	(Lugnasad)
Year 5	SAMAIN/FRI	(Imbolc)	(Beltane)	LUGNASAD/FRI
Year 6	(Samain)	(Imbolc)	BELTANE/FRI	(Lugnasad)
Year 7	(Samain)			

YEAR ROUND III   **KEYNOTE DAY: MONDAY**

Year 7		IMBOLC/MON	(Beltane)	(Lugnasad)
Year 8	SAMAIN/MON	(Imbolc)	(Beltane)	LUGNASAD/MON
Year 9	(Samain)	(Imbolc)	BELTANE/MON	(Lugnasad)
Year 10	(Samain)			

Using Western astrological associations, it could be said that the first Year Round is under the influence of Mars, the Keynote Day of each Feast being Tuesday (Mars being the equivalent of the Old English god Tiw after whom the day was named). The character of the second Year Round is set by Venus (Freya), the presiding influence of Friday. The rest of the Grand Cycle follows in order:

Year Round I	Keynote Day: TUESDAY	Influence: MARS
Year Round II	Keynote Day: FRIDAY	Influence: VENUS
Year Round III	Keynote Day: MONDAY	Influence: MOON/DIANA
Year Round IV	Keynote Day: THURSDAY	Influence: JUPITER
Year Round V	Keynote Day: SUNDAY	Influence: SUN/APOLLO
Year Round VI	Keynote Day: WEDNESDAY	Influence: MERCURY
Year Round VII	Keynote Day: SATURDAY	Influence: SATURN

This may seem to be simply a haphazard arrangement of the days of the week, but nothing could be further from the truth. In a manner analogous to the families of Celtic Oghams, the seven 'planetary' celestial bodies have, as we have seen, their equivalents in the days of the week and tutelary deities. They also have corresponding sets of colours, musical notes, gemstones and metals. Looking at the traditional associations of metals with the planets, we find that Mars represents iron; Venus, copper; Moon, silver; Jupiter, tin; Sun, gold; Mercury, quicksilver; and Saturn, lead. In a brilliant example of the encrypting of knowledge in traditional lore, this arrangement sets out the metals in atomic weight order. Iron, the least massive of the series, comes first and is followed by copper which is more massive than iron. Copper is followed by silver which is more massive than copper, and so on until lead, the heaviest of all, is reached as the following table shows:

DAY OF WEEK	PLANET	METAL	ATOMIC WEIGHT	ATOMIC NUMBER
TUESDAY	MARS	IRON	55.864	26
FRIDAY	VENUS	COPPER	63.54	29
MONDAY	MOON	SILVER	107.87	47
THURSDAY	JUPITER	TIN	118.69	50
SUNDAY	SUN	GOLD	196.97	79
WEDNESDAY	MERCURY	QUICKSILVER	200.59	80
SATURDAY	SATURN	LEAD	207.19	82

I am not suggesting that the ancient Celts or indeed their contemporaries knew of such things as Atomic Weights, but it is certainly true that Archimedes was aware of the relationship of mass to volume, as his demonstrations of displacement show, and that the Celts and other northern peoples were in direct or indirect contact with Hellenistic Greece. My own opinion is that there is no conscious human agency behind the encoding of such information for later ages to disentangle. Rather, it is an affirmation that all things spring from the One Source and all things are interrelated, even if our inadequate intellects can only see the more glaringly obvious connections. I do not see savants of a bygone Golden Age frantically encrypting the sum of their scientific and esoteric knowledge in architecture and fairy tales, while their civilization crashes round their ears. What I do see are the fingerprints of God.

Coming back to the Year Round and the influence of the Keynote Days, it seems that each Feast bestows a different gift or blessing for each of the seven days of the week it falls on. Only after every combination of four Feasts and seven Keynote Days has been celebrated and a full set acquired can a person properly progress from one social state to the next.

This Grand Cycle of 21 solar years is so deeply rooted in the social fabric of Britain that it is still kept in most families. Completion of a person's first Grand Cycle marks the end of childhood and adolescence; the change of state from minor to adult. The right to full citizenship in Britain was earned only after each of the four quarter-feasts had been kept on each of the seven days of the week; a full 21 years, Birth-day to birthday. The traditional 'key of the door' at 21, always more symbolic than actual, represents the turning of one complete Grand Cycle.

The Grand Cycles themselves are still quite firmly embedded in the way we structure our lives in Britain. The first Cycle, that of pre-adult, used to be set legally and socially at 21. This, the Cycle of Preparation, is the time to grow physically and intellectually from the egg in the womb to the full personality; mature, skilled and responsible. Although the legal age of responsibility was lowered to 18 some years ago, the 21st birthday is still widely celebrated for no apparent reason other than a deep rooted sense of it being 'the right thing to do'.

The second Grand Cycle, that of Domestication, has no legal status. It runs symbolically from the ages of 21 to 42. This is the time of forming partnerships, mating, breeding and creating a secure home. This is the time of high energy, the energy needed to bond with another human being, raise children, carve a career, build a home and maintain all this against the vicissitudes of the big, wide world.

As the turning of the first Grand Cycle is celebrated at the 21st birthday, so the nominal ending of the second is held at the 40th. Implicit in the encouraging tone of 'life begins at forty' is the acknowledgement that an earlier stage of life is, in fact, drawing to a close. In the archetypal family, this is when children no longer need nurturing and are preparing to leave home and move on to their own second Grand Cycle. Homes and careers have long been established and now only need maintenance to run smoothly. There is a sense of loss, but also of new beginnings.

The Cycle of Realization runs from 42 to 63. The end marker of official retirement at 65 is obvious. In this Cycle there is, at last, the time to look back and take pride and satisfaction in the achievements of the second Cycle. There is also time to look within and embark on a journey of discovery into our own spirituality. This is the time to

The Grand Cycle
The outer wheel represents the Grand Cycle of twenty one years with Keynote
Days in the outer ring, (here starting on Sunday, but can start anywhere,
depending on the date of birth). The inner wheel is the Year Round wheel
(p. 169) which rolls round seven times in a complete cycle.

reap what we have sown. The personal development of the third
Cycle is impossible without the achievements of the second. The
achievements of the second Grand Cycle are impossible without the
skills and talents developed in the first.

It is now clear that these are not true cycles. They do not come
back to their point of origin. Each may be seen as a turn in a continu-
ously widening spiral, although it may be more accurate to visualize
these as turns along a helix. The best picture is that of a spiral staircase. Each complete turn does not bring us back to our start point,
but to one level above where we started; one stage further along the

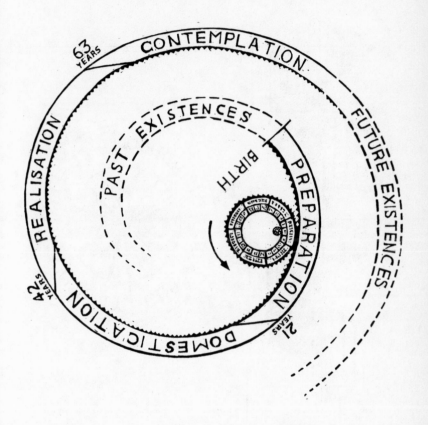

The Spiral of Life
This diagram shows the wheel of the Grand Cycle rolling round the
Spiral of Life. Each revolution marks off a complete Cycle: Preparation,
Domestication, Realization or Contemplation. Shown here is the position
of the Grand Cycle wheel for a child of eleven years.

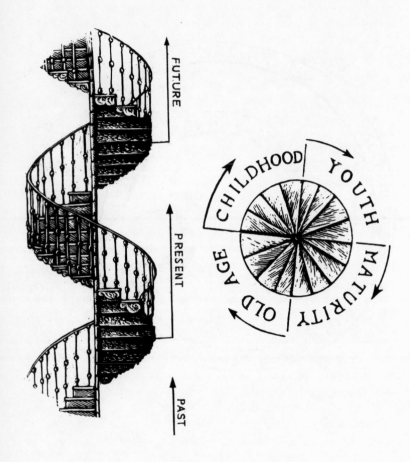

The Cycle of Life (Right)
Because of our naturally egocentric view of life, it often appears to be a one-off
closed cycle. The *apparent* direction is circular; coming from nowhere and
leading to nowhere.

The Helix (Left)
The diagram on the right represents the view of a spiral staircase from above.
On the left we see the same spiral staircase from the side.
It is now clear that the *true* direction of travel is not round and round, but
upward from the past and on to our ultimate destiny.

true direction of travel which is not round and round, but onward and upward. It is implicit in this image that the turns of the spiral will continue ahead in some way beyond the transition we call 'death' into future lives and existences. By the same token, we can see that the small fragment of the spiral that we are working our way through in this present lifetime is only a natural extension of the cycles of our many past lives and existences that we barely remember, even in dreams.

This sets the tone for the fourth and last Grand Cycle in this series: the Cycle of Contemplation. The fourth Grand Cycle is open-ended and runs from the age of 63 or thereabouts, to the end of this incarnation. Personal mortality can no longer be ignored and the withdrawal from much of the active business of life promotes a contemplative outlook. The position in this Cycle of Contemplation is threefold. First, there is a change of social status to Elder. A lifetime's experience is a precious gift that can now be offered for the good of the community. Second, there is an assessment of life so far. How did you do? What did you leave undone? This line of enquiry-naturally leads to the third: What next? In Prospero's words, 'every third thought shall be my grave'. This is a time of preparation for the next, invisible Grand Cycle and the others that lie beyond.

Here, within the Sacred Calendar of Britain, we have an ever-expanding structure of cycles within cycles that encompasses the whole human experience, from the annual cycles of the Sun, to the great cycles of the human lifespan, and on into the greater mysteries of the cosmos. These are the great lessons of our Tradition, but they are ones not to be learned as much as lived.

It is their gift to the world that the ancient Druids of Britain preserved their Sacred Calendar long enough for it to become a light and a guide to the increasing numbers of enlightened people who are striving towards a more meaningful spiritual and holistic relationship with their universe.

Chris Turner was born on the Isle of Wight in 1940. A childhood devoted to beachcombing and skywatching developed into a career skipping from one job to another. On Midsummer's Day 1992 he met a gifted psychologist and married her on Midsummer's Day 1993. He started a much belated BA Hons course in Fine Art and has lived happily ever after. Chris Turner is a fine-art printmaker and poet; designer and builder of labyrinths, stone circles and land-art installations.

Robert Mills

THE WHEEL OF CHANGES

At first glance there seems to be little to connect the major festivals of the Druidic calendar with the Chinese 'Book of Changes', the *I Ching*. Both systems are ancient and venerable, but there seems no reason for any fundamental connection between their underlying philosophies. Yet think for a moment of the foundations of the two systems. The major festival days of the Druidic calendar are an eight-fold expression of the continuous cycle of the seasons, of the inter-play between darkness and light, decay and growth, *yin* and *yang*: a fitting description of the eight trigrams which form the basis of the *I Ching*.

By considering together the 'Book of Changes' and the 'Wheel of the Year' comprised by the festivals, valuable new insights into each are obtained through knowledge of the other. Combined they form the 'Wheel of Changes'.

The Book of Changes (*I Ching*)

The *I Ching* is a Chinese book of wisdom and oracles. Its precise age is open to debate, though its origins are certainly several thousand years old, dating back to pre-Confucian times. It has its roots in duality, regarding the universe as a manifestation of the interactions between a pair of polar energies. These energies are in turn but expressions of ultimate unity, *t'ai-chi*. The strong, active, solar energy is called *yang*, and is denoted by a solid line; while the weak, recep-tive, lunar energy is called *yin*, and is denoted by a broken line.

The *I Ching* is primarily concerned with the 64 hexagrams obtained from all possible combinations of six *yin/yang* lines. However, each hexagram is considered as being the synthesis of two more fundamental units: trigrams. There are eight of these, constructed from all combinations of three *yin/yang* lines, and each represents an important phase in the interaction of the two energies.

The figure below shows the trigrams arranged in the Sequence of Earlier Heaven which, according to tradition, was established by the legendary emperor *Fu Hsi*, who is also credited with the original construction of the trigrams from markings on a dragon-horse and a turtle. There are other possible placings of the trigrams, but *Fu Hsi's*, which correspond with the cardinal points and the seasons (Summer – South; Autumn – West; Winter – North; and Spring – East), are the most cogent and symmetrical, offering great rewards when overlaid with the Druidic festivals.

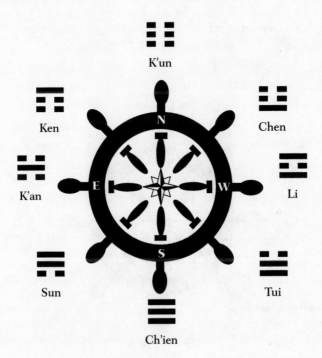

Fig 1: *Fu Hsi* arrangement of the trigrams

The Wheel of the Year

The eight Druidic festivals constitute an ever-turning eight-spoked wheel of the year that marks the changing of the seasons and the ebbing and flowing of light and darkness, heat and cold, growth and decay, throughout the year. The eight are comprised of four movable festivals tied to solar events (the two solstices, Alban Arthuan and Alban Heruin; and the two equinoxes, Alban Eiler and Alban Elued), and four fixed fire festivals on cross-quarter days between them. Each festival marks an important phase in the natural cycle of the year.

Figure 2 shows the festivals arranged in sunwise order around a circle, the 'Wheel of the Year'. For the northern hemisphere, placing midwinter (Alban Arthuan) in its characteristic position of north produces a natural ordering which gives an impressive correlation with the *Fu Hsi* arrangement of the eight trigrams.

Fig 2: The Druidic Festivals

The Wheel of Changes

Simply combining the circle of the trigrams with the circle of the Druidic festivals gives figure 3, the 'Wheel of Changes'. The accord between the two systems seems remarkable; yet it is also understandable, given that both elucidate the critical phases of a bipolar dynamic at eight points.

With a form of equivalence between the systems established, the time-honoured practice of occult correspondence can be employed, allowing knowledge of either system to be used to enhance understanding and appreciation of the other. For example, the trigram symbols themselves could be incorporated into festival observance, and their form and underlying philosophy used to enrich meditation upon the light-dark dynamic of each festival, and how it stands in relation to the others in the wheel of the year. Conversely, knowledge

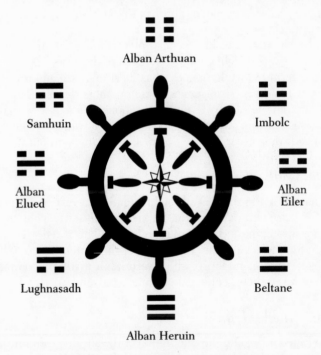

Fig 3: The combined "Wheel of Changes"

of each festival's motivations and place in the natural cycle of the seasons may allow a richer, less abstract empathy with the cyclical flowing of *yin* and *yang*, and consequently with the *I Ching* itself.

As a starting point for this synergy, let us end by considering briefly in turn each of the eight festival-trigram correspondences, starting arbitrarily with Alban Heruin – *Ch'ien*.

Alban Heruin – Ch'ien

Alban Heruin is the Druidic celebration of the summer solstice, the longest day of the year. The name means 'Light of the Shore', an appropriate title for this turning point of the year, lying at the mid-point between 'Light of the Earth' and 'Light of the Water' (the Druidic terms for the equinoctal celebrations). This midsummer festival celebrates the apogee of the strong, active, solar force; symbolized in the crowning of the Oak King, god of the waxing year. The trigram *Ch'ien* represents the apogee of the same force: it consists of yang lines alone, and has the epithets creative, strong, heaven, and father.

It is in the nature of the cyclical interaction of *yin* and *yang* that either force at its height contains the seed of the other, into which it will transform. So while *yang* reaches its strongest manifestation in *Ch'ien*, it can get no stronger and therefore must weaken. This truth is mirrored in the Alban Heruin celebrations, where it is recognized that, at his crowning, the Oak King falls to his twin, the Holly King, god of the waning year: days will grow shorter from now on.

Lughnasadh – Sun

Lughnasadh marks the time of the first (grain) harvest, and is named after Lugh, a Celtic deity of light. Summer is still at its height, but the days are shortening and autumn is on its way. This is reflected in the trigram *Sun*, formed by the weakening of the bottom line of *Ch'ien*. The light (*yang*) is no longer all-powerful, but it still predominates. *Sun* has the epithets gentle, penetrating, wind, and wood.

Alban Elued – K'an

Alban Elued is the Druidic celebration of the autumnal equinox, the pivot between the light and dark halves of the year: day and night are of equal length. It also marks the time of the second (fruit) harvest. Alban Elued means 'Light of the Water', and 'water' is one of the main titles attached to the trigram *K'an*.

K'an is formed by the weakening of the top line of *Sun* to give, appropriately, one of only two symmetrical mixed trigrams, the other corresponding to the vernal equinox. Though symmetrically balanced, *yin* lines for the first time outnumber *yang* lines: autumn is here and winter is on its way – from now on nights will be longer than days. In keeping with the idea of ascendant darkness, *K'an* has the epithets water, danger, abysmal, and moon.

Samhuinn – Ken

Samhuinn marks the time of the third and final harvest when, in earlier days, cattle were slaughtered and their meat smoked or salted for winter. It is an occasion for divination and honouring the dead, for at this time the veil between the mundane and subtle realms is considered to be particularly insubstantial.

The trigram *Ken* is formed by the single strong line of *K'an* moving forward and blocking the two remaining weak lines beneath it. The winding down aspects of Samhuinn are expressed in the epithets of *Ken*: stillness, rest, and mountain. And a mountain may bridge the gap between two worlds, between Heaven and Earth, just as Samhuinn does.

Alban Arthuan – K'un

Alban Arthuan is a celebration of the winter solstice, the shortest day of the year. The name means 'Light of Arthur'; King Arthur being identified here with the sun god who is reborn on this day (from now on days will grow longer).

The midwinter nadir of the light is also the zenith of the dark, passive, receptive force; and this is perfectly reflected in the trigram *K'un*, which is formed from *Ken* by the weakening of the final strong line to give *yin* lines alone. *K'un* has appropriate epithets for this time of rebirth: receptive, yielding, earth, and mother. As with Alban Heruin – *Ch'ien*, the supremacy of one half of a cyclical duality can only result in the decrease of itself and the increase of the other. Thus the bottom line of *K'un* must soon strengthen, just as the victorious Holly King falls to the reborn Oak King at Alban Arthuan.

Imbolc – Chen

The waxing of light and the ascent towards spring are celebrated at Imbolc, which is considered to be the first of three spring festivals in the Druidic calendar. Winter still has its grip on the land, but the days are lengthening: the darkness of the trigram *K'un* has been lightened by the strengthening of its bottom line to form *Chen*. The usual representation of *Chen* is thunder, which the Chinese consider to erupt from the depths in early spring to awaken the dormant seeds to new life. *Yin* lines still outnumber *yang* lines (nights are still longer than days), but now the bottom line is strong and able to move forward through the weak lines above it, giving *Chen* suitable epithets for the earliest stirrings of spring: arousing, awakening, movement, and thunder.

Alban Eiler – Li

Alban Eiler is the Druidic celebration of the vernal equinox, the second of the spring festivals. It is the pivot between the dark and light halves of the year: day and night are again of equal length. Alban Eiler means 'Light of the Earth'.

Li is formed by the strengthening of the top line of *Chen* to give the remaining symmetrical mixed trigram (the other corresponding, as already seen, to the autumnal equinox). Though symmetrically balanced, *yang* lines now outnumber *yin* lines: spring is here and summer is on its way – from now on days will be longer than nights. In keeping with the idea of ascendant light, *Li* has the epithets luminous, sun, lightning, fire, and clinging.

Beltane – Tui

The third and final spring festival marks the beginning of summer and is called Beltane, the 'Good Fire' or 'Bel-fire', named after the solar deity Bel. At this time, cattle were driven between Beltane fires and led out to summer pastures until Samhuinn. Fruitfulness in all its forms and the celebration of the ascent towards summer are the main themes of Beltane.

The trigram *Li* has become *Tui* – now only the top line is weak and cannot impede the two strong lines below. The celebratory and life-giving aspects of Beltane are expressed in the epithets of *Tui*: joyfulness, pleasure, and lake.

And then the wheel turns once more, as *Tui's* remaining weak line is strengthened, the sun reaches its peak, and we again find *Ch'ien* at Alban Heruin.

Robert Mills has studied Kabbalism and the Western Mystery Tradition with several esoteric societies, and Druidry with The Order of Bards Ovates and Druids. A graduate in mathematics, and a published writer and poet, he currently works in the software industry.

Madeleine Johnson

CAER ARIANRHOD – THE FESTIVALS AND THE STARS

The Starry Wisdom Of The Druids

'Behold a Bard who has not chanted yet, but he will sing soon - and by the end of his song he will know the starry wisdom'

FROM *The Hostile Confederacy*
TRANSLATED BY JOHN MATTHEWS

So sang the sixth century bard Taliesin, Primary Bard of Britain, in one of the many tantalizing glimpses in Celtic literature into the star knowledge of the Druids. As this verse intimates, the starry wisdom was contained within the oral tradition of the ancient Bards and Druids, who were the wisdom keepers of this land, handing down their knowledge in poetry and song from teacher to pupil in an unbroken tradition. To find evidence of the star knowledge of the Druids, we must look both without and within; we must seek the song of the stars hidden not only in the art, literature and archaeology of the early Celts, but within the Land itself. We follow the thread of the Goddess Arianrhod, Lady of the Silver Wheel, from the circle of stars – the *Caer Sidi* – to the circles of stone upon the land, for the song of the stars is also the song of the stones, the song of the cyclic nature of life.

The Spirits Of The Circle

'Whatever is born or done this moment of time, has the qualities of this moment of time'

CARL JUNG

Life is about cycles, and the ever-weaving synchronicity that occurs within those cycles. Life is a journey, and we walk our soul-walk through the interweaving energies of the Spirits of the Circle. Our individual, tribal and ancestral journeys are honoured within Druidry through these Spirits – the Spirits of Time, Place, Ancestors and Tribe. We travel around the wheel of existence, the wheel of the zodiac and the Celtic wheel of the year, in the Spirit of the Journey. The Spirits of the Circle have formed and continue to form us into who and what we are, and who and what we will become, and they are also a part of ourselves. We are born at the meeting of the Spirits of Time and Place, when Sun, Moon, Earth and Stars are at a particular point in their respective cycles, and in their relationship to each other. And as every planet and star sounds its own note and vibrates at its own level, their song, their position around the circle of the zodiac, as perceived from earth, encapsulates at any moment of time the very essence of that moment in time. And 'whatever is born or done' is born or done in the Spirit of that moment.

Astrology – star knowledge – is a perfect representation of these Spirits of the Circle. We bring into each lifetime the lessons we have learned and need to learn during this particular phase of our Soul Journey. In the Spirit of Time and Place we are born at 'a moment in time' and place, with the songs of the stars imprinted into our Beings. As a seed within the earth we are born, bringing with us lessons from previous incarnations, and aspects of ourselves which have not been fully assimilated and integrated into the whole. Our companions are the Spirits of our Ancestors and Tribe – we are born into a family whose ancestors and sociocultural environment (the Tribe) endow us with the genetic and cultural inheritance required for us to work out those lessons.

Whether we follow our destiny, align ourselves with the Spirits of the Circle, and are willing to walk with them through pain and sorrow as well as health and joy, or whether we attempt to avoid our obligations and choose a different path, is our choice, and also, still, our Journey.

Circles And Cycles

'Great is the Mystery of the Circular Course'

FROM *The Chair of the Sovereign*
TRANSLATED BY JOHN MATTHEWS

The early Celts understood the cyclical spiralling nature of the Universe. Looking up into the skies, they watched the rhythmic rising and setting of the stars, sun and moon, and noticed their rela-tionship to one another. They saw that as the sun rose, culminated and set, he traced an arc which expanded and then contracted throughout the year, appearing as a spiral tightly wound at Midwinter, rising higher in the sky as the heat of the sun increased and the days grew longer, until Midsummer, when the spiral once more began to rewind, like a flower opening its petals to rejoice in the day, then closing them as the hours of daylight decreased. The early peoples of Britain carved vivid representations of this spiral path over rocks and boulders, together with discs and crescents, representing the sun and moon, and their interweaving paths. We know too that they built circles of stone to represent the circle of stars, and aligned these and their passage graves, stones and dolmens with the rising and setting times of sun and moon at particular times of the year. Many stone circles and carved stones acted as calendars, some predicted eclipses as well as the phases of the moon. Dowsers have discovered that certain stones are connected to the phases of the moon at an energetic level, acting as conductors of moon and star energies from sky to earth, and to the stars within the land.

Sun, Moon and Integration

'On High God made the planets, he made the sun,
he made the Moon'

FROM 'Song of the Macrocosm' BY TALIESIN
TRANSLATED BY JOHN MATTHEWS

The Sun and the Moon, and their rhythmic relationships to each other were of primary importance to the Celts in their understanding of the rhythms of their lives. To the early Celts, the sun and moon were of equal importance for a very obvious reason – they appeared equal in size in the sky. But whilst the disc of the Sun God remained constant, the Moon Goddess changed her shape, waxing and waning in a cycle of change that itself contained regularity and rhythm; the moon's phases. We must never forget that the phases of the moon are not just about the moon. They are about the ever- changing relation-ship between Sun and Moon, as seen from earth, and as they can only be seen from earth, *they are uniquely related to human and plan-etary consciousness*. The phase of the moon reveals the manner in which the solar energy is transmitted to Earth, through the lens of the zodiac. When we look up and see the moon in partial darkness, we see the light of the sun and the shadow of the earth cast upon the moon's surface: Sun, Moon and Earth working in combination as an integrated whole.

The course of our outer lives can be correlated with the course of the Sun. We rise with the light of day and perform our outer, daily activities, and no matter how introspective we become at night, dwelling upon our concerns and worries, with each new dawn there is new hope, as the dawn of the year at spring brings expectation of new beginnings. The Sun calls to the Earth and she responds, the Moon calls to the Waters upon the earth and the waters within ourselves, and they and we, respond; rhythmically, subconsciously. For the Moon exerts influence upon ourselves and our inner lives; our reactions, emotions and responses; calling to us from our child-hood, our parenting and our past; whether that past be of our ances-tors, our present life, or our previous incarnations. We recognise her influence upon the tides of the ocean, but her influence is also over the inner tides, the cycles of inner expansion and contraction, wax and wane of our lives.

Integration, making whole, is both the keynote of astrology and the Path of the Druid. The relationship of Sun and Moon as revealed in the phases of the moon is a key to our understanding of Nature and of the Self, our inner nature, the relationship of the masculine and feminine, linear and intuitive aspects of each one of us. Just as a study of the sun and moon in a birth chart, by sign, position and their relationship to one other (the phase), can reveal much about ourselves, so a study of the continuing relationship between the sun and the moon during the months and years around the wheel of the seasons and the year, can tell us much about life and Nature, and our place within the whole.

As the sun travels through one zodiac sign each month, the quali-ties of that sign are emphasized, in the seasons and in the individual. But that is only part of the story. The moon takes around two and a half days to travel through each zodiac sign. When she gets to the same degree of the sun, we have a dark moon (called 'new moon' in astrology), and when she is in the same degree but the opposite sign of the sun, we have a full moon. It is important to realize that in astrology there is always balance, so that if one sign is emphasized, then its polar opposite will also be involved. Each month, then, we have a dark and full moon reflecting the element and quality of the sign of the sun and, in balance, its polar opposite. Dark and full

moons are power points, for sun and moon both collect and dissemi-
nate the energy of the sun sign; dark moon is a time of beginnings,
the birth of an idea or focus; building to full moon when these energies are released, seeded, disseminated.

The Zodiac And The Eightfold Year

'I know the names of the stars from the North to the South'

FROM *Primary Chief Bard*
TRANSLATED BY JOHN MATTHEWS

We can follow the paths of the sun and moon through the twelve
signs of the zodiac and the Druidic wheel of the year, and discover a
story – the journey of the seasons.

The Sun's apparent path around the earth is called the ecliptic,
which at present we divide into twelve, although many divisions from
eight to over 40 have been used by different cultures. But whatever
system of signs we use, this path does divide naturally into four: the
quartered circle. Our system of twelve signs fits into this quartered
circle in many ways. The signs fall into two basic groups, the qualities
and the elements, and are designated alternately masculine and
feminine in character; Water and Earth are feminine, Fire and Air
are masculine. An understanding of the four elements of Fire, Air,
Earth and Water are fundamental to both Druidry and astrology.
There are three signs to each element, and four signs to each quality,
two interweaving circles within the whole. The qualities are
Cardinal, Fixed and Mutable. Each season and each quarter of the
circle of the zodiac commences with a Cardinal sign, progresses
through a Fixed sign and proceeds to a transitory stage, the Mutable
sign, progressing at the same time through the elements. These fit
perfectly into the eightfold year.

The Cardinal signs of Aries, Cancer, Libra and Capricorn are
motivated by the Will – to act and to initiate. They are full of the
energy of the element which they represent; eager to begin, to
continue, to manifest. As the Sun enters the first degree of a cardinal
sign, leaving the last degree of the preceding mutable sign, it marks a
Solstice or an Equinox; the commencement of a new season.

The Fixed signs of Taurus, Leo, Scorpio and Aquarius fall at the
centre of each season, each again manifesting a different element.
These signs concentrate the energy and consolidate the element.
They are stable, intense and profoundly potent. They are immensely

powerful and sustained expressions of energy, so that it is not surprising that each of the four 'fire' festivals fall wholly in these four fixed signs.

The Mutable signs of Gemini, Virgo, Sagittarius and Pisces lead to the close of each season. Their energy is moving, breaking down, shapeshifting towards a new cycle, seeking new forms of expression. They are ruled by the planets Mercury and Jupiter, planets signifying the search for knowledge and wisdom, the power to communicate on all levels, from the mundane to the divine. Their shifting energies signify the move towards the next quarter of the circle, they are ever in transition, each in their own way.

As Druids today we celebrate eight festivals of the year – the four solstices and equinoxes at the turn of the seasons, and the four fire festivals at the centre; two interlocking cycles in one, a solar and a lunar. The solar cycle is that of the solstices and equinoxes, as the sun moves from the end of one quarter of the zodiac to the next, reaching a point of tension and transition, ending one season and beginning a new. The sun has travelled through the last sign of one quarter, the mutable phase, and enters a Cardinal, initiatory sign.

The lunar cycle is represented by the four fire festivals, which fall roughly in the central portion of each season, where they are at their most settled and also their most powerful – the prime of life for each season. It is appropriate therefore that these four festivals should fall in 'Fixed signs' of the zodiac: the signs of Aquarius, Taurus, Leo and Scorpio, who are also the four creatures of the apocalypse of biblical legend: Man, the Bull, the Lion and the Eagle. This all becomes clear when we place the signs of the zodiac upon the Wheel of the Celtic/Druidic year, and see that the equinoxes and solstices begin with a Cardinal initiatory sign in each of the four elements, and the four cross-quarter festivals fall in the fixed signs, the central, settled portion of the season.

Within each sign too, and within each season, are the new and full moons, further concentrating the energies of the signs at particular times of each month. The phases of the moon may also be correlated with the journey of the sun throughout the year, from Dark Moon at Midwinter, to Full at Midsummer – circles within circles, and cycles within cycles.

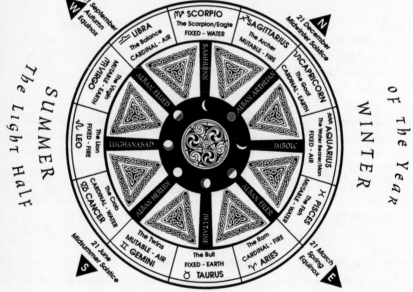

The Wheel of the Year

The Solstices And Equinoxes – The Solar Festivals

The Festival of Alban Eiler – Spring

> *'Now are day and night in perfect balance. We stand at the doorway of dark and light'*
>
> FROM *the Festival of Alban Eiler, of the Order of Bards Ovates & Druids*

Around the 21st March the Sun enters the Cardinal Fire sign of Aries, and we celebrate the festival of Alban Eiler, 'Light of the Earth'. This is truly the time when the light of the earth blesses us with her gifts. Days and nights are equal; the fire of the Goddess Brigid bursts from the land in sheer exuberance and joy of living. The sun enters the sign whose symbol resembles the curled horns of the Ram, the sprouting first growth of the seed, two tongues of fire born from the womb of the Goddess. The time of Aries, like those born under the sign of Aries, is full of energy, love of life, desire to achieve, to win, to be first. Their enthusiasm has an innocent, childlike quality. Nature knows no courtesy, there is only the desire to Be, to Manifest. The sun has left the mutable water sign Pisces, whose keynotes of service, sacrifice, and a desire to merge with the whole, like a fish within the sea, lead us to a truer understanding of the redemptive powers of spring. Now Niwalen, Goddess of Spring, treads softly upon the earth, leaving behind her the imprint of her footsteps, the trefoil, symbol of the festival of Alban Eiler. The corresponding phase of the moon is waxing towards fullness, at first quarter.

The Festival of Alban Heruin – Summer

> *'Born out of the darkness of the womb of the Earth Mother, the Mabon, Child of Light, travels the circle of time, until he stands in the centre, at the zenith of the year, in full and life-giving radiance'*
>
> FROM *the Festival of Alban Heruin, of the Order of Bards Ovates & Druids*

At the Midsummer Solstice, around 21st June, the spiral of the sun's path is fully unwound as the sun enters the Cardinal Water sign of

Cancer, from the dual Air sign of Gemini. At this time of the height of the Sun's power, comes the festival of Alban Heruin, the Light of the Shore; that meeting place of sea and land. Cancer, a Water sign, is in polarity with Earthy Capricorn, the opposite sign of Midwinter. I never quite understood the meaning of Light of the Shore until I stood one Midsummer morning on a high Derbyshire moor, awaiting the rising sun. As I looked over to the west, for a moment I thought I was looking upon the sea, for the distant skyline with its thin covering of cloud shimmered, shifted and changed in the distance, like the shifting meeting of land and the sea, or the meeting place of this world and the otherworld. It reminded me too of the duality of Gemini, the sign the sun had just left; the divine twins who in Celtic mythology can be equated with Nissyen and Evnissyen of the Mabinogion; the latter full of anger and violence, the former the peacemaker – two parts of the whole, two people in one – and of the chattering, quick, nervous movements and restless energy of the natives of that sign.

The symbol of Cancer is that of a double disc or the centre of two spirals, meeting together from opposite directions. The spiral is fully unwound, and the tension and sensitivity inherent in Cancerian natives reflects the knowledge that whilst now the Sun is at the height of his powers, the return journey is about to begin. The double disc has been carved on stones in these islands for millennia. The Pictish stones of Scotland, in particular, display this symbol over and over again. The disc or wheel is the symbol of the sun, and it is very likely that this is a symbol of the sun at its optimum power, Midsummer. In her excellent book *In Search of the Picts*, Elizabeth Sutherland recounts the story of an anthropologist working with native Americans on the Oregon River. A study of the Edderton Stone, with its impression of a salmon and double disc, evoked a response from one of the native Americans of the party who said, 'My chief can tell you what that means – it tells you the times of the year when the Salmon are running'. The double disc told the time of the year and possibly the time of the month, as the corresponding phase of the moon at this time of the year is the Full Moon.

The Festival of Alban Elued – Autumn

'As the sun sets in the West, so the year sets in Autumn. Night falls for each one of us; tonight and in our lives.'

FROM *The Festival of Alban Elued, of the*
Order of Bards Ovates & Druids

At the Autumn equinox, around 22nd September, the Sun enters the Cardinal Air sign of Libra. Libra is the sign of the balance, of the return of equal days and nights; the festival of Alban Elued, Light of Water when, as the Celts believed, the year descended into the ocean. The urge of the Libran is ever towards harmony and balance, reflecting exactly this special time of balance within the year. The eternal battle of light and dark has been fought once more, and dark has the victory – for a while. In Celtic lore, the Lady Keridwen prepares her cauldron for the great festival of Samhuinn. The sun has left the Earth sign of Virgo and the land has yielded its harvest of grain and fruits and is already preparing for the following spring. Receiving the seeds of new life within her womb, protecting them with a covering of fallen leaves, she feels more fulfilled at this time than at any other. There is a restfulness about Autumn, despite the obvious outer activity and preparation. Virgo natives are constantly preparing, sifting and organizing, but their need is to serve and to heal, to fulfil the needs of others as well as themselves. They use the fruits of their work in service, constantly fine-tuning and improving, like nature. This is the sign of the harvest goddess and of the sacrificed corn king, who must now concede to the dominance of the dark, as does the corresponding phase of the moon, now at waning quarter.

The Festival of Alban Arthuan – Winter

'In every death is the seed of birth, and in the darkness of the longest night we await the dawn of the waxing year.'

FROM *The Festival of Alban Arthuan, of the*
Order of Bards Ovates & Druids

At the Midwinter Solstice, around the 21st December, the Sun enters the Cardinal Earth sign of Capricorn from the Mutable Fire sign of Sagittarius, whose arrows point ever upward, aiming to the

top of the Capricornian mountain, always seeking to move higher
and deeper into knowledge and wisdom and the understanding of all
things. This is the festival of Alban Arthuan, Light of Arthur. Arthur
the Sun King begins his return from Annwn, the child newborn, as a
weak flickering light that nevertheless holds all the promise of
Midsummer in his grasp. Now the sun appears to stand still for a few
days on his lowest arc over the horizon, as the spiral of his path is
tightly wound. Capricorn is the sign of the mountain goat, whose
dogged persistence achieves the slow, steady climb from mountain
base, Midwinter, to pinnacle, Midsummer, and whose people born
under this sign show the same steady perseverance towards their
goals. At the celebration of Alban Arthuan we extinguish our lights
and wait awhile in silence and darkness, in the stillness of time,
before rekindling the light for a new sun, the Mabon. The phase of
the moon is Complete Dark, but like the promise of Midsummer that
is inherent within the dark, so here is the promise of Full Moon, and
of growth.

The Four 'Fire' Festivals

The four 'cross quarter' fire, or lunar festivals, were celebrated traditionally at specific phases of the moon, although as modern Druids
we now tend to celebrate them on fixed days of the year. They fall
between the Solstices and Equinoxes, and in Fixed signs, and they
concentrate the energy of each season, reflecting the energy of the
sign and element through which the sun manifests itself.

Samhuinn

> 'We have reached the time of Samhuinn which is no time. The old
> year has ended, yet the new year is not begun. We stand without
> time and the veil between the Worlds is thin'

> FROM *The Festival of Samhuinn, of the Order
> of Bards Ovates & Druids*

Samhuinn is the true beginning of the Celtic year, drawing on the
distant time when the year was divided into two halves, light and
dark; for the Celts reckoned their days from sunset, and their year
from the dominance of the dark. This is the month of Scorpio, the
water scorpion who is also the serpent, and the eagle or phoenix.
Deep, still, fixed, silent water, whose depths are unknown. Inherent

within the meaning of this sign and this festival, held on or near 31st October is the power of transformation. The serpent, dragon energy of the earth, has the power to regenerate, as we are flung into the Cauldron of Keridwen and like Gwion/Taliesin we are reborn to take flight as the eagle, transformed like the phoenix rising from the fires of the earth. The Moon is now a crescent waning into dark, as the year sinks deep into the Cauldron of Annwn.

Imbolc

'Brigid, guard your fire, this is your night'

FROM *The Festival of Imbolc, of the Order
of Bards Ovates & Druids*

The tight spiral of Midwinter unwinds and the sun god begins to open his arms to welcome the beginnings of spring, touching the earth with his soft pale rays. We reach Imbolc at the beginning of February, the time of the triple goddess Brigit, lady of smithship, poetry and healing. She is Goddess of the Land, her milk-white outer radiance hides the deep dark fires of the dragon within. For as smith, she is lady of Alchemy; the frost and ice burn our exposed fingers with white fire, and her elements of fire and water are those used to temper and shape steel. Brigit is lady of the sacred internal fire, whose time is the time of the Fixed, Air sign Aquarius, the humanitarian sign, whose cool, detached exterior hides the urge to serve the group, to work for the good of the whole. The dragon breath of Brigit breathes life into the re-awakening Spring, and the Moon reaches first crescent, waxing towards first quarter.

Beltaine

'The Goddess has appeared. In green has she dressed the land, scenting the breeze with blossoms'

FROM *The Festival of Beltaine, of the
Order of Bards Ovates & Druids*

At Beltaine, May day, the Rite of Spring is at its height, and the sun enters the sensual, Fixed Earth sign of Taurus the Bull, who is also the Ox; both animals are sacred to the Celts. This is the polar opposite of the dark time, Samhuinn – summer's end – for now we reach

the beginning of summer. The natives of Taurus are attuned to their
senses, loving the rich scent of the blossoms and the earth, revelling
in abundance and richness, seeking the security of the land through
firm foundations, possessions and beauty. The rising powers of spring
are present in the sheer joy and abundance of nature; exuberance
and sexual activity without responsibility. The urge is to procreate
and perpetuate; the Maypole, like the phallus, is erect, and the
Goddess of the Earth opens like the flowers of the May to join in
joyful sexual union with the God of the fertile, growing Land:
Cernunnos, the antler-headed God. Now the Moon is like the full-
bellied Goddess, past first quarter and waxing towards fullness,
following her impregnation by the Lord of the Land.

Lughanasadh

> 'Let us be glad of the Mothers gifts. She bears us as She bears
> wheat in the field. Remember as we harvest, that we shall be
> harvest in the field of stars. Let us be glad of the Father's gifts.'
>
> FROM *The Festival of Lughanasadh, of the*
> *Order of Bards Ovates & Druids*

The spiral slowly begins to rewind as we reach the first of the
autumn harvest festivals, Lughanasadh, the time of Lugh the Sun
King who is married to the Goddess of the Land, awaiting his sacrifice at the Equinox. This is a time of dissemination, revealed in the
first soft fruits of the harvest, the cutting of the first ripened corn.
The Sun King is in the sign of his rulership, the Fixed Fire sign of
kingly Leo the Lion, whose natives exude warmth and sheer joy
in life, and also the desire to be 'king' or centre of their world. The
Sun rules and is at home in the sign of Leo, which connects to the
heart *chakra*, the centre of love. *Chakras* can be seen as wheels, and
the symbol of this festival is the fiery wheel. Lugh is the main deity
of the Light, but now he is the setting sun, the colour of deep
orange red, descending in a blaze of orange glory. The Moon too
disseminates, past her fullness but not yet at waning quarter,
releasing the fruits of her belly for the sustenance of the land and her
creatures.

Cycles Within Cycles

The ancient Celts, guided by their astronomer-astrologer priests, the Druids, lived and worked within this system of cyclical activity. They spent much of their lives out of doors with the trees and plants, birds and animals, stones and stars. They experienced and responded to their call, to the rhythmic pulse of life; observing this pulse in their celebration of the annual round of festivals and in the phases of the moon. Their lives were bound up with the cycles of life, death and rebirth, seeing them ever-present in the natural world, in the life of the tribe and in the round of their own successive earthly existences. They observed that within each cycle is a time of waxing and waning, growth and release, light and dark. This system permeated every aspect of life and death; for life and death, like light and dark and masculine and feminine, depend upon one another and walk hand in hand at all times. Theirs was no dualistic view of the Universe – all was, and is, seen as a valuable, welcome, necessary part of the whole. The Celts lived out their lives working with the rhythms of the planet, the land and the heavenly bodies, recognizing that the apparent separateness of these bodies was illusory. Their stone circles and groves of trees, and the meetings, courts of law and cere-monies held within them, reflected the wheel or spiral of existence. They recognized the existence of a single life-force or energy which they named *Nyvwre*, which pervades all creation and all realms of existence, including the mineral, planet, animal, human and star realms. There was no separation; every part of the whole reflecting every other part of the whole; the microcosm within the macrocosm.

As modern Druids we seek to find once more that sense of inte-gration, to become whole and to heal the aching sense of separation within ourselves and within the Land. Modern society searches for ways in which we can understand ourselves and our relationship to the whole, attempting to find its way back, and yet forward, to that sense of wholeness. But we cannot do this without acknowledging all parts of ourselves and our place within the scheme of things; not as controllers, but as participants in the cosmic dance.

In 1927, Freud said, 'The principal task of civilization, its actual *raison d'être*, is to defend us against nature.' We try psychology and tech-nology, but find that all we have done is build ourselves a defence: a defence against nature, like the castles and walled cities of old, to keep the enemy, the uncontrolled part of ourselves and of nature, out.

The more 'advanced' we become, the more complicated become our lives, and the less time we have to worry about what is 'out there' – chaos. We attempt to control, and when we find that we cannot, we shut it out: physically, emotionally, mentally, and spiritually, like the way we annihilated the wolf from most of the world, because her cries to the moon, the shadow, made us fearful. So we attempt to shut out what we see as the evil, dark, unwanted part of the world, of society, and of ourselves as individuals. But we cannot, we can only pretend. And whilst Wolf no longer cries outside our homes at night, those products with which we have replaced her howl instead – the police sirens, the car and burglar alarms, the whine of traffic on a not-too-distant bypass – serving only to remind us of our fears.

The Druids knew that shadows are as valuable as light. They recognized the use of shadow to reveal that which is hidden by the light, in many ways. The sun, rising on a particular day of the year, can cast his light behind a stone whose shadow points to a distant horizon or landmark; as at Castlerigg, where at sunset at the summer solstice the shadow cast by the tallest stone traces a path towards the Imbolc sunrise at the opposite end of the alignment.

Our own shadow-paths can lead us to the light of our souls, the light of hidden wealth; spiritual wealth; like the Wolf, our shadow, who is recognized by both Druids and Native Americans as a valued guide. The most valuable use of starlore is as a tool for development; to heal, to integrate and to make whole by bringing ourselves back into touch with that which we have lost over centuries of increasing separation and alienation from nature. If we can connect with the seasonal cycles and the festivals and the energies of sun and moon, and discover that they are within ourselves, we begin the path back to integration and wholeness. That is the only creed we need. As we become aware of our place within the whole, we learn the value both of ourselves and of the whole, and in such awareness we find a growing eagerness to serve and work for all. And then we are no longer alone. For Druidry is a path of service; service to the Land, to the planet, to humanity.

The Land is sacred, the stars are sacred, the stones are sacred, you and I are sacred, a sacred part of the sacred whole. Walk with aware-ness around the wheel of the eightfold year, and whether you stand under the stars in your own backyard, or climb a windy hilltop to an ancient circle, you begin the journey towards integration. You begin to respond to the Song of the Land, re-connecting with nature, with life, with Mother Earth and Father Sky; joining your song with the sacred Song of the Earth as it rises to meet the Song of the Stars.

And, like the Bard who has not chanted yet but who will sing soon, when you have come to the end of your song, you will know the starry wisdom.

Madeleine Johnson is both a practising solicitor and an astrologer. She is also an active member of the Order of Bards Ovates and Druids, working with her local grove to celebrate the eightfold year and walk the Druid path. She edits the Order's monthly magazine, *Touchstone*, to which she also contributes a regular astrology/starlore column. She is one of a number of astrologers dedicated to bringing true astrology or star awareness into the everyday lives of all people. Her own way of doing this is through the Celtic and Druidic heritage of the Land of Britain, for Druidry and astrology are in many ways one and the same, they celebrate and work with the cycles of life, they encourage the practice of the art of sacred living.

Graham Harvey

HANDFASTINGS, FUNERALS AND OTHER DRUID RITES OF PASSAGE

Every year Druids, Witches and other Pagans celebrate eight festivals. Not only do these festivals honour the natural cycles of the Earth and her relationship with the Sun and the Moon, they also celebrate common experiences of ordinary human people. In celebrating the seasons of the year, with their beginnings, middles and ends, we celebrate the seasons of our lives.

My intention here is to explore some rites of passage, more or less public or communal celebrations of some events natural to human life-cycles. I will talk about actual celebrations that have taken place among Druids of one Order or another, particularly concentrating on Handfastings (or Weddings) and Funerals, and other ceremonies surrounding death. The eight festivals that most Pagans celebrate are not unrelated to these rites of passage and I will refer to them often in the course of this exploration. I begin with some notes on rites of passage and human life-cycles.

Rites of Passage

If for a moment we consider that life begins with conception and ends in death, we can draw a straight line between these two events. Between the two events human life progresses: the individual grows from fertilized egg to foetus, to baby, then child, adolescent, adult, elder and eventually to death. Disease and untimely death can interrupt this cycle but, just for now, let us assume a complete progress from a happy conception to a peaceful death.

The transitions between these phases are not often abrupt and immediate. You do not go to sleep as a child and wake in the morning as an adult. Nor do the changes take place at the same rate for every individual. Most cultures have found ways of marking the changes in more or less public ways. For example, a girl's first menstruation may be taken to mark her move from childhood to adulthood. Before she can enter the full responsibilities and restrictions her new status brings, she undergoes a rite of passage: a guided move through a passage from one room – childhood, to another – adulthood. In our society this particular event is not celebrated, it is rarely honoured as a positive experience and initiates neither parties nor pleasure. This is in part due to the patriarchal devaluing of womens' experience, womens' bodies and indeed women in any sense. It is also part of the wider ignoring of the passage into adulthood; in our individualistic society we are expected to 'make it' on our own.

A rite of passage that is celebrated is the transition from 'single person' to 'wife', 'husband' or 'partner'. This event is celebrated with a series of increasingly public celebrations: proposal, engagement, stag or hen parties, wedding. Our society then allows the couple a return to privacy for their 'first night'. In some other societies the couple's first sexual intercourse is a fairly public event, especially where it is necessary for the new bride to 'show proofs of her virginity'. The degree to which a culture stresses the relative value of the individual or the community, strongly affects its celebrations of marriage, as it does other rites of passage. In our society, marriage is generally seen as a relationship between two people. However, many people experience their wedding day almost passively while family and friends control and direct what, when and how things happen. Only rarely do people get married with only the minimal requirement of a state recognized official (priest or registrar) and witnesses. In some religions, a wedding emphasizes the relation between marriage and procreation, family, lineage and descent. The couple being married are at the centre of a web of relationships: their parents and families (sometimes including distant ancestors) are involved, and the couple are expected to provide that family, clan or nation with children who will themselves continue this complex process of human living. All of these understandings (of the couple's role in their society, of sexuality, family, power relationships between the genders and so on) will be reflected in some way in the ceremony that marks the passage into married life.

In short, human societies often express their complex understandings of life in the context of ceremonies marking the times and places at which people, as individuals or groups, move from one state or status into another.

Anthropologists studying rites of passage in many societies have noticed that they typically follow a similar pattern. The pattern is a three-stage one: separation, transition and reincorporation. For example, the child moving through the passage to adulthood is often separated from those things most associated with childhood, such as mother, home and village. The children are taken out of their normal environment, sometimes without warning and in frightening ways, and taken elsewhere – physically, emotionally and spiritually – to undergo the central phase of the rite. Here a particular ceremony takes place, perhaps including an ordeal and the learning of new understandings, responsibilities and stories. The one who was once a child is taught what their society expects an adult to be and to do. The rite of passage must then reincorporate the new adult into normal everyday life again. The new adult cannot return to the things of childhood, cannot expect the kind of comfort they might have received as a child. They are, almost literally, a new person, a different person; a stranger to their people and to themselves. They must learn and practise what they have learnt in their rite of passage and their people must learn to treat them differently also.

Our society does not, of course, put people through ordeals in this way. In fact rites of passage are almost completely ignored, often along with many calendar and seasonal festivals. Perhaps the rebirth of Druidry and Paganism is assisting a re-enchantment of life and therefore of such celebrations.

Life cycles

In a recent group discussion of rites of passage, we noted typical events in people's lives between Birth and Death and produced the following chart (in the almost random order and positioning dictated by the space and spontaneity of the discussion).

Birth →	.... →	Death
naming	weaning	first menstruation	funerals
voice breaking	first sexual experience	croning
first word	first love	birthdays	marriage
first disappointment	coming out	parenting	divorce
potty training	first violence	first job/dole	grandparenting
joining group/club	legal maturity	major illness
first drink/drugs	first experience of death	retirement
first awareness of self	leaving school	anniversaries
first awareness of world	first responsibility	divorce
teething	first school day	first car	moving house
first disenchantment		first accident

Naming, marriage, retirement and death are often marked in some way in contemporary British society by a group larger than the individual's immediate family. Significant birthdays and anniversaries are sometimes similarly marked. Some clubs or associations (Cubs, Guides, Freemasons, Churches, Bardic Orders and so on) have ceremonies to mark an individual's joining and perhaps progressing. These are also likely to have symbols or regalia marking the person's position within the group, as may be true also in certain jobs or careers, such as the military. Otherwise, we rarely mark status with outer symbolism. Perhaps the wedding ring is the most common, if not the only such symbol of a person's status, outside of club or career associations. We no longer cut or grow our hair to mark transitions into different age groups. Only some British people (usually Jews and Moslems) practise circumcision. Not everyone in mourning follows the tradition of wearing sombre clothes for an extended period. Menstruating women are not expected to withdraw themselves from their normal occupations (except in some religions) nor do they publicly mark these periods.

Not only do we not mark significant events with symbols, we rarely mark them with celebrations or rituals. These have become the preserve of religious groups or other associations we voluntarily participate in, rather than part of normal day-to-day living. In the following section I introduce the ceremonies that some Pagans have produced for some of the above events. Then I will say something more specific about Druid Rites of Passage.

First I want to note that the above chart contains some events which some people consider negative and certainly not something 'respectable' people, religious or otherwise, would celebrate. Druidry might have a very different attitude to some of these events, especially those that can be labelled 'natural'. I will say more about this later. I will also say more about some other negative events which are not in that list but which are certainly major experiences in many people's lives, and these too should be taken into account in thinking of rites of passage. Sexuality is a useful context for illustrating both these points. Some religions insist that a first sexual experience should follow a marriage ceremony and can be acceptable only within heterosexual, monogamous marriage. But conversely, many people's first sexual experience may be abusive.

Paganism and Rites of Passage

Paganism is a name many people have chosen to use for a spirituality (religion or way) of honouring Nature, including both the Earth and the individual's body. In giving honour to ordinary, physical, mundane reality, Paganism is different from many other religions – though it is perhaps no more different from them than they are from each other. It is also a growing tradition, in which diversity and pluralism are themselves seen as natural and positive. This celebration of Nature and diversity gives Pagans the opportunity to rethink, recreate and re-enchant their life-cycle. Some events in ordinary life which are celebrated by non-Pagans, whether religious or secular, can be seen in new ways. Other events ignored or denigrated by non-Pagans, perhaps especially religious non-Pagans, can be rescued and celebrated as good and even sacred. Some events which Pagans consider unnatural or wrong can also be responded to in ceremonial ways.

Pagans have developed distinctive ways of honouring birth, naming, first menstruation, sexuality, adulthood, marriage, giving birth, honouring the dead and receiving death. It is no accident that these are related to the Pagan festival cycle. In at least one of the festivals, and often in several of them in different ways, the events of ordinary life – human and other-than-human – are incorporated into a response to the whole of Life. Paganism does not divide reality into the 'Sacred' and the 'Profane'. In the words of William Blake, 'all that lives is holy'. Everything is *both* profane and sacred, ordinary and special, mundane and spiritual. (This is part of the meaning of the name chosen by the Secular Order of Druids.)

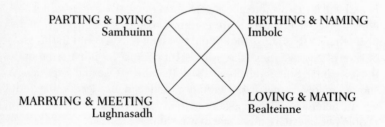

PARTING & DYING — Samhuinn

BIRTHING & NAMING — Imbolc

MARRYING & MEETING — Lughnasadh

LOVING & MATING — Bealteinne

One way that the Rites of Passage and the Festival Cycle can be related

There are also Pagan ceremonies that aim to enable people to deal in some way with abuse, rape and other violence inflicted on them. Paganism is not alone in developing responses to these events. It does, however, have advantages over certain other spiritualities and secular therapies. Seeing that which is natural as good enables the celebration of the body and does not denigrate 'the flesh' as something inherently opposed to deity, perfection, health and well-being. Clearly it will take a long time for survivors of abuse to be able to enjoy their sexuality – they are often driven to blame and punish themselves for their abuse. But not being encouraged to deny the body's moods, desires, fears, dislikes and needs may be considerably more enabling than such self-denial.

I think it also needs saying clearly that Paganism may encourage people to honour Nature, but it does not demand that you like or accept everything. No-one says you have to like mosquitoes. You can honour them without having them drinking your blood. Death is a fact of life, part of the cycle of life that Pagans celebrate, particularly in the harvest festivals of Lughnasad and Autumn Equinox, and also at Samhain. AIDS and malaria are also 'natural'. This does not mean we have to enjoy or celebrate such things. But we can see them as part of Nature, and deal with them in that light. We kill to eat (even vegans are life-takers in this sense) and find ways to cope with our daily violence against other living beings. Similarly, we can find ways to cope with things that we do not like, or things which endanger us.

If killing is necessary to living, then certainly anger is sometimes necessary. In order to survive the passage from victim of abuse, or survivor of rape, into safe, independent, growing, whole person, it may be necessary to express anger, bitterness, hatred and sorrow. If this sounds trite, you might consider reading some of the advice given by evangelical Christians in such cases. Such 'counsellors' have been known to tell victims or survivors that they must first forgive and love their abuser or attacker before God or God's people can or will help, heal and forgive them. What is there to forgive the survivor for? Pagans have produced rites of passage helpful in the process of living beyond survival. They have also faced AIDS, cancer and other invasive forms of death with ceremonies.

Druids and Rites of Passage

The contemporary Druid Orders appear to be becoming increasingly Pagan. That is, the existing orders are evolving in Pagan directions and new, explicitly Pagan Orders are being established. I am aware

that some Druids are unhappy with this evolution. From the eighteenth century up until perhaps the 1930s or even the 1960s,
Druidry has been the preserve of decent Christian gentlemen, with
occasional token roles for women, as is traditional in Christianity of
any sort. Ancient Druidry too is distinguishable from the ordinary
Paganism of ancient non-Druids. If the Romans were telling the
truth (and if they weren't, we have little or no evidence for the existence of Druids in their period), what the Druids did and thought
was quite different to what archaeology shows Iron Age religion to
have been like. Modern Druidry, when it looks to that period at all,
tends to draw on a blend of what the Romans said about Druids and
what archaeologists say about wider Iron Age culture. Hence
contemporary Druidry is becoming less like ancient Druidry and also
less like the Druidry of the last two centuries. In a positive way, it is
becoming more like ancient Paganism and is playing a leading role in
the continuing evolution of contemporary Paganism.

This is important firstly because Paganism speaks to the contemporary age in a way that ancient and eighteenth-century Druidry
cannot. Secondly, because Druidry can draw on the rich heritage of
the whole of the past (including the recent Christian past), while
freely developing responses to the world as it is now. Finally, it is
important because the rites of passage of ancient Druids are lost to
us, and those of past Druids may not be appropriate to the less hierar-
chical, less formal, more Earth-centred Druidry attractive to many
people today.

Weddings and Handfastings

Every Beltain, Druids celebrate the height of spring and the beginning of summer. They blend traditions from English, Welsh, Irish
and Scottish folklore with understandings gained from the surviving
literatures of these lands. To this they add the recently born understanding that the festival is one of eight in an annual seasonal cycle.
Out of this potent cauldron comes a celebration of vitality and fecundity, in which garlanding lovers and homes, dancing and sexuality,
music, drinking and laughter express the intimation that all that lives
is holy and all of life is holy. 'Summer is a coming in', indeed it is
brought in by those who go maying. What better way to celebrate the
marriage of the vigorous Sun and a bountiful Earth than by rites of
love and marriage?

Though Beltain is both an appropriate time for Druid marriage
ceremonies and provides abundant festive symbolism, other festivals

also yield appropriate contexts for such occasions. The Summer Solstice and Lughnasad continue the themes of vitality and fertility. A wedding incorporated into these festivals of summer's beginning, middle and end could, for example, include the participation of summer Kings and Queens, or Oak Kings and May Queens or Sun God and Earth Goddess. The couple being married might play these roles themselves or they might supplement those playing these roles, evoking powerful resonances and establishing rich harmonies.

A number of recent Druid weddings have indeed been included in the celebration of these festivals. They can, of course, also take place as separate events. Some Druids prefer to call a wedding by the name handfasting. It has been suggested that a handfasting is different to a wedding, in that it is not necessarily intended to be permanent. It might be a sort of trial marriage of 'a year and a day', after which the couple may either reaffirm their love and commit themselves to each other for life, or they may separate without prejudice. My impression, however, is that people getting handfasted are no less committed to the hope of a life-long relationship than people getting married. I suspect that the name is preferred only because it is different, being both new to most people and bearing rumours of those mythical romantic days of Merry England. It also stresses a central symbol of the ceremony: the binding of the hands of the happy couple.

There are three things to be considered in the production and conducting of Druidic weddings or handfastings: The understanding of Druidry held by the couple and their friends; the couple's understanding of their relationship; and the understanding of others who are participating or observing the celebration. Legal issues are also of some significance, but at the present time the law here is fairly straightforward – Druid ceremonies are not recognized. If a couple wish their marriage to be legally recognized they have to make use of those places and people that are legally recognized, that is, Registrars or Christian ministers, although changes to the legislation have been proposed which may change this situation.

Before addressing the actual handfastings, I will briefly consider these three matters. Consideration of the couple's understanding of Druidry includes both practical matters (can the ceremony take place indoors or must Druid ceremonies take place 'beneath the eye of the sun'?) and theological ones (are deities, elementals and such other-than-human persons included in any way in the relationship, and therefore the ceremony?) The question of who else is involved in the ceremony might also occur here. Does a Druid handfasting need

to be led by a senior Druid, an Archdruid for example, or can any
friend officiate? The question of the couple's understanding of their
relationship clearly affects what words they will say to each other in
the ceremony. What kind of vows are appropriate? What expressions
of love and faithfulness should be expressed? In other societies the
marriage is not just a relationship between two individuals, but is
inclusive of wider family and clan relationships. Should Druid celebrations form, at least in part, a critique of individualism, or are we
happy with this new way of being human? The consideration of those
participating or observing relates to these previous considerations.
Do the couple's parents – or indeed children – have a role to play in
the ceremony? Does it matter whether everyone at the ceremony
understands what is happening? People invited to a wedding might
expect to wear formal clothes – will this be appropriate to a ceremony
in the open, in uncertain weather? How do you allay some people's
fears about a Pagan and potentially arcane event? Is it actually
possible to merely observe a Druidic event or are people expected to
participate in some way?

Once these issues have been dealt with to the satisfaction of the
couple and, hopefully, of those participating, the ceremony can now
be produced. Those handfastings which have taken place have
usually followed a pattern similar to other Druid ceremonies, especially as they have often occurred during other ceremonies. A circle
is formed, the Quarters, or cardinal directions, are greeted in some
way and the intended rite takes place, including the couple's actual
wedding or handfasting. The proceedings end with a farewell to the
Quarters, and so on. The threefold pattern of separation, transition
and reincorporation recognizable here is no accident, but seems to
arise naturally from something deep and deeply shared in humanity.

Druid ceremonies typically include a number of significant participants. For example, only rarely in any Pagan celebration does a single
person invoke all four Quarters. This is particularly valuable at more
public events such as marriages, when to have a sense of carnival and
celebration engendered in the gathering is no bad thing – formality
seems especially misplaced at rites of love, such as of marriage or
summer, when the tone of the occasion should be joy and pleasure.
At a Druid gathering, when so many people are wearing white, the
bride might consider wearing a different colour. Green, for example,
could aptly link her with the land in summer. The groom too might
find a complementary costume, rather than the drab formality of the
typical wedding suit. If the couple are playing the part of summer
King and Queen their attire could reflect these roles.

In a Gorsedd of the Bards of Caer Abiri handfasting, the couple represent Lleu and Blodeuedd, described as 'Sun God' and 'Earth Goddess'. Other existing handfastings tend to express honour, in some appropriate manner, to deity or deities, but give a more active role to the four elements. In a ceremony used by some members of the Order of Bards, Ovates and Druids, four people represent the four Quarters and their associated elements. They ask the couple questions, recognizing that marriage is not always an easy relationship, and expect the couple to face the difficulties of 'the clear light of day', 'the fires of change', 'the ebb and flow of feeling' and 'the times of stillness and restriction'. On hearing affirmations of loving commitment from the couple, they also offer the blessing of their element and its associated season. East, for example, offers the 'Blessing of the Element of Air in this place of Spring. May your marriage be blessed by the Light of every new Dawn'.

Often more than just the blessing of the element is given – the physical elements themselves can be incorporated into the ceremony, with the couple being sprinkled with water, for example. This occurs in other traditions, too – fire is central to Hindu weddings, and a Burmese tradition has the couple's hands immersed in water, 'so that their love be as indivisible as water'. The family tree need not be a mere verbal metaphor, an actual tree can be planted or replanted, depending on the season, to honour the occasion and the Earth. The couple can be censed with incense for Air, or can themselves place grains of incense on a prepared burner. At our handfasting, Molly and I replaced incense with bubbles, delighting the children (and hopefully the adults too). Those tending the elemental objects (water bowl, fire pot, urn for repotting the tree and bubble blower) also asked a suitable question, the reply to which affirmed our love and commitment to each other.

In a legal wedding, the couple have to affirm that they have come willingly and do desire to be united in marriage. In Druid ceremonies these things can be replaced by more poetic declarations by the couple to each other. It is of course possible to use set words, but people should be encouraged to find their own way of expressing their love and commitment. In fact, the couple should be encouraged to put as much of themselves as possible into the ceremony, remembering again that this is not just a private affair and therefore what happens has to make some sense to other participants. Appealing to all the senses is one way to make sense. The real presence of the four elements, inviting everyone to drink from a shared cup or mead horn, different costumes, movement, drama and

perhaps, as in our handfasting at Beltain, the use of traditional characters like Jack-in-the-Green and the Hobby-Horse enable people to
enjoy the event and experience re-enchantment.

Rings are widespread symbols of marriage and resonate harmo-
niously with other symbols of significance to Druids and other
Pagans (like the stone circles, the circles of Earth, sky, life, eternity,
rebirth, and so on). The exchange of rings and kisses are central
moments in most weddings. A handfasting will also highlight the
ceremonial binding together of the couple's hands. The rite of the
Church of England also has a binding, performed by the officiating
priest with part of his own ritual regalia. In a Druid ceremony the
couple might prefer to provide their own binding; Molly and I used a
strip of cloth on which our totemic symbols had been embroidered by
a friend.

In much of what I have said about weddings it might be assumed
that the happy couple are heterosexual. However, there is no reason
why Druidry should have any difficulties celebrating the love and
commitment of any couple who wish to affirm it publicly. Some
Druids and other Pagans seem obsessed with matching the gender
and sexuality of divinities with that of those who represent them in
ceremonies. When we represent the Quarters in animal form, for
instance the Salmon or the Stag, we have no problem with gender – a
woman can portray a Stag. It seems churlish then to insist that a
Goddess can only be represented by a female human being. Gender
and sexuality are not peripheral to the celebration of marriage and
they are, of course, central to our experience of embodied life.
Though some religions have problems with this, based on their
devaluing of the body in favour of something more 'spiritual', Druidry
does not. Nonetheless, our cultural assumptions about gender roles
and sexual preferences should not be imposed on the greater realm of
'all that is'. In short, gay weddings, gay embodiment of the divine, and
envisaging of the divine as gay can be incorporated into Druid celebrations and into Druidry itself.

Funerals and Remembrance of the Dead

Death is a rite of passage for both the one who dies and for family and
friends 'left behind'. This rite enables the mourners to express their
loss, and begin to find new ways to relate to the one who has
departed. Inability to do these things can be damaging and shocking.
(I say more about this in an article called 'Death and remembrance in
modern Paganism', (*see bibliography*) which includes discussion of

the deaths of a young child and of Wally Hope, the founder of the Stonehenge People's Free Festival.)

Nothing in Druid tradition demands a particular method of disposing of the body, although in our society burial or cremation are the accepted choices. Funeral directors now deal with most of the necessary preparation of the body, perhaps lessening the trauma, but also perhaps distancing us from that great fact of life: death. The increasing trend towards the beautification of the deceased, in French and American style, also seems to contradict the Pagan acceptance of death and decay as a natural, if not always welcome, part of our life-cycle. The keynote of Druid dealings with the dead should be the attempt to accept that which is natural.

Although people can chose the day of their handfasting, they do not usually have the privilege of choosing their dying day. Sometimes, however, they can make certain choices about how they would like their funeral to be conducted and how their physical remains should be treated. Whether their wishes are carried out or not is partly deter-mined by legal concerns and partly by the desires and capabilities of their families, and perhaps friends. If our society inculcates a general respect for the dead, it might not always insist that the previously expressed wishes of the deceased are enacted. It is conceivable that a Druid with Christian parents might receive an explicitly Christian burial service. Perhaps few Druids would object to being buried in Christian 'holy ground' but, for those that do, it is actually very hard to avoid this; even supposedly secular municipal burial grounds are by law 'consecrated' by the Church of England. And a funeral may not be the correct occasion to query whether one piece of land is any more sacred than every other place.

Summer celebrations express the kinship between the bonds of human affection – sexuality, love, marriage, fertility – and the increasing vitality and fecundity of the land. Similarly, autumn and winter celebrations explicitly refer to death in various manifesta-tions. At Lughnasad, the cutting of grain is honoured. John Barleycorn is cut down in his prime, sacrificially feeding people and animals. (Mythology and rites of passage can do things otherwise impossible: Christians can 'drink' blood in the Eucharist, Pagans can 'sacrifice' the corn king). The Autumn Equinox balances growth with decrease by pausing at the end of harvest to look back to the height of summer and forward to the depths of winter. At Samhain, the begin-ning of winter and of the year, the primary focus is the honouring of the human dead, both 'the ancestors' and recently-deceased loved ones. At Winter Solstice, before we rejoice in the rebirth of the sun and her turning northwards once again, we wait in the cold dark and acknowledge the sleep and death that are part of Nature's life-cycle in Midwinter. Winter also enables us to see that in Nature, death is not always a complete end. Trees shed their leaves which provide life for myriad teeming lifeforms. In spring new leaves form. Even when a tree does die it continues to provide life to others. Life continues.

Among these celebrations, Samhain is the one most closely associated with human mortality. This is the time when Druids honour their dead and take the opportunity to contemplate their own death. In his novel *Reaper Man*, Terry Pratchett (who seems to know more about contemporary Paganism than anyone else I know of) powerfully links Beltain and Samhain. A Morris dance at the beginning of summer is not unusual, at least in literature, but in this novel it has an equally important counterpart in a dance at the beginning of winter. The clappers of the dancer's bells are removed and they wear sombre clothes: honouring death does not encourage the exuberance that celebrating sexuality does, (although wakes and bell ringing might remind us that making a lot of noise is not alien to mourning and can be central to human dealings with death). However, both the dances of death and of life should be danced to honour the whole cycle of the year and of Life. Beginnings and ends, summer and winter, birth and death, growth and decline – all unite in the cycle. Such dances can incorporate ideas into physical experiences, and people can return to ordinary daily life with renewed understanding.

At Samhain, Druids honour the dead because they are thought to maintain a relationship with the living, and vice versa. Whether our dead return at that time, or whether they are in fact 'dead and gone', celebrating their gifts to us is a powerful experience. Their gifts are indeed worth celebrating, especially the gift of life and the gift of their own death, without which life on this planet would be difficult, it not impossible.

If the eight festivals provide resources for understanding death in more than purely intellectual ways, the test comes in the actual experiencing of death or dying. Hopefully, facing Death at Samhain is a valid preparation for an individual's own dying. Hopefully, beliefs about what happens after death will be proved reasonably accurate, although of course, not all the conflicting human beliefs in this area can be correct, some hopes are going to be disappointed. What is clear is that Druid approaches to death do bring about valuable ways of honouring the dead.

The ancient Celts and Gauls are said to have believed in the transmigration of souls. When people died, their souls – some separable, continuing, essential part of them – took up residence in another physical form. Other sources intimate an Otherworld of bliss: the land of youth, the summer lands. This can be seen as a permanent paradise or as a temporary rest between incarnations. Arthur's rest in Avalon and Taliesin's initiatory births and transformations provide support for such popular beliefs. Another ancient view is that when someone dies, that is the end of them, except for the memories and artefacts they leave behind. The body returns its nutrients to the land and life continues (though not the individual's consciousness or separate existence). All these understandings, and others, are valid options for contemporary Druids and have indeed played their part in recent rites of remembrance for the Dead.

Most Druids, I suspect, live in the hope of continuing life beyond death. It should be said that unlike other religions, I have heard no Druid or Pagan suggesting that the individual's post-mortem existence in any way depends on beliefs or deeds in this life. There is no heaven, hell or purgatory, there is no judge but the self, no reward or punishment is imposed. The afterlife, like death, is democratic – everyone gets it equally. Whatever deities Druids believe in, none of them seem particularly concerned with directing human affairs in the afterlife. Having said this, a generalized belief in the doctrine of *karma* is probably held by most contemporary Druids.

Philip Carr-Gomm describes a Parting Ceremony for Lucie in his book *The Druid Way*. This is a deeply moving honouring of the untimely death of someone who meant a great deal to those who knew her. It wishes Lucie well as she leaves our world, celebrates the new life that her soul has been born into, celebrates her time on Earth, expresses the sorrow of the mourners and aims to enable them to say 'farewell'. Lucie is envisaged as journeying towards the Otherworld, 'the Summer Isles, the Isles of the Blessed'. She journeys with various Otherworld beings towards the heart of all things (and is therefore always near, always present), but is expected to be born again on Earth 'when it is right, in your own time'. The ceremony intricately weaves together various hopes about the afterlife with honouring the life recently ended. I imagine it will form a valuable model on which other funerals will be built.

Rounding off

Life is not a straight line nor does it always progress smoothly. An individual's conception is preceded by generations of life with considerable significance to this new beginning. The individual's death relocates them in a longer history and a wider ecology of human and other-than-human relationships. The eight festivals enable Druids to locate their ordinary, individual experience in the wider spirals of seasonal and annual growth and decay. As the Druid Renaissance develops, it will continue to explore ways of marking the rites of passage which move people into the new phases of their current lives. It will also face traumatic abrupt interruptions into the circle of life, recognizing that these too are part of the experience of being human. Druidry will continue to honour ordinary physical existence because everything that lives is holy, and all of life is holy.

Suggested Reading

For discussion of Rites of Passage see Arnold van Gennep, *The Rites of Passage* (University of Chicago Press, 1960); Victor Turner, *The Forest of Symbols* (Cornell University Press, 1967) and Maurice Bloch, *Prey into Hunter: the Politics of Religious Experience* (Cambridge University Press, 1992).

For more discussion of Druid rites of passage, including the complete texts for a Druid naming ceremony, wedding and funeral, see Philip Carr-Gomm, *The Druid Way* (Element Books, 1993). Also see my article, 'Death and Remembrance in modern Paganism', in *Ritual and Remembrance: responses to death in human societies* (edited by Jon Davies; Sheffield Academic Press, 1994), pp. 103–122. The whole book is worth reading.

For death as a part of Nature, see Annie Dillard, *Pilgrim at Tinker Creek* (Picador, 1974).

For practical information on Pagan funerals, and Pagan approaches to dying send SAE to *The Pagan Hospice & Funeral Trust*, BM3337 London WC1N 3XX.

For Paganism in antiquity see Ronald Hutton, *The Pagan Religions of the Ancient British Isles* (Blackwell, 1991). For more recent seasonal celebrations see his *The Rise and Fall of Merry England: the ritual year 1400–1700* (Oxford University Press, 1994).

For modern Paganism see Terry Pratchett's Discworld series (published by Corgi). Death makes his best appearances in *Mort* and *Reaper Man*. There are more serious books about Paganism, but seriousness does not make them any more insightful.

Graham Harvey is a lecturer at King Alfred's College, Winchester, with interests in Paganism, Judaism, Sacred Geography and Ecology. His major contribution to Paganism so far is the insight that since we more often meet hedgehogs than deities, we should be more concerned for their well-being than that of Goddesses and Gods who seem to be doing ok anyway. Although he and his wife, Molly, normally live a quiet life, they enjoy celebrating with the Secular Order of Druids, among others. Graham is currently writing a book on Paganism in Britain which he hopes will become a text book for the growing number of students interested in Paganism and for the lecturers who probably know less than the students.

V

FINDING OUR ROOTS – FINDING OUR FUTURE

The cup is filled the cup has power
the waters of new vision flow

The Cosmic Legend, ROSS NICHOLS

The value and relevance of a spiritual tradition can partly be judged by the degree to which it empowers the people who follow it. The patriarchal religions have tended to disempower people, who were taught to follow with little questioning those with power – the priests, bishops and mullahs. Esoteric and occult groups of the last few centuries have tended to follow the same pattern – with the power residing in 'inner circles' and 'Secret Chiefs', or, in Eastern systems, 'Gurus'. The Nature religions, by contrast, stress the power that resides in Nature Herself. Although they do suffer from the inevitable existence of strong personalities and the rise and fall of power structures, they tend to encourage decentralized, non-hierarchical groups that hand responsibility to the individual rather than to a 'leader'. This seems completely in tune with the Spirit of the Times, which is urging us to find new ways of working and relating to each other.

The Druid's duty is to be sensitive to the needs of the present time, and the promptings of the Future, while at the same time honouring their heritage. A triad for a modern Druid might read:

The three tasks of a Druid:
to live fully in the present;
to honour tradition and the ancestors;
to hear the voice of tomorrow.

Caitlín Matthews

FOLLOWING THE AWEN:
Celtic Shamanism and
The Druid Path in the Modern World

'As the true method of knowledge is experiment,
the true faculty of knowing must be the faculty which experiences.'

All Religions are One
WILLIAM BLAKE[1]

The preoccupation of Celtic peoples with sets of triplicities is a
constant throughout their history: threefold deities like Brighid and
the Morrigan; triadic sayings by which memory is preserved; the
threefold elements of sky, earth and sea; the threefold motifs of the
triskel and triple spiral which recur in Celtic art, myth and culture. It
has been suggested that even the theological and mystical concept of
the Christian Trinity was influenced by Celtic thinking.[2]

In considering the course of my own life thus far, I have been
drawn to the emblem of the *awen*. Awen means 'inspiration' in
Welsh; it is specifically associated with the divine inspiration which
comes upon the poet in his Bardic trance. It is depicted in the motif,
(depicted on the cover of this book) by three rays emanating from
three drops of inspiration, an emblem which has come to stand for
the unity of the three Druidic functions of Bard, Ovate and Druid.
But Awen encompasses something greater and wider than this.

The three drops which in legend fall upon the fingers of Gwion
from the cauldron of inspiration brewed by the Goddess Ceridwen
and the three drops of juice which spurt from the salmon of knowledge upon the thumb of Fionn MacCumhail, are direct encryptions
of the primal powers which inform Celtic and Druidic spirituality.
These powers have not changed down the ages, although the perception of their influence has been interpreted in many ways and been
ascribed to different manifestations.

The threefold constants of Celtic mysticism include conception, creation and exposition; the elemental powers of the heavens, earth and sea; the interconnective family unit of mother, father and child. The Sacred Threefold may be greeted in its divine, human, or natural forms but is always welcomed as the great inspirational, healing and reconnective power which animates life and which is accessible to anyone who follows Druidry and the Celtic path.

From an early age, I have been drawn to the Celtic spiritual path, a pathway which has been interwoven by a triplicity of its own: by mystical, ancestral and environmental strands which have teased my feet to follow them. For me, these have been the *awen*: the three sacred drops which have touched me and shed their own light upon my life and that of others.

Looking at these three strands, I will begin with my ancestry, since the ancestors are the bridges of our lifeline. My mother was the youngest child of a large Irish family which had lived in Britain for two generations. My grandmother was quite ill after my mother's birth, and as a result my mother was fostered with an elderly aunt. The custom of fosterage, once common in Ireland and in rural communities throughout the world, was not, however, well understood in Britain. The aunt moved away from her immediate family and so my mother grew up without the proximity of mother, father or siblings – a fact that she deeply resented, having taken her fosterage as a kind of rejection. In consequence, I grew up without access to or contact with my maternal family.

This roused in me a great curiosity: all I knew was that my mother's family were Irish. So it was that I was predisposed to do some detective work and discover what being Irish (and being Irish in Britain) really meant. This was the beginning of my conscious research in matters Celtic: it began when I was thirteen and eventually led to the reunion of my mother with her family when I was twenty-one, and undergoing my own ancestral coming home. The study begun then has never ceased.

The mystical strand of my pathway was laid down even earlier. As a small child, I was aware of and communicated with spiritual presences whom I called 'the Shapers.'[3] They were my peers and mentors, my reference point when life seemed incomprehensible. As a lonely child, I spent hours speaking with the Shapers. I perceived them as geometric shapes which combined in complex patterns; I heard their voices in my head; I felt their vibration and resonance within my body as a physical sensation. Needless to say, there were no human beings with whom I could share this experience. I learned to keep silent about them, but would continually 'give the game away' by knowing things that I, as a child, could not know. I was regarded as a kind of infant prodigy or freak by some people, although my parents treated me as an ordinary child.

While I was young, this communication with the unseen worlds seemed perfectly normal to me. Only as I grew older did I realize that no-one else would think so. I began to experience the very human longing to be with others of my kind when I was a teenager: a need that was very hard to satisfy. I explored the Society of Friends, Catholicism, Judaism and world religions at large. Where did the Shapers and my experience of them fit into this picture?

I was also in dispute with the religions I encountered at first hand, because they all seemed to be headed by a totalitarian male God. My experience of the divine seemed to differ greatly from everyone else's, as I experienced the divine as manifesting in many forms, but most particularly as female. The divine was, and still is for me, more often Mother than Father.

Enter the environmental strand of my story: the land itself. Love of the land, especially the North-West end of Europe where I was born, has been the one stable and nourishing factor of my life. Even though I have been through terrible confusion and strife in attempting to reconcile my personal spiritual experience with the conventional views of the rest of the world, the land has ever been my mother and sustainer. I was fortunate that my father considered it his duty to drive us out and explore a new part of the country every Sunday, whatever the weather, so I got to see and know the land in all its moods and seasonal phases. My family lived under the South Downs, overlooking the Solent, and I would walk out alone and commune with the chalky hills and the quiet woods near my home (now alas felled to provide a golf-course.)

It was here on the South Downs that I began to reconcile all the factors of my Celtic path. Fuelled by my ancestral search, I had begun to read about Celtic mythology. Suddenly, whole areas of my life leapt into definition. The Shapers ceased to be geometric patterns and musical resonances, they began to appear in the shapes of Celtic deities and spirits; the land which had always moved me to tears of yearning love and homage began to speak to me with an ancestral voice. Words are not adequate to describe the extraordinary clarity of comprehension that illuminated my life at that point. I had been socially marooned on an island of personal spirituality for thirteen years; now I was no longer alone, I was *accompanied*.

My ritual life formally began at thirteen, when I went out into the woods at night to speak to the spirits of the land, taking offerings, candles and home-made incense to celebrate my true coming-home. This was the moment when the three drops of the *awen* coalesced within me. The rest of my life is and will be the realization of its influence.

Such moments of clarity do not usually last long, and so it was with me, for 'still she wished for company.' I began to feel an urgent need to find others of my kind, whom I felt must be out there somewhere. When I left home and went to drama school in London, I went looking. I found Wiccans very easily, but, although they were very welcoming, I felt that little that they did accorded with my experience. I also went and spoke to the leaders of the two main orders of Druids then operative, first to Thomas Maughan of the Ancient Druid Order, a wonderfully urbane and charming man who made it clear that, in his order, actual communication with Celtic deities was not standard practice. I then visited Ross Nichols of the Order of Bards, Ovates and Druids and found his poetic and mystical approach to spiritual exploration much nearer to my own. I consequently attended his meditation classes for a short time until a great change suddenly fell upon my life.

Unfortunately, I made an unhappy marriage in which my life became further restricted by illness. Significantly, the illness lasted the exact duration of my marriage, during which time my natural creativity was forced into deeper and deeper channels until I began to feel that the tide of creation had gone out forever. These years of exile from emotional happiness and health were a descent to the underworld for me from which I was rescued by John, now my husband. I had somehow lost my story-line and he helped to restore it. My return to health was also aided by the Shapers, who returned in their former guises and helped re-route me.[4]

From the mid 1970s onwards, John and I have pooled our joint experiences of spiritual reality and explored its limits and freedoms in many ways. We have been fortunate in having the opportunity to work esoterically with many of the foremost hermetic and Pagan practitioners as colleagues. Latterly, though, we have concentrated on the wisdom of the British, Arthurian and Celtic traditions. For me, this has meant going ever deeper into the Celtic and ancestral traditions of Britain and Ireland and discovering how my personal otherworldly connections can be of benefit to the world. This work inevitably brought me to a consideration of both Druidism and Shamanism.

I had always been drawn to Druidry but seemed unable to find a group that resonated with my own spiritual path: modern Druidic orders seemed too narrow or exclusive to accommodate me and I had been unable to re-contact the Order of Bards, Ovates and Druids. However, in the Spring of 1988 I had the good fortune to meet Philip Carr-Gomm, who I learned was the successor of the same Ross Nichols whom I had met back in the early 1970s. With the satisfaction of someone picking up a dropped thread in a weaving, I heard him announce that he had been asked to reform the Order of Bards, Ovates and Druids, which had lain dormant since just after Ross's death in 1975. Without any sense of why and how, I immediately offered my services in any way that Philip felt appropriate. Shortly afterwards, Philip invited myself and John to become the first presiders of the reformed order and, with others, to help with the training work of the Order.

The OBOD postal training course enables people to connect with their native spiritual tradition through study, meditation and a personal implementation of the principles embodied within it, in their own time and at their own pace. It also provides the option of meeting with fellow members, at regular grove and seed-group meetings, as well as at seminars, courses and retreats run by Philip Carr-Gomm and other OBOD teachers.

In parallel with this work, John and I had been studying ways in which individuals might practically re-connect with the wisdom of the Celtic tradition. I had long since learnt how to journey into the Otherworlds in order to consult with and learn from ancestors and spiritual teachers, drawing upon my experience with the Shapers, while John was now looking at the ways in which Celtic seers and poets used their inner vision in shamanic ways. Now we worked together to devise a course which would teach a form of Celtic Shamanism to a small number of students every year.

Shamanism is practised throughout the world, and North-West Europe has its own localized shamanic manifestations. Our joint experience as teachers of Western wisdom traditions had taught us that many people were exiled from their own native tradition and were seeking to kindle their spiritual flame at the camp fires of other traditions, usually those of the First Americans. As one who had spent most of her life seeking out the roots of the British and Celtic wisdom traditions, I felt that my experience might help people of European ancestry connect with their own spiritual roots.

The Celtic Shamanism courses which John and I run consist of experiential workshops where a small group of people have the opportunity to work together and learn how to become 'walkers-between-the-worlds', able to make spirit-journeys between this world and the otherworld. These spirit-journeys are for the purpose of healing, understanding ancestral lore, and working more closely with the spirits of the land and of nature. In all cases, the wisdom that is learned through these journeys is received through personal experience and perception, from the spirits themselves, and not through formal tuition.

Having been involved in both forms of teaching, from a student's as well as a teacher's perspective, I believe that the Druidic and Shamanic ways of training are not mutually exclusive but, in fact, complementary. Each seeks to awaken personal perception and spiritual awareness in ways that lead us to use our innate gifts and abilities more effectively for the benefit of the world. In both cases, students make their own spiritual contacts and progress upon their own spiritual path.

The spiritual pathway is not a neat or linear one: we seek and find our spiritual nurture in many places and our quest has no ending. Yet it has become obvious to me that, whatever the parameters of our quest, whatever our expectations and desires, we cannot proceed without drawing upon our ancestry, our environment and our own natural mysticism. Indeed, unless we acknowledge this triplicity as a matter of urgency and discover what nurtures our soul, we risk spiritual malnutrition or that pernicious form of self-deception which obliges us to abide within the confines of a spiritual tradition due to family, social or religious pressures and which becomes, in actuality, the poisoning of our soul.

One of the challenges for anyone who undertakes a formal course of esoteric study or who becomes part of a group in order to maintain their spiritual direction, is the practical application of that study and those meetings to their everyday life. Joining an esoteric group can sometimes mean one enters a kind of mental ghetto in which one relates spiritually and intellectually – and sometimes socially – only with fellow members of that group. And there can also be the problem of idealized projection, whereby the past is viewed with nostalgic delight or judged to be invested with current politically correct views.

The Druids of Celtic history are often retrospectively regarded as the professional custodians of Celtic spirituality, where their role is understood as being roughly parallel to that of the priesthood of modern churches. This is not a helpful or accurate parallel. We would do better to understand the ancient Druids (as opposed to the modern orders of Druidry) as an intellectual and professional élite, involved at all levels of daily life and not merely as the sacerdotal guardians of spiritual transactions, as most religious priesthoods are today.

We may imagine Druids living and associating in large bands, but the historical reality shows us individual Druids, Seers and Bards, some attached to training schools, but most serving in their appropriate capacity within the community as judges, healers, remembrancers, reconcilers, seers, diagnostic problem-solvers, and keepers of knowledge. What each Druid shared was access to a common wisdom-pool; not only of historical and ancestral knowledge, but of natural history, geography, story, verse and memory. Each Druid was a walking terminal of knowledge, accessible to members of his or her society, as any qualified professional is in our own world.

The specialist and professional work of the Druid was particularly concerned with the way in which Otherworldly reality impinged upon everyday reality. The accessing of Otherworldly reality was professionally taught in Druidic schools and this is where it is relevant to discuss the role of shamanism:

Shamanism is the art of effectively bridging the worlds of physical and subtle reality so that they are brought into harmony and wholeness. A Shaman can access Otherworlds at will, ask questions and find answers of Otherworldly spirits and beings. One of the major ways in which such information is discovered is by means of a spirit flight or journey, whereby the shaman's spirit journeys forth into the Otherworlds, returning to the body to act upon the information or healing gained. Unlike most forms of divination, the shamanic journey accesses an unseen Otherworld which is understood as having as real a life as that which we call reality.

Shamans exist and have existed all over the globe under a variety of local names. Celtic names for people exercising Shamanic roles include *awenydd* (inspired one); *taibhsear* (vision-seer) and *fili* (poet).[5] Where shamanism is practised there are normally two modes of training and initiation; either the subject is born into a family gifted with shamanic skills and trained by a practitioner, or the subject is chosen by the spirits and trained by them.

Among the Celts, both methods of initiation seem to have been current. As with modern-day public schools, Druidic colleges were often the training grounds of the rich and nobly-born who would go on to become rulers in their own right, but they also trained gifted children who went on to become Druids in turn. Individual Druids are known to have been teachers who took personal apprentices, like Nede Mac Adna, who was sent from Connacht by his father to be trained by the Alban (Scottish) Druid, Eochu Echbel.[6] Similarly many continental Celts sent their children to Britain to be trained by the pre-eminent Druidic schools of this island, suggesting a long Druidic scholastic tradition. Even Pliny commented on the way in which Britain was a by-word for magical doings: 'Even today Britain is still spell-bound by magic, and performs its rites with so much ritual that she might almost seem to be the source of Persian ritual.'[7]

But we also know of individuals who, without recourse to the Druidic or Bardic schools, were innately gifted by the spirits with shamanic abilities which they used to help heal and divine for others. Such people operated outside of Druidry. It is still common to encounter Celts from all over the world who have innate Seership, the second sight, or healing powers of some kind.

There were no schools of 'Celtic Shamanism', only eclectic and localized traditions of healing, divination and diagnostic problem-solving, practised by individuals. Such shamanic abilities were also possessed by the Druidic class who practised divination, prophecy and healing by means of accessing the spirits.

After the destruction of formal Druidic foundations in Britain at the Roman invasions, the historical picture is confused and frag-mented. But we see from Ireland that, even after the inception of Christianity and the waning of Druidic influence as a political and social force, the Druidic teachings flowed directly into the Bardic schools where poets were taught.

Although Julius Caesar classified the Celtic intellectual élite as one category, Strabo defined them as three categories: the Bards or 'panegyric poets', the Ovates or 'sacrificers and diviners', and the Druids who practised natural and moral philosophy. Within the Order of Bards, Ovates and Druids, contemporary members study these three categories in turn.

Our modern understanding of the word poet or Bard is severely limited, usually meaning either a versifier living on subsidies from the arts council or an itinerant musician. The Druidic poet or Bard was one of the gifted people, trained over at least twelve years, not only in the laws and applications of verse, prosody and music, but also in memo-rizing the equivalent of many books of wisdom and lore, and in the arts of prophecy, divination and seership. The exercise of their craft involved not just the evocation of images by means of words and music, but the manifestation of truth in both physical and subtle reality. We can see this exercized in the ability of poets to satirize anyone who had insulted them by means of a specially composed satire: if the satire was justified, boils and other blemishes would appear on the face of the insulter. Latterly, the profession of poet in Celtic countries was still regarded as more than a little magical.

The historical training of the Bard or poet was in the word, the oral tradition. The modern training of the Bard does not deviate from this in any respect, but although there are many accomplished poets in the modern Druidic orders, there is no modern esoteric order with the equivalent of the compendious knowledge of complex metres and rhyme schemes of the ancient orders. The Bards of the Welsh Eisteddfodau, the Cornish Gorsedd, the Scots Gaelic Mod and the Irish Feiseanna, where literary competitions in traditional verse forms are still held, alone retain part of this ability.

The modern Bard is required to speak the truth and to represent its living beauty in all times and places, as well as to maintain the spark of creativity: to uphold 'the perpetual choirs of song' which continually utter the note of the universe, maintaining the harmony that renders chaos into order and keeps the balance between the worlds. These duties are still maintained by every person who seeks for and fulfils their spiritual vocation.

Shamanically, the Bard is 'a voice of the spirits', able to extend the bridge of the imagination between this world and the others, able to invite healing and reconciliation through the word which unites and does not divide.

The historical training of the Ovate was to prophetically divine from whatever signs the universe provided. Divination from nature has always been at the root of native spirituality. It is not without significance that representations of Celtic divinities were minimal until contact with the anthropomorphic depictions of the Classical world. The deities of the Celtic world were nearer in concept to those of the Japanese Shinto world which sees all manifestations of nature as the residencing places of the *kami,* the spirits. Thus, in the Celtic world, people did not bring offerings to statues of gods, but to lakes, springs, mountains, trees and hills. What the modern eye now sees as uninhabited countryside or spectacular views, our ancestors read with a deeper eye. But, with them, we are still able to commune with the spirit of place and respect the power and beauty of what we experience.

The modern Ovate is still encouraged to learn from the wisdom of nature and to look beyond the circle of the self; to learn from that which is enduring; to discern the spark of life in situations that seem dead; to discover, celebrate and defend the beauty of the natural world in all its manifestations.

Shamanically, the Ovate uses nature as her touchstone, able to divine through any part of the natural world, by proximity to and

understanding of the earth, plants, animals and their inter-relationship with all life-forms.

The historical training of the Druid was informed both by a deep
connection with the oral traditions of the Bard, and by the perceptive
prophetic ability of the Ovate, so that the giving of judgements and
decisions – even when determined by means of the drawing of lots or
by reference to historical precedents – was squarely based on the will
of the gods. The Classical commentators on ancient Druidry
frequently remark that the Druids were concerned with spiritual
astrology, with discovering the will of the gods, with learning about
the metaphysics of the soul. We know that the observation of the
elements, weather and the stars played an important part in ancient
Druidic teachings, for these observations revealed the intrinsic
nature of the universe.

The respect accorded one whose study of the universe brought him
or her into harmony with all life was immense: we must imagine how
we would each feel if brought into the presence of a great scientist
and mystic who was also versed in the humanities. We have a potent
description of the chief Druid of Ulster, Crom Deroil, which is one of
the nearest contemporary accounts of a Druid from Irish culture:

> 'a sedate, grey-haired man ... with a fair, bright garment about
> him, with borders of all-white silver. A beautiful white shirt next
> to the surface of the skin; a whitesilver belt around his waist; a
> bronze branch at the summit of his shoulder; the sweetness of
> melody in his voice; his utterance loud but slow.' He is 'sage and
> judicial' and is 'the most eloquent man of the men of earth and the
> peacemaker of hosts.'[8]

It is this ability to make peace, to bring harmony and reconciliation
amid conflicting elements, that seems to me the most important
function of the modern Druid. It is also the most important feature of
the shaman: the ability to reconcile the worlds so that the threefold
powers of the *awen* are able to flow once more.

> Deep within the still centre of my being
>   may I find peace.
> Silently within the quiet of the Grove
>   may we share peace.
> Gently within the greater circle of humankind
>   may we radiate peace.
>
> A Druid Prayer for Peace BY CHRISTINE WORTHINGTON

The training of the modern Bard, Ovate and Druid is based on an understanding of the deep integrity of life; of how thought, feelings and action have real influence on the course of events; and on an understanding of the responsibility we must have for any knowledge we gain.

The most powerful oath that the ancient Celts could swear was, 'May the sky fall upon us, may the earth rise up and swallow us, may the sea overwhelm us if we break our oath.' In the Western Highlands of Scotland, invocations for healing call upon the clouds, the mountains and the seas to bear a portion of the illness far away. Celtic cosmology was a tripartite one that encompassed the powers of these three elemental witnesses of air, earth and water and saw them as active in the skies, hills, rivers and seas. Indeed, the Christianized Celts squared their ancestral dread of the elements collapsing upon them by acknowledging Christ under the title of 'the King of the Elements.'

The ancient Celtic oath has more ominous and immediate connotations in our own times since humankind has made it more than possible for the sky to fall upon us, the earth to swallow us and the sea to cover us forever.

Modern followers of the Celtic spiritual path are of many persuasions: Pagan, Christian, or of other or no fixed spiritual abode. Some combine their spiritual path with an active promotion of Celtic sovereignty, with the learning of Celtic languages, music and poetry; some are more interested in the practical application of Celtic wisdom or mysticism in the modern world. Whatever our backgrounds, whatever our direction, we all live upon the planet and are bounded by the elements.

The ancient triplicity of elemental powers was bounded by a fourth: all actions, especially first motions, must proceed *deosil* or sunwise, as the sun governs the life of all things. The Celtic triskel, the three-legged or three-spoked wheel which comprehends this understanding, always rolls *deosil*. Traditionally, to move *tuathal*, or widdershins, is to invoke power which proceeds contrary to the life-flow.

Whether we follow a Druidic, Shamanic or individual spiritual path, the responsibility upon us all is to act, think and imagine with integrity, so that we in no way hasten the collapse of the elements, so that the flow of life is upheld, so that the laws of nature are maintained. The manifest world is the receptacle of the threefold *awen*; if this vessel of the universe is shattered, then the *awen* cannot be reflected by any of nature's life-forms but must return to its source.

The *awen* does not cease to be, but continually abides, just as the regenerative essence of the Grail abides within the Otherworlds, ready to be dispensed. Ancient Celtic mysticism does not posit a doomsday or an end-point, only the successive ebbing and flowing of life into many forms. Nor do Druidic and Shamanic wisdoms vaunt the pre-eminence of humankind but accept instead that any natural form can be a repository for the lifesoul.

Those who seek direct knowledge of the universe from the elemental powers, the spirits of land, air and water, and who live the seasonal round of the sun's circuit with observation and humility, arrive at the same place as the Druids and Shamans of old: realizing that there is no division between life and life, between form and form. This is the initiation of the *awen*, the three mystical drops of inspiration which touch us to make us aware that the universe is as a cauldron,and that our composite lives are as the liquor within it. Once we have experienced this mystical knowing, we can never again be mindlessly uncaring about anything which happens around us.

In my own life, the inspirational, healing and re-connective rays of the triple *awen*, as well as the three functions of Bard, Ovate and Druid, have come together in my teaching, my writing, and in my shamanic practice. My use of voice and resonance in truth-speaking and the imparting of information have been inspired by the Bardic ray of the *awen*; my connection with the spirits of nature, land and ancestry has given me access to the inner coordinates of dreams, prophecy and oracular divination which emerge as the vatic ray of the *awen*; and my work as a 'midwife of the soul', shamanically helping people untangle the thread of their life-story, I regard as the Druidic ray of the *awen*, since this work makes peace with the soul.

The three rays of the *awen* are the pathways which have continually reasserted their influence in my life, sometimes leading me where I least wanted or expected to go. Shamanism has been the fulfilment of my Druidry, bringing me into direct contact with the needs of people to be re-inspired, reconnected and regenerated. Like most of the ancient Bards, Ovates and Druids, my practice has been largely solitary; but the fellowship I have experienced with other practitioners of Druidic, Celtic, Shamanic and other wisdom traditions has been a great encouragement in hard times. It has shown me who my soul-friends really are. I cannot doubt that many of them have walked these pathways before and will again, for their wisdom and support has been inspired by the eternal truth, insight and spirit of the *awen*.

Following the rays of the *awen* has led me to conclude that both

Druidism and Shamanism are ancient spiritual professions which have currency today.

The reformed orders of modern Druidry have created a community of like-minded people who are willing to be responsible for remembering and building the creative, resourceful and spiritual frameworks of life. The capacity for memory, imagination and resourceful implementation is the hallmark of the modern Druid. The image of the stereotypical nightshirted Druid who scoots about at sacred sites at festival-time, dwelling in a hinterland of atavistic nostalgia, has nothing to do with real Druidry.

The members of The Order of Bards Ovates and Druids maintain a living watch on their environment, and effect spiritual transactions for their community by way of seasonal ritual celebrations, and by providing ritual frameworks for namings, marriages and deaths. By a great variety of different means, they maintain the universe in the way traditionally upheld by the ancient wisdom; by living lives of integrity and inspiration, which are the ancestral pillars of peace – the essential spirit embodied in the three drops of the *awen*.

Those who follow a Shamanic Celtic pathway are directly exposed to the teachings of their ancestors, their environment and the spirits of the universe. Although they may seem to follow an individual pathway, in reality they are deeply enmeshed in their immediate society and locality. Their ability to effect spiritual transactions in their community is being called upon in many ways: to heal deep-seated ancestral and national problems, to address the spiritual cause of physical illness, to re-forge the bridges of help, reconciliation and reconnection so that the powers of the Otherworld can heal the individual soul.

I see no dichotomy between these two pathways. Ultimately, the Shamanic and Druidic pathways of the Celtic tradition can be travelled only by means of our personal experience. The practical application of their wisdom has to be manifested in our lives in whatever way our skills and abilities allow.

The Celtic spiritual path is elusive and elliptical; it does not offer neat explanations or easy directives. I have fought with it as often as I have embraced it, railed against it as much as I have praised it; been comforted, uplifted and inspired by it, and driven to speechless rage and irritation by its inability to stay still for a minute; but it has shaped and trained me as the wind and rain sculpts the rock. I do not know where it will next lead me, but I am willing to find out, as long as the *awen* accompanies me.

NOTES

1. Blake, William *Poetry and Prose,* ed. Geoffrey Keynes, Nonesuch Library, 1975.
2. Hiliary of Poitiers, author of *De Trinitate,* influentially promoted the mystical idea of an indivisible, yet triple-aspected deity. See *The Celtic Inheritance* by Peter Berrisford Ellis, Muller, 1985.
3. See the introduction to *Singing the Soul Back Home,* by Caitlín Matthews, Shaftesbury, Element Books, 1995.
4. A biographical account of this descent appears in *Voices of the Goddess,* ed. by Caitlín Matthews, Aquarian Press, 1990.
5. These roles are discussed in *The Encyclopedia of Celtic Wisdom,* by Caitlín and John Matthews, Shaftesbury, Element Books, 1994.
6. *The Celtic Tradition* by Caitlín Matthews, Shaftesbury, Element Books, 1995.
7. *The Druids* by Nora Chadwick, Cardiff, University of Wales Press, 1966.
8. From 'The Intoxication of the Ulstermen', in *Ancient Irish Tales,* ed. T. P. Cross and C. H. Slover, Dublin, Figgis, 1936.

Caitlín Matthews is the author of 25 books, including *Singing the Soul Back Home* and *The Celtic Book of the Dead.* With John Matthews, she is past-presider of OBOD and with him, she has collaborated on many books and projects, including *The Arthurian Tarot* and *The Encyclopedia of Celtic Wisdom.* She has a shamanic practice in Oxford.

Her quarterly newsletter of forthcoming books, events and courses, Hallowquest, is available from BCM Hallowquest, London WC1N 3XX at £6 (Europe), or £12/$20 (World): sterling cheques or sterling travellers cheques payable to Graal Publications.

Dr Gordon Strachan

AND DID THOSE FEET?

Did Jesus come to Glastonbury and Cornwall with Joseph of Arimathea? If so, was it only to accompany his uncle when tin trading or were there Druidic and Megalithic connections?

And did those feet in ancient time
Walk upon England's mountains green?
And was the holy Lamb of God
On England's pleasant pastures seen?

And did the Countenance Divine
Shine forth upon those clouded hills?

What did William Blake mean by these questions? Were they symbolic or literal? Set to Parry's inspiring music, his famous 'Jerusalem' has become Britain's second national anthem, taken symbolically by some, literally by others. Blake believed that Jesus symbolized a human and divine perfection which in ancient time had originated in the land of Albion. In this sense he *had* walked 'upon England's mountains green'. This was a modern version of a tradition that the teachings of Christ, as the eternal Logos or Word of God, had been accepted by the Druids in pre-Christian Britain. [1]

But Blake was also steeped in the legends which claimed that Jesus had literally come to Britain with Joseph of Arimathea. The most distinguished product of the Celtic revival of the late eighteenth century, in which extravagant claims had been made linking the ancient Welsh to the ancient Jews and even suggesting that the religion of the Old Testament had come from Britain, [2] Blake was not alone when he proclaimed: 'To the Jews: Your Ancestors derived their origin from Abraham, Heber, Shem and Noah, who were Druids, as the Druid Temples (which are the Patriarchal Pillars and Oak Groves) over the whole Earth witness to this day.'[3]

The Glastonbury Legends

Blake's theories, like those of his fellow Celticists, have long been consigned to the dustbin by scholars, who have branded them as at best romantic eccentricities, and at worst, fraudulent nonsense. However, despite such condemnation, his 'Jerusalem' continues to be sung as lustily as ever, and Glastonbury has grown enormously as a centre for mystical Christianity.

At the heart of the Glastonbury mystique lies the belief that Jesus came to Britain as a youth during his silent years with his rich, tin trading uncle, Joseph of Arimathea, and that he built a church later called 'the Old Church'. Further, that shortly after the crucifixion, Joseph returned with twelve disciples and built a hutted encampment on land gifted by King Arviragus; that he brought a staff which he planted on Wearyall Hill which became the famous thorn, which has blossomed ever since; that he also brought two cruets containing the blood and sweat of Christ, which later turned into the Holy Grail; that his first encampment was at Chalice Well near the Tor, but that his more permanent dwellings were around the Old Church, built by Jesus, on the site of which is now St Joseph's Chapel at the west end of the Abbey ruins.[4]

Scholars are almost as dismissive about the Glastonbury legends as they are about Blake's Judeo-Druidism because of the lack of historical evidence. Joseph of Arimathea isn't mentioned in connection with Glastonbury until 1240, which is very late. Jesus isn't mentioned at all until the eighteenth century and even then only by inference, with regard to his building the Old Church. If he had come, argue sceptics, then surely the Abbey monks would have mentioned it. His supposed visit is thought to be no more than the product of Protestant propaganda to establish a primacy for the early British Church over Rome.[5]

Yet, despite this lack of early evidence, even Professor R. T. Treharne, the most severe critic, cannot bring himself to deny that Joseph *might* have come, suggesting that if this were so, it would have been by sea up the Bristol Channel.[6] Also, leading historian Geoffrey Ashe thinks that the Grail romances of the later Middle Ages, which feature Joseph so prominently, could not have sprung out of nothing: 'There must have been a prior belief lurking somewhere, a belief too stubborn to dismiss, a belief which there was good reason to use.'

Ashe compares the dormant Joseph stories to those of Arthur: 'Throughout the Dark Ages the English had many scribes and scholars, but not one so much as hints at the existence of Arthur, or … Arthurian legend. Yet there was such a legend: the Welsh hoarded it for six hundred years before the English discovered it … So with Joseph of Arimathea … I find it easier to believe that such a fancy existed from early times than to accept the sudden contrivance of the whole business in the Middle Ages.'[7]

If Professor Treharne is prepared to say Joseph could have come and Geoffrey Ashe that he possibly did, could it not also be proposed, in principle, that Jesus might have come with Joseph on an earlier occasion? The fact that the evidence is oral, not written, need not be an insuperable obstacle if we are dealing, as in the Arthurian legends, with a lost tradition. Traditions get lost because they are politically or ecclesiastically 'incorrect'. They are persecuted and prohibited by the winners and hidden away secretly by the losers. Thus the Arthurian tradition was hidden by the Welsh from the English. Similarly, the tradition of Joseph in Britain may have been hidden by the Celts from the Roman church. Traditions can be lost for longer than 600 or 1200 years, as we have seen from the discoveries of the Gnostic texts at Nag Hammadi and the Dead Sea Scrolls at Qumran, which were lost for 1600 and 1900 years respectively.

If it is 'Protestant' to maintain that the Roman Catholic hierarchy ruthlessly suppressed many legitimate spiritual movements over the millennia, classing them heretical, when actually their only sin was to challenge power and threaten authority, then so be it. The Protestants succeeded. Many before them failed. Could it be, that, for all their eccentric and dubious scholarship, Blake and his mentors sniffed out, as much by psychic intuition as by historical research, a lost-Jesus-in-Britain tradition to complement that of Joseph of Arimathea? After all, the Druids' tradition was not just oral, it was secret. Jesus' visit as a youth would have been a closely guarded secret – except to the psychics, to those with the second sight. Blake had 'the sight' as many stories about him testify. Had he seen Jesus in Britain as other psychics since have claimed? While it cannot be proved, it is certainly not beyond the bounds of possibility.

The New Evidence

In recent years new evidence has emerged which indicates that Blake's Judeo-Druidic mysticism may not have been so eccentric after all. This new evidence has to do with the discovery that the people who built the megalithic monuments in Britain in the Neolithic and Bronze ages may have been proto-Pythagoreans. This claim rests on the work of the late Professor Alexander Thom, who showed that some of the stone circles were egg-shaped or elliptical and had been constructed around Pythagorean triangles. Thom's surveys show that the megalithic monuments can be interpreted as being the remnants of an advanced proto-Pythagorean civilization.[8]

This being the case, it is of great significance that Hippolytus, Polyhistor, Clement and other Classical writers thought that the Druids were Pythagoreans, while Caesar, Pliny, Strabo and others listed, as Druidic, such subjects as natural philosophy, astronomy, astrology, cosmology, magic, reincarnation and the immortality of the soul; all subjects also known to be Pythagorean.[9] This new Pythagorean evidence from the stone circles, taken together with these Classical texts, indicates that not only were the Druids Pythagoreans, they were the heirs of a tradition which went back at least to the first phase of circle building around 3300 BC. If this were so, then the Druids would have been well worth a visit.

Objections among archaeologists to the belief that there was continuity of culture over the 2500 years from Neolithic to Druidic times are not as strong as they used to be. For instance, John Wood says that when the Beaker Folk came to Britain, around 2500 BC, there was 'apparently no break in continuity'[10] with earlier Neolithic culture. Likewise, Euan Mackie has shown that the dimensions of the Iron Age brochs of Scotland show a 'unity of length almost identical to the megalithic yard', as proposed by Professor Thom.[11]

The case for continuity is further strengthened by Professor Thom's histogram of alignments at stone circles, which shows that while most are aligned to the solstices and equinoxes, a substantial number are also aligned approximately to the first day of February, May, August and November. These are what are still known as Quarter Days in Scottish law; they refer back to the four Celtic fire festivals of Imbolc, Beltane, Lughnasadh and Samhain. Professor Thom's analysis thus shows that these Celtic festivals must in fact have originated with the Neolithic or Bronze Age builders and not with the Celts.

There is therefore a strong case for a continuity of culture; a case for the Druids as Pythagoreans and for Megalithic Britain as probably the earliest expression of a proto-Pythagorean civilization. Our inherited notions about our 'primitive' and 'inferior' prehistoric ancestors now seem absurd, and Blake's notion of the primacy of Albion now seems more than half sane.

If the Druids were Pythagoreans and the megalithic culture was proto-Pythagorean, who were the Pythagoreans themselves? They were the followers of Pythagoras, who was born at Samos around 570 BC and who went to Croton in South Italy to start a political and religious commune, which was as social as it was spiritual, as mystical as it was mathematical. To his contemporaries, Pythagoras was larger than life and was accorded divine status. He was generally thought to be the incarnation of the God Apollo from Hyperborea and to have magical gifts. Hyperborea, the land beyond the North Wind, was thought in early times to be in Central Asia in the Altai mountains, but as geographical knowledge improved it moved west until by the third century BC it was considered to be Britain. Diodorus Siculus, following Hecateus, tells us that Apollo was honoured among the Hyperboreans above all other Gods. Thus we find an unexpected link between Pythagoras and ancient Britain. Behind the mythology of Hyperborean Apollo, we can detect the belief that Pythagoras embodied a wisdom that had originated in Britain. And in the story which Diodorus also tells, about Abaris the Druid who exchanged gifts and skills with Pythagoras, we can see that this wisdom had been inherited by the Druids.

Diodorus also said that the Hyperboreans had 'both a magnificent sacred precinct of Apollo and a notable temple which ... is spherical in shape. Furthermore, a city is there which is sacred to this God.'[12] Could the sacred precinct be Avebury, the spherical (pertaining to the sphere of the heavens) temple be Stonehenge, and the sacred city Glastonbury? If he is describing Pythagorean 'cathedrals' and Druidical centres, then this would seem a distinct possibility.

The Pythagorean Bible

What has all this Pythagoreanism got to do with Jesus or the Judaic tradition? The answer is simple. The Bible itself, both Old and New Testaments, whatever else it is, is a Pythagorean text-book. It is an enormous expression of the fourfold Pythagorean paradigm of number. The four aspects of this paradigm are: number as such, geometry which is number in space, musical harmonics which is number in time, and astronomy-astrology which is number in space-time. The fact that the Bible has not been seen in this way in recent centuries does not detract from the Pythagorean interpretation which can be given to the pervasive presence of symbolic numbers, from the 6 days of creation to 666, the number of the beast, via an

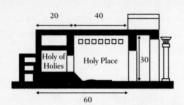 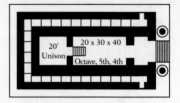

Temple measurements and proportions

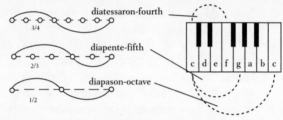

The ratios of musical intervals

overwhelming quantity of references to such key numbers as 7, 10, 12, 40, 50, 70 and 144. It is the same for geometry, and for musical harmonics. These two disciplines were usually expressed together, and were manifest in the architecture of temples, where the architectural proportions embodied geometric ratios, which were themselves the equivalent of the string-length ratios of musical intervals. The proportions of Solomon's Temple are perfect examples of this.

It is also the same for astrology-astronomy. It is clear to those who have studied the Precession of the Equinoxes and the consequent Ages of the Great Year, that in the Old Testament the battle between Jahweh and the Goddess was the battle between the Age of Aries the Ram, ruled by Mars, and the Age of Taurus the Bull, ruled by Venus. It is equally obvious in the New Testament that this battle was carried on between the new Age of Pisces the Fish, ruled by Jupiter-Neptune, represented by Jesus, and the Old Age of Aries the Ram, whose protagonists are the Jews.[13]

The life of Jesus agrees to a remarkable degree with this interpretation. In his miraculous or magic powers, in his calling of a group of followers, in his teaching by parables, in his belief in the greater reality of the unseen world, and in the immortality of the soul, Jesus was like Pythagoras. He is also shown as using numbers in a Pythagorean way, in his choice of 12 apostles, 70 disciples, 40 days in the desert, forgiving 70 times 7, 153 fishes caught in the net, and so on. This is particularly the case if we look at the numerology of his own name.

In the Hebrew of the Old Testament and the Greek of the New, each letter is equivalent to a number. The Greek alphabet is given below:

Aα	Bβ	Γγ	Δδ	Eε	F*	Zζ	Hη	Θθ
1	2	3	4	5	6	7	8	9
Iι	Kκ	Λλ	Mμ	Nν	Ξξ	Oo	Ππ	Q*
10	20	30	40	50	60	70	80	90
Pρ	Σσ	Tτ	Yυ	Φφ	Xχ	Ψψ	Ωω	⌐*
100	200	30	400	500	600	700	800	900

* F, Q, ⌐ – numerals only

Reading numbers for letters was called Gematria in the Classical World. In Gematria, among other practices, the total number for each word was analysed in terms of its prime and its divisors. Symbolic meanings then emerged. In Greek, the name of Jesus Christ is spelt Iesous Christos. If the value of each letter is added up we get 888 plus 1480 which comes to 2368:

$$\begin{array}{ccccccc}
I & E & S & O & U & S \\
10 & 8 & 200 & 70 & 420 & 200 & = & 888
\end{array}$$

$$\begin{array}{ccccccccc}
CH & R & I & S & T & O & S \\
600 & 100 & 10 & 200 & 300 & 70 & 200 & = & \underline{1480} \\
& & & & & & & & 2368
\end{array}$$

If we then divide 888, 1480 and 2368 by their highest common factor, which is 296, we get 3, 5 and 8. So the ratio of these numbers to each other is 3 to 5 to 8. Now it so happens that the ratios 3 to 5 and 5 to 8 are part of a most important number series which in recent centuries has been known as the Fibonacci Numbers, with the code letter ø or phi. This series is formed by adding each number to the one before; thus 1, 1, 2, 3, 5, 8, 13, 21, 34, 55, 89 and 144. These numbers form ratios to each other which are close, whole number approximations to what is known as the Divine Proportion or the Golden Section. This was so important to the ancient Greeks that they called it simply 'the section'. The Divine Proportion was, and is known to be, the proportion embodied in all growing things throughout the cosmos, from the spiral nebulae to the nautilus shell, from the proportions of the human body to the pattern of sunflower seeds and daisy heads. It is the spiral of life and the essence of harmonics, from the inner ear to the shape of musical instruments. It was called the Divine Proportion because the character and signature of the Creator could be seen in it throughout creation.

Return to the Source

It is this Divine Proportion which is embodied in 888, 1480 and 2368, the numbers for Jesus, Christ and Jesus Christ. Expressed as 3 is to 5 as 5 is to 8, the numbers 3, 5 and 8 represent the most important proportion among the 10 principle proportions favoured by the Pythagoreans. It is therefore impossible to escape the conclusion that whatever else Jesus was actually called in his lifetime, by the time his name appeared in the gospels, it had been tailored to fit a Pythagorean interpretation. Jesus may have been called Iesous, Iesus, Iesu or some other variant of the Greek Septuagint translation of the Hebrew for Joshua. Likewise Christos, the Septuagint translation of the Hebrew for Messiah, is known to have been sometimes spelt Chrestos, Christus or Chrestus. But the fact that *only* the numerology of Iesous Christos fits the Divine Proportion points very strongly to Pythagorean influence and interpretation. From a Pythagorean point of view, the reason for this would be clear: Jesus, as the heir to, and embodiment of, the Pythagorean wisdom, had to have a name which in itself expressed the essence of that wisdom. Names were not chosen at random. They had to express the identity of, to actually *be*, that which they named. The meaning of Iesous Christos as *words* was Joshua the Messiah. But as *numbers* – which had given rise to the particular spelling selected – according to the ancient wisdom of the Pythagoreans, it was the embodiment of the Divine Proportion, the character and signature of the creator throughout creation.

We cannot say definitely whether or not Jesus was himself a Pythagorean. All we can say is that the evidence leads that way, and that the numerology of his name, like the gospels themselves, has been constructed so that we shall come to the conclusion that he was. That the gospel writers were unanimous in their *belief* that he was, would seem to be conclusive from this numerological analysis.

We can take this a little further and suggest that, working within a Biblical tradition which was itself pervasively Pythagorean, the gospel writers had come to the conclusion that Jesus was not just a Pythagorean among Pythagoreans, but was in fact *the* Pythagorean; that is, the new Pythagoras. But who was Pythagoras? As stated earlier, he was thought to have been the incarnation of Hyperborean Apollo. But where was Hyperborea and who was Apollo? Well, well, this all begins to sound familiar. It also begins to look very obvious why Jesus should want to come to Britain.

Whether Jesus understood himself to be *only* the new Apollo of the Hyperboreans, or much more besides his obvious fulfilment of Old Testament prophecies, I think that the facts now before us make it difficult to deny that he saw himself as *at least* that. To make such a denial would be tantamount to proposing that there was no connection at all between who he understood himself to be and those who later spun mythology around him. It is fashionable in certain circles to do precisely that, but I believe that the Pythagorean symbolism is so central to the Old Testament that it would have been impossible for Jesus not to have understood himself *at least* in terms of that tradition. It was nothing new. Nothing had to be dreamt up in terms of maths, mystery, magic or mythology. All Jesus had to do was to fit, fulfil and renew it. This I believe he did, and in order to equip himself for the task, I believe it was important for him to return to the source of that tradition – to Britain.

Was Blake right after all? It looks remarkably like it. Everything I have put forward here points to the possibility that Britain might well have been 'the Primitive Seat of the Patriarchal Religion'[14] if by that we mean that the Old Testament was a later manifestation of the proto-Pythagorean Druidism which had originated in the cult of Hyperborean Apollo in Megalithic Albion.

Have we lost our senses? Has some Druidic spell been cast over us? Do Blake's bizarre notions still exert a fatal fascination? How have we moved from criticizing to endorsing them? Surely there must be some trickery. We can't really be saying 'And those feet did' – can we?

Perhaps we can. Perhaps we have all been the victims of history as told by the winners. Perhaps Blake accurately sensed the presence of a lost tradition which it has taken others to expose through more pedestrian researches. Perhaps we have pieced together a scenario which could be the basis for a new historical perspective. If this were the case, then another very good reason for Jesus to have come to Britain might soon emerge. This would centre around a fresh interpretation of the meaning of human sacrifice as allegedly practised by the Druids, and as put forward by Anne Ross and Don Robins in *The Life and Death of a Druid Prince*.

The Life and Death of a Druid Prince

Lindow Man or 'Pete Marsh' as the media nicknamed him, was
discovered by a peat cutter in Lindow Moss, south of Manchester,
in 1984. He was identified as dating from the first century AD. This
was almost unbelievable because he was so well preserved that the
police had to be convinced that he was not the victim of a recent
murder! The tannins in the bog had mummified the body so
completely that wrinkles, fingerprints, beard, stubble, eyelashes and
fingernails could still be identified.

Experts soon found that Pete Marsh had died extremely violently.
His neck and jaw were broken and his skull fractured. Because there
were no signs of resistance, binding with ropes, or swollen wound
margins on the scalp, the team began to suspect he had been killed as a
human sacrifice. When they discovered that he had also been
garrotted and a sharp blade had been stabbed into his jugular, this
suspicion was confirmed. He had suffered a threefold sacrificial death.

Who was he? His finger nails were smooth and manicured. He
was therefore not a peasant or a craftsman but an aristocrat. His 'O'
blood group showed he was an insular Celt. His physique was
unblemished and therefore he could not have been a warrior. The
only possibilities were that he was a Bard or a Druid. As he had no
callouses or roughening of fingers or thumb from harping, he must
therefore have been a Druid. If so, then 'He was the first physical
trace of the mysterious cult that had ever been discovered.'[15]

The body was naked except for a fox-fur armband. Because 'fox',
or 'lovernios' in Celtic, was a synonym for a nobleman at that time, it
was deduced that he had been a prince. Put together, the conclusions were that he was a Druid Prince who had been ritually put to
death. The next question was 'Why?' The dating of his death to 60
AD, the Black Year, gave the answer.

The Roman invasion of Britain under Claudius had begun in 43 AD.
This invasion was only seriously resisted by the tribes north of the
Thames in East Anglia, the Midlands and the West, and was
encouraged by the Druids. In 54 AD, the Emperor Claudius was
succeeded by Nero, who was greedy for British copper, lead and
gold. In 58 AD he ordered Suetonius to strike at Mona (Anglesey)
which was considered to be the spiritual and material heart of the
Western tribes. In the spring of 60 AD he successfully destroyed the
whole island, massacring the Druids, laying waste the farms and
burning the sacred oak groves.

Then news came of Queen Boudica's (or Boadicea's) uprising. Catus, Nero's procurator, had tried to sequester the famed wealth of Prasutagus, the recently deceased king of the Iceni, who had been Boudica's husband. Boudica rebelled, raised a huge army, sacked Colchester, London and St Albans and was only defeated by cunning at Mancetter. But her defeat meant the end of all hope of ridding Britain of the Romans. 60 AD was a blacker year for Britain than 1066 or 1940.

Anne Ross and Don Robins came to the conclusion that the Druid Prince had been sacrificed to placate the Gods Taranis, Esus and Teutates and to stop the Roman advance: 'His high rank fitted him for this supreme sacrifice. Lovernios knew he was going to die and composed himself for the solemn and sombre occasion'.[16]

They also liken his death to that of Christ: 'He died naked, with the fox-fur armband as the only token of kingly rank, as subtly marked as Christ, who had died in torment a generation before.' They believe that the sacrifice achieved its purpose: 'Despite their navy and despite the consolidation of their grip on Britain in the decades that followed Lovernios' death, the Romans never did go to Ireland'.[17] Neither did they discover that Anglesey was really only a staging post on the sacred gold route from the Wicklow mountains to the lands of the Iceni. This secret was never revealed. Lovernios, the Druid Prince, had been a holy and sufficient sacrifice.

He Died to Save His People

There could not be a sharper contrast between the Romans' attitude to the Druid practice of human sacrifice, and that of Anne Ross and Don Robins as outlined. The Romans were completely negative: 'Barbaric rites' (Lucan), 'savage' (Pomponius Mela and Tacitus) and 'monstrous' (Pliny) are typical examples of their response. To a great extent, we have inherited their opinion.[18]

Caesar however, although just as negative, inadvertently made an observation which gives us an unexpectedly positive link with *The Druid Prince*: 'The Gallic people are extremely superstitious. Consequently, people suffering from serious illnesses, and people involved in the dangers of battle, make or promise to make, human sacrifice; the Druids officiate at such sacrifices.'[19]

Now it is precisely a situation involving 'the dangers of battle' that Ross and Robins maintain was the context of the Druid Prince's sacrifice, but unlike Caesar they do not think it was 'extremely superstitious'. Quite the contrary, for Anne Ross believes that:

'Human sacrifice in order to save the people is an important factor. The victim seems always to have been willing.'[20]

Her phrasing 'in order to save the people' is very reminiscent of the New Testament, when Caiaphas the High Priest, discussing the advantages of letting Jesus be crucified, says to the Jewish council: 'it is expedient for you that one man should die for the people, than that the whole nation should perish'. With one bound, we appear to have left the 'savage' and 'monstrous' 'barbaric rites', and entered the heart of the Christian religion. What the Romans rejected, the Christians accepted. Here indeed is a complete reversal of values.

Although Caiaphas was referring only to the immediate political situation, St John extends it to the spiritual: '... and not for the nation only, but to gather into one the children of God who are scattered abroad'.[21] Elsewhere in the gospels, this is extended still further into a theory of atonement in which the sacrificial death of Jesus, because he was the son of God, was sufficient for the sins of the whole world. It would thus appear that the sacrifice of the Druid Prince and that of Jesus Christ differ only in degree, not in kind.

Where did Jesus get his theory of human sacrifice? The Jews had banned it for many centuries. Even the Romans had recently done so. But, as we have seen, the Druids still practised it. Thus, if Jesus had been a Druid, his determination to be a willing human sacrifice would have been entirely consistent with this tradition, but if he was only Judaic, as we have been led to believe, it would not have been. Christians have become so used to thinking of Jesus as the Passover Lamb, they have forgotten that he was only symbolically a sacrificial animal. He was, quite literally, a human sacrifice. So the question remains, where did he get his theory of human sacrifice?

In answer, Biblical scholars cite the Akedah, the almost human sacrifice of Isaac, replaced by a ram or lamb; the suffering servant of Isaiah, and the concept of martyrdom among the Maccabees. While these analogies are acceptable in the Jewish context, they fall far short of explaining the full profundity of the ancient Christian theories of atonement. They also do not explain the mythology of the God who dies and then rises again. If Jesus had been a Druid, his sacrificial death would have had a cultural and religious context which would have seen him as a legitimate voluntary human victim and not just as a symbolic lamb, or suffering servant, or martyr. Indeed, if Jesus' self-perception was not just that of lamb, suffering servant and martyr, but if he perceived himself also as the incarnation of the God who dies and then rises again, then, because he did rise from the dead, he fits the Druidic context better than the Judaic.

The Comparison with Odin

Ross and Robins maintain that the Druid Prince suffered a threefold death. Nicolai Tolstoy in *The Quest for Merlin* proposes the same fate for Jesus, comparing the Crucifixion to the death of the Norse God Odin. He tells us that there are seven points of similarity between the deaths of Odin and Jesus: One: Odin dies hanging on the World Tree, as does Christ. Two: Whilst on the tree, Odin is wounded with a spear, as is Christ. Three: Odin hangs for nine full nights, a multiple of three reflecting the three days between Christ's death and resurrection. Four: Odin thirsted in his agony, as did Christ. Five: Odin screamed at the moment of truth, just as Christ 'cried with a loud voice'. Six: Odin was sacrificed to himself as Christ laid down his life of his own accord. Seven: Odin, like Christ, rose from death, fortified with occult wisdom which he communicated to Gods and men.[22]

This impressive list has a considerable bearing on the question of why the gospel was so well received when it came to Northern shores. Tolstoy's answer is that the stories of Odin and Jesus were so similar that 'it has been believed to be a principal cause of the relative ease with which the North was converted to Christianity. Christian Anglo-Saxon poetry describing the death of the Saviour unself-consciously employs Odinic terminology at every turn.'[23]

Tolstoy considers the threefold aspects of the Crucifixion as, one, hanging on a tree; two, being pierced with a spear; three, being drowned or poisoned with vinegar. Had Jesus not just been like Odin but an actual Druid Prince, his three deaths would have propitiated Esus by hanging, Taranis by spear thrust and Teutates by drowning.

Tolstoy also notes the threefold symbolism which saturates the Christian story. 'After three days I will rise again'; 'from the sixth to the ninth hour' there was darkness; 'Jesus yielded up his spirit' 'about the ninth hour', and he was hung between two other victims. When we remember that the number three was much more central to Celtic than Judaic numerology, and that the number nine was avoided by the Jews because of its association with the triple Goddess, but popular with the Celts for the same reason, Tolstoy's observations add strong support to the case that even if Jesus was not a Druid, he could have been. There seems to be as much

evidence to link him to the Druid Prince and the Odinic mythology
as there is to link him to Old Testament heroes. And there seems to
be enough evidence to believe that he might have come to the North
to learn about the Druids' profound understanding of the purpose of
a perfect, voluntary, human sacrifice.

The Oak-Grove Calvary

Ross and Robins describe the Druid Prince as 'the divine victim
coming down from his own oak-grove calvary'.[24] This image links his
sacrifice to that of Jesus in a most striking way. It also reminds me of
the many visits I made to Caesarea Philippi, or Banias as it is now
called, when I was working in Tiberias. Caesarea Philippi is an
ancient town, now only ruins, in the far north of Israel on the slopes
of Mount Hermon, at the source of the river Jordan. Its old name
was Panias because its shrine was sacred to the god Pan. It was an
ancient centre of gentile religion and it still abounds in oak trees.
Acorns litter the pathways by the river. What if Panias was Jesus'
'oak-grove calvary', for it was there, we are told, that he first 'began to
show his disciples that he must go to Jerusalem and suffer many
things from the chief priests and scribes, and be killed, and on the
third day be raised'.[25]

Peter's response 'God forbid Lord! This shall never happen to you',
and the stern admonition he received, may have obscured the importance of the remote, wooded location of this exchange. If Jesus had
learnt from the Druids about the supreme importance of human
sacrifice and had chosen to begin to tell his followers about it in the
oak groves of Panias, it isn't surprising that Peter didn't understand.
We are told that the disciples continued not to understand until after
the resurrection. If this teaching had been in any way obvious in the
Old Testament, Jesus would have referred to it, if indeed he had
needed to because, had that been the case, Peter, James and John
would have known of it already. They would soon have understood.
But they didn't, which suggests that Jesus' teaching, at this point, did
not come explicitly from the Old Testament.

The disciples' inability to accept the centrality of suffering and
death in relation to their Messiah may thus have been because it
wasn't central to their own tradition. Human sacrifice and the
mythology of the dying and the rising god were alien to Judaism.
They were heathen. But Jesus' Calvary could be said to have *begun*
among the heathen oaks at Panias and to have had as much to do
with the fulfilment of gentile spiritual expectations as with Jewish.

St Just – 'The Just One'

When we look at the legends surrounding the visit of Jesus to Britain, it is strange that none of these give any reason for him coming, other than that he accompanied his 'uncle' Joseph in the tin trade; as if, like some aspiring royal, he was merely filling in time until his Messianic call came through. This is so unsatisfactory it suggests an alibi hiding more serious reasons. In this essay, I have proposed two potentially profound motives for his possible visits. Firstly, that he wanted to return to the source of the wisdom tradition which he had come to embody. Secondly, that he wanted to learn about the exalted theory of human sacrifice from the Druids.

While none of this can be proved and is in a sense pure speculation, there is no more reason to doubt this theory than to doubt that he spent his 18 silent years doing carpentry, as has traditionally been believed. There is no more evidence that he was in Nazareth for much of that long period than that he was away travelling in Britain, Egypt, India or elsewhere. In fact the very silence itself suggests that either no-one knew, or that it was a closely-guarded secret. It has been proposed that the story of the flight into Egypt was concocted to defuse Jewish criticism that he had been away in Egypt learning magic.

It has also recently been shown, by Professor Fida Hassnain in *A Search for the Historical Jesus*, that there is a tradition in the East that he went to Kashmir, and that while there he was strongly influenced by Buddhist teaching. The evidence for this is strong and centres around ancient references to a certain St Issa who is believed to have been Jesus.[26]

The Kashmiri tradition of St Issa is strangely reminiscent of our own Cornish story that Jesus and Joseph landed at St Just.[27] No-one really knows who the St Just of Roseland or Penrith really was. There is a story that he was one of a group of monks, sent by Pope Gregory to England in 596 with St Augustine. This is probably no more than Roman Catholic propaganda. The most authentic source indicates that St Just was the son of St Erbyn, son of St Gerent, son of Lud. But since King Lud, of Ludgate fame, was a humanized version of the king of the fairies, the God Nodens, (or Nudd, or Nuedu of the Silver Hand), we may take it that this is pure mythology. Judging by the likeness of many other Cornish saints to the old Celtic gods and goddesses, we may take it that his forebears were probably canonized Celtic deities. Even if St Just himself was actually an historical figure, like St Brigit of Kildare, behind him lay the Celtic pantheon.

Yet might that pantheon have included a late arrival who was as much at home among Celtic deities as Christian saints? Someone who was twice called 'the Just One' in the Acts of the Apostles, and who was said to have come with his uncle, also called 'just and good'? In both the Hebrew and the Greek world, to be 'just' was to be righteous, holy and thus godlike. Like St Sophia, St Cross and St Creed, could the name St Just represent the veneration of the prime attribute of Godliness? Could St Just in fact be the memory of the one who embodied that godliness, who was said to have landed in the Fal estuary, at the site of that name, and to have visited Falmouth, St Anthony Head, Place Manor and the tin mines west of that area? Was St Just a synonym for the Just One? And do the many wayside crosses of West Cornwall, which seem to depict a young Jesus wearing a knee-length tunic, testify to this?[28] If so, it would fit a Pythagorean interpretation perfectly, for Plato's concept of the 'just' man was derived from the metaphor of the proportions of the musical scale which came straight from Pythagoras. As we have seen, Pythagoras represented a wisdom which can be traced back to megalithic Britain. If Jesus had come to 'tune in' to that wisdom, he could have had no better pseudonym than St Just, for to be 'just' was to be in tune with the sanctity of all things.

The Golden Bough

The comparison noted earlier between the deaths of Jesus and Odin comes much nearer home when we remember that Balder was the son of Odin. The story of Balder's death by a branch of mistletoe is well known. His mistletoe is even better known as a Christmas decoration. What is not so well known is that, according to Sir James Fraser in *The Golden Bough*, Balder was the tree spirit of the oak, and the mistletoe growing on the oak was his soul. It was believed that once this mistletoe was cut, the host oak would die. At the same time as the lightning of Odin gave birth to the mistletoe, it struck death to the oak.[29]

But the mistletoe had to be cut in order to be of use. It was known to have great medicinal properties and was called All Heal. While growing on the deciduous oak it was observed to be evergreen, which made it seem immortal; it was only during the months after cutting that it turned golden. Hence the Golden Bough was not just mistletoe as such, it was *cut* mistletoe. Only as *cut* mistletoe could it heal. Only in its own death could it give life.

It is easy to see how close this mythology of the Golden Bough is to that of the death and resurrection of Jesus. In its own way, it comes closer to it than that of Odin because it clearly exemplifies the principle of sacrifice for healing purposes. It also exemplifies the ancient theory of the external soul, in which the soul had to be kept somewhere safe to avoid vulnerability. Balder's soul was in the mistletoe. By sympathetic magic, only mistletoe could kill him. As the mistletoe kills the oak while it produces its miraculous healing powers, so it too must be 'killed' or cut, before those powers can heal others. Thus the Golden Bough is a powerful symbol for the health and salvation that come from the sacrifice and resurrection of Jesus. In this sense, Jesus is Balder and the mistletoe is the symbol of his all-healing power. There is also a possibility that Jesus is Esus, for while that shadowy Celtic deity has been sometimes likened to Mars and Mercury, Anne Ross points out that Esus is equated with Odin, Balder's father, in so much as both were 'commonly offered human sacrifices in which victims were hanged from a sacred tree and had their throats slashed'.[30] The fact that grains of mistletoe pollen were found mixed into the burnt bannock which the Druid Prince ate just before he died, adds an eerie link to the Odin, Balder, Jesus and Esus connection.

The theory of the external soul was taken over by Christianity.[31] When St Paul said 'Your life is hid with Christ in God',[32] he meant that the soul of the Christian was safe as long as it was hidden away in God's care, together with the risen Christ. Hymns such as 'Rock of ages, cleft for me, let me hide myself in thee' and 'He hideth my soul in the cleft of the rock' have popularized this in more recent times.

Yet for the ancients, this theory was literal as well as spiritual, in a way that has not been the case with the Christian interpretation. The external soul was as much to do with the actual, physical world as with the gods. It was descriptive of a process in nature that was regarded as central to the life of the community. For the oak was the best timber in the forest and was therefore the king of the wood, and the mistletoe was known as the All Heal.

For many centuries, mistletoe has only been good for stolen kisses at Christmas time, thought of as a symbol of harmless fun on the one hand, and as a remnant of a Pagan superstition on the other. Likewise, the Druidic cutting of the mistletoe is now associated with the ludicrous obsession of Getafix, the friend of Asterix. Even the details of Pliny's famous description of how it was reverently cut with a golden sickle, on the sixth day of the moon, without ever touching the ground, has long since been dismissed as magical nonsense.

Yet the theory of the external soul continues to haunt modern man, despite his superior scientific detachment from quaint customs and ancient lore. It comes out in the growing perception that there is a fateful link between technological progress, environmental irresponsibility and soullessness. Alienation from nature, pollution and spiritual emptiness are now seen to be connected. In the arts, this has been a recurrent theme for generations. Matthew Arnold's *Thyrsis* and Coleridge's *Ancient Mariner*, for instance, locate the external soul in an elm tree and an albatross respectively:

> *That single elm-tree bright*
> *Against the west – I miss it! is it gone?*
> *We prized it dearly; while it stood we said,*
> *Our friend the Scholar-*
> *Gipsy was not dead;*
> *While the tree lived, he in these fields lived on.*[33]
> *For all averred, I had killed the Bird*
> *That made the Breeze to blow.*[34]

Attitudes to mistletoe have also changed in recent years. Anthroposophical medicine claims that it does, after all, have very remarkable healing properties. It has been used extensively in the treatment of epilepsy, high blood pressure, rheumatoid arthritis and cancer. It is beginning to look now as though the Christian era has been quite wrong to draw such a sharp distinction between the physical and the spiritual. Such a division was not seen by Jesus, who constantly saw in nature, parables of the spiritual life. For him, the kingdom of heaven was like a grain of mustard seed; God's magnanimity, to which we should aspire, was like the rain falling (significantly) on just and unjust alike; the simple trust we should have in his providence was like the lilies of the field and the birds of the air. Even his own death and resurrection he likened to the seed that must die: 'Truly, truly, I say to you, unless a grain of wheat falls into the earth and dies, it remains alone; but if it dies, it bears much fruit'.[35] In the light of this teaching, how could it ever have been thought among the followers of Jesus, that he had separated creation from salvation, and that they therefore had permission to do the same? How could it ever have been denied that he fulfilled the gentile mythologies of the dying and the rising god? How could it ever have been doubted that the real church was the whole of creation, and that all things were part of his being and holiness?

For Jesus, nature demonstrated the character of the creator more clearly than anything else. God had taught him about his own being through nature. Nature, in that sense had been his teacher. If not a Druid, he was certainly like one as, indeed, was Wordsworth:

> *And hark! how blithe the throstle sings!*
> *He, too, is no mean preacher:*
> *Come forth into the light of things,*
> *Let Nature be your Teacher.*[36]

Until the followers of Jesus look directly to his teachings, rather than those that teach the ecclesiastical dualism between matter and spirit, these sentiments will be marginalized as pantheistic moonshine. They will not be seen as practical until the earth is once again held sacred.

Jesus the Pythagorean Druid?

It cannot be proved that the young Jesus came to Britain in the flesh. There is no sound historical evidence for it – only legends of dubious authenticity. But equally, it cannot be proved that he did not come. We have always known there was plenty of time for him to do so, during the silent years, but no serious motives for his coming have ever been given. In this essay I have presented two motives which are serious and new. Firstly, that he wanted to return to the source of the Pythagorean tradition, which there is good reason to believe was megalithic Britain. Secondly, that he wanted to learn about the Druid's wisdom, which, according to Ross and Robins, included the theory of voluntary human sacrifice. Both of these propositions are based on recent archaeological discoveries and have not been put forward before. I believe they are therefore worthy of serious consideration.

I am proposing a new model for Jesus Christ. One which would honour the Megalithic-Celtic preparation for the gospel, and put it on a par with the Jewish Old Testament. One which would respect the Pythagorean tradition and make it central to our understanding of the Bible, especially the New Testament. One which would find a legitimate parallel to Jesus' sacrifice in Druidic practice and, by extension, in the mythology of the dying and rising god, especially of Odin and Balder.

The Celtic-Druidic connection would give us a green, alternative Jesus and the Pythagorean connection would give us a cosmic Christ. Both these emphases already exist in the Bible, but have been so marginalized by historic christianity that only by adopting a new model could they possibly be made central. It is important that they are made central because it is clear that traditional understandings of who Jesus was have largely failed to address the environmental issues of our day or the need for an holistic system of knowledge, which Pythagoreanism could offer. If we were to adopt such a green, alternative, Pythagorean Jesus, we would find him highly relevant to the future welfare of our planet.

NOTES

1. In more recent times, this tradition has been fostered by a frequently cited quotation that is almost certainly not authentic and can be traced no further than the work of Eleanor Merry (*The Flaming Door*, 1936). In it the Welsh bard Taliesin is reputed to have claimed in the sixth century: 'Christ, the Word from the beginning, was from the beginning our Teacher, and we never lost his teaching. Christianity was in Asia a new thing; but there never was a time when the Druids of Britain held not its doctrines.'

2. Ashe, Geoffrey. *Camelot and the Vision of Albion*, Panther, 1975, Chapters 9 and 10.

3. Blake, William. 'To the Jews'. From *Jerusalem*.

4. Lewis, Lionel Smithett. *St Joseph of Arimathea at Glastonbury*, James Clarke, 1988.

5. Ashe, Geoffrey. *Avalonian Quest*, Fontana, 1982, pp. 96, 97, 252.

6. Treharne, R. F. *The Glastonbury Legends*, Cresset, 1967, p. 128.

7. Ashe, Geoffrey. *King Arthur's Avalon*, Fontana, 1957, p. 45.

8. Thom, A. *Megalithic Sites in Britain*, 1967; *Megalithic Lunar Observatories*, 1971; with A. S. Thom, *Megalithic Remains in Britain and Britanny*, 1978, Clarendon.

9. Cited by Nora Chadwick. *The Druids*, University of Wales, 1966.

10. Wood, John Edwin. *Sun, Moon and Standing Stones*, O.U.P., 1978, p. 30.

11. MacKie, Euan W. *Science and Society in Prehistoric Britain*, Paul Elek, 1977, p. 229.

12. *Diodorus Siculus* II.47. Trans. C. H. Oldfather, Heinemann, 1967, p. 37–41.

13. Strachan, Gordon. *Christ and the Cosmos*, Labarum, 1986, Chapters 2 and 6.

14. Blake, William, op. cit.

15. Ross, Anne and Robins, Don. *The Life and Death of a Druid Prince*, Rider, 1989, p. 52.

16. Ross and Robins, op. cit.
17. Ibid. p. 125–126. (This theory has been weakened by recent archaeo-logical discoveries, near Dublin, of a Roman presence in Ireland.)
18. Cited by Nora Chadwick, op. cit.
19. Caesar, Julius. *The Battle for Gaul*, Book 6:16, trans. A. and P. Wiseman, Chatto and Windus, 1980, p. 123.
20. Anne Ross in an unpublished letter to the author.
21. John 11:50–52.
22. Tolstoy, Nicolai. *The Quest for Merlin*, Hamish Hamilton, 1985.
23. Tolstoy, Nicolai. op. cit., p. 181.
24. Ross and Robins, op. cit., p. 99.
25. Matthew, 16:21, 22.
26. Hassnain, Fida. *A Search for the Historical Jesus*, Gateway, 1994.
27. Lewis, Rev H. A. *Christ in Cornwall, Legends of St Just-in-Roseland and other parts*, Lake, Falmouth, 1939.
28. Langdon, A. G. *Old Cornish Crosses*, Joseph Pollard, Truro, 1896.
29. Fraser, Sir James George. *The Golden Bough*, Macmillan, 1922, Part 7, chapter 9.
30. Ross and Robins, op. cit., p. 47.
31. Fraser, Sir James, op. cit., Part 7, chapter 8.
32. Colossians, 3:3.
33. Arnold, Matthew. *Thyrsis*, lines 26–30.
34. Coleridge, S. T. *The Ancient Mariner*, lines 91–92.
35. John, 12:24.
36. Wordsworth, William. *The Tables Turned*, lines 13–16.

Gordon Strachan studied history at Oxford and theology at Edinburgh before being ordained in the Church of Scotland. After some years of parish work in Glasgow, he completed a doctorate at Edinburgh on *The Pentecostal Theology of Edward Irving*, published in 1973. From 1974 to 1980 he ran the Netherbow Arts Centre in Edinburgh, after which he and his wife Elspeth took a five year sabbatical to write *Freeing the Feminine* (1985) and *Christ and the Cosmos* (1986). They then worked in Tiberias, Israel for two years, returning to Scotland in 1989 with their young son Christopher. Since then, Gordon has been lecturing at Edinburgh University in the Centre for Continuing Education and the Department of Architecture where he is an Honorary Fellow. He is at present completing a manuscript on Jesus and the Druids.

Dr Christina Oakley

DRUIDS AND WITCHES: HISTORY, ARCHETYPE AND IDENTITY

Introduction

Druidry and Wicca are two of the most articulated traditions within the esoteric nature-spirituality movement today. In some ways they can seem quite similar. Both reverence nature, both acknowledge the divinity within the human soul, both worship in the open landscape in the ancient ritual form of the quartered circle. Yet all who have some familiarity with them, and many who know of them only through the vivid images of popular culture, sense that there are profound differences between these two spiritual paths.

As I write, I remember that my first contact with the Pagan current in Britain was through Druids. One sunny September day many years ago, whilst I was travelling alone on the isle of Arran, I went to the stone circles of Machrie Moor as a small pilgrimage to the sacred site. It was a remote place, and I was surprised to meet another person there. I got talking with the young man and it transpired he was a Druid. We spoke of the spiritual journey and he told me about the Druidic way. I could almost physically see the pure, green energy of wisdom permeate his aura, a quality about him that almost smelled of dawn mist and was as cool as the granite of the megaliths of a stone circle. We became friends, and through my acquaintance with him I attended open Druidic rites and meditations over the next two years. I found that same cool quality even more strongly present in the auras of the older members of his Order, some of whom had been involved in the Druidic spiritual disciplines for at least twenty years.

During this period I moved to London, and, through a series of strange coincidences, landed in the midst of a network of people who followed the old path of initiatory Witchcraft, more commonly called

Wicca. While uninitiated I was unable to attend their inner rites, but I was invited to join in some of their exoteric meetings. The priests and priestesses of Wicca had auras less cool and green than that of my Druid friend; rather, they had a presence about them which I sensed as ruddy-gold in hue, and the atmosphere around them seemed ineffably tinged with smoky sandalwood incense, musk and warm candlelight. Amongst the men I sensed the presence of the dancing God Pan, and in the women I could almost see the rodstraight integrity of a sword blade and the clear crescent moon shining on the brow of the midnight sky.

In the years since I met the young Druid, I have learnt a great deal about the respective cosmologies, identities and ritual forms of Druids and Witches. And yet, my sense of a profound difference between Druidry and Wicca remained until very recently an intuitive matter. I had not thought to challenge or explore with intellectual or academic tools.

However, as I am an historian, such an enquiry was eventually bound to press itself upon me. In 1993, Philip Carr-Gomm's *The Druid Way* (Element Books) raised questions of comparison between the Druidic and Wiccan paths, their histories and identities. This work proposed a rare if not new thesis – that Witches and Druids might have an underlying commonality which might be accessed by getting hold of a shared history, or at least a single history wherein both fit.

The link between history and identity is fundamental. Human beings the world over form their sense of identity through building and retelling instructive stories of the past. Teaching English school-children about the British Empire is a way of giving them an identity of greatness, for example. Two different groups, even though they may live in the same land and during the same centuries, can have profoundly different histories. Why? Because they have profoundly different identities. Events which are considered important are kept in the forefront of the retellings, so that the next generation will inculcate the qualities which were used by the group in the 'important' events. Thus the identity of the group is maintained, strengthened and passed on. If we are to understand the sense of identity held by Witches and Druids, we must explore their history; but the reverse is also true – to understand their history, we must also study their sense of identity.

Witches and Druids both inhabited Britain from before Christianity and their histories span the prehistoric age up to the present day. Yet those histories seem so different that they are

virtually mutually exclusive. In the course of this article, I will
explore the reasons why, and will touch upon the parts of their historical myths which are used in the formation of their respective identities today. In doing so, I hope to show why I believe these two
traditions are almost certain never to develop a common historical
mythos.

Meeting the Druids

The written sources of the antique and dark ages say that the Druids
were the priesthood of the Pagan Celts, and that they were the
keepers of the wisdom and knowledge. They knew history, science,
and poetry. They were judges, lawgivers, and advisors to kings. They
were magicians and 'shamans'. It was said that they knew the inner
meanings of the landscape, could read the stars, and could commune
with the spirit of the land. Druids of the modern era view themselves
as scions of this great ancestry. Different groups draw on different
elements within the broad panoply of images, for a wide variety of
people have identified themselves as Druids over the past 250 years.
But whether Pagan or Christian, the spiritual Druids of today see
themselves as being part of the heritage of a legitimate social order.
This is true of Druids religious and non-religious, Christian and
Pagan.

The first modern Druids to apply the term to themselves were
eighteenth century Christian gentlemen interested in theology and
philosophy. For these men, the Druids were Christianity's spiritual
forerunners. William Stukeley (1687–1765) claimed that the Druids
were 'of Abraham's religion and their religion was so extremely like
Christianity, that in effect it differ'd from it only in this; they believed
in a Messiah who was to come, as we believe in him that is come.'
(Quoted in S. Piggott, *The Druids*.)

There are Christian Druids to this day. But what is their sense of
identity? When speaking to them, one finds a recurring reference to
nativism, to Britishness, to 'our own' roots. The Christian Druid
seeks to find his centre simultaneously in Christianity and in the
landscape. The Druid is, for the Celtic Christian, the perfect embodiment of the land, rightful authority, nature, and Christ. As to their
view of history, they assert that there was a continuity of tradition
between Pagan Druidism and early Christianity. They conceive that
Druids, having been centrally important in Paganism, became
centrally important in the new 'Celtic' Christianity, which is thought
to have been a complementary syncretism of the deep wisdom of the

old and the new religions; the Druids acknowledging and participating in the society's religious conversion.

Historical sources have long been used to support this thesis. In a
few early medieval Irish tales, Druids foretell the arrival of
Christianity. For example, one Christian Irish story from the Middle
Irish period recounts that the Chief Druid of the Ulster king knew
when the passion of Christ was occurring, and could psychically
sense it. (Myles Dillon, *Cycles of the Kings*, 1946). A second example
often cited is an early medieval Irish prayer (dated to the early
seventh century) wrongly attributed to St Columcille, which refers to
Jesus as the poet's personal Druid:

> *An army marches round a cairn*
> *'tis the son of the storm that betrays them*
> *He is my Druid who denies me not*
> *The son of God it is who will work with me.*

The Annals of Tigernach

Pagan Druids

Given the wide quotation of this sort of material by modern Druids,
one could get the impression that all are 'universalist' Christians of
some variety. Many indeed are. However, with the rise of Pagan spirituality, the 1990s have seen an ever-increasing number of Druids
who identify themselves as Pagan. Paganism, loosely defined, is a
spiritual orientation which celebrates the divine in nature, and which
draws its roots from pre-Christian religions and pantheons. Most
Pagans are either pantheist or panentheist. Whilst Druids who
consider themselves Pagan are a new phenomenon, Druids of a
proto-Pagan leaning existed as long ago as the eighteenth century, an
era that gave rise to a fascination with 'Primitive Man' and the then
radical idea that 'savages' could be worthy of admiration. Some
educated Europeans took up the idea that the original state of native
tribes was perhaps not brutish but idyllic. Polynesians and South
Americans were the first to be regarded this way, and it was but a
short step to the corollary notion that ancient Britain had also been a
nation of 'noble savages'. Indeed, some actively developed this idea.

Twentieth-century Paganism has a wide streak of the 'Noble
Savage' doctrine. Many Pagans feel a cousinly kinship with the
Native Americans and other tribal societies, and a sense of
spiritual descent from the historical tribal cultures of Europe – Celts,
Anglo-Saxons, and the people of the Neolithic Age. The Magical

techniques, implements and ceremonial structures of primitive cultures are often adopted or adapted. Pagans consider them valid, and include them as part of a world-wide fraternity of nature-oriented religions which value supernatural, magical and 'shaman-istic' activities. Pagan-oriented Druids often show such inclinations: Elizabeth Murray of the Council of British Druid Orders has produced a Druidic ogham divination pack, for example, and Philip Shallcrass, head of the British Druid Order, is notable for his ceremo-nial dress which heavily features animal skins.

Like their mystic-Christian fellows, Pagan Druids are also informed by historical sources, which are useful not only in shaping practice but also in forming their sense of Druidic identity. One well-known story from Ireland, from around the eighth century AD purports to tell of one sort of practice amongst Druids:

> *The men of Eriu then assembled at the bull feast: a*
> *bull was killed, and one man ate his fill and drank its*
> *broth and slept, and an incantation of truth was*
> *chanted over him. Whoever this man was in his sleep*
> *became king.*

> '*Da Derga's Hostel*'

A specific divinatory technique attributed to Druids is ogham-divina-tions, or divinations by rowan sticks, or 'hurdles'. Medieval Irish sources attribute this practice to pre-Christian Druids. For example, in one tale Druids gain information for their king through this means:

> *King Aidan said to his Druids, 'find out who is responsible for*
> *these strange doings'. The Druids went on to their rowan*
> *hurdles and new beer was brought to them.*

> *Irish Life of Berach*, C. 23

As these examples show, the magic of the Druids was legitimate; that is, it was legally sanctioned, it served the king, and in turn it helped the social order. In this it is very different from the magic of Witches, who were in the service only of their Gods, their honour code and their consciences.

As I mentioned earlier, Christian Druids look to a time when a synthesized religion, 'Celtic Christianity', reigned in the British Isles, a time coincident with the age of King Arthur. Ironically enough, so too do Pagan-oriented Druids. For one of the best articulated examples of this modern belief, I quote the founder of OBOD, Ross Nichols:

> *Finding out (or knowing already) all about the high standard of life and learning set by the Druidic colleges, he [St Patrick] proceeded to the rather easy conversion of the Druids to what must have seemed to them only a more dramatic version of their own ideas; after all, both cults taught survival of death, both believed in an in-dwelling supreme spirit, only represented for the vulgar by the stones now called 'idols' and Druidry had an essential spirit called Hesus or Esus, linked with the oak tree, which seemed a plain anticipation of Jesus upon the tree of the cross. So the Druidic training colleges were taken over and called monasteries or nunneries, with schools keeping intact most of their internal arrangements.'*

Book of Druidry (1990, AQUARIAN)

This view can be heard again and again: Tim Sebastian, Chief of the Secular Order of Druids, restated it at a Talking Stick lecture in January 1995. Here he said that when early Christian missionaries came to the Celtic lands they found a learned Druidic priesthood who assimilated Paganism into the new faith, forming 'Celtic Christianity'. This flourished in the fifth to seventh centuries, but was eradicated by the Synod of Whitby.

Druids of both Pagan and Christian persuasions assert that, for a few centuries, Christianity could and did incorporate the Druids' love of nature, reverence for the divine, promotion of the creative arts, and respect for history and tradition. Throughout the modern period, Druids have asserted a historical harmony between these persuasions. They believe there was even a time of synthesis between the two, and an underlying shared wisdom between them.

It is fascinating to observe Pagan Druids arguing along these lines, when Paganism has a long established mythos of persecution at the hands of Christians. But the Druidic mythos of a golden age of syncretism has been taken completely on board by Pagan Druids. So they share with Christian Druids this belief, and as a result are able to work in harmony with them in such organisations as the Council of British Druid Orders. But I think there is another reason too: the ancient sources reiterate that the Druid works within society's order, not outside it. Accommodate and integrate seem to be watchwords. Pagan Druids are doing just that.

The ecumenical tone taken by today's Pagan-slanted Druids is reflected very noticeably in their use of historical sources. They shy away from reprinting, citing or quoting from some of the most abundant and interesting extant textual material portraying Druids; this is the material which shows Druids violently resisting Christian missionaries and their message.

Taboo Sources

Because so little exposure is given to it elsewhere, I will take the liberty of digressing to say a bit more about these marginalized sources. Far and away the most abundant are the Saints' Lives of early medieval Ireland, which fill four volumes of *Irish Saints' Lives*, edited by Charles Plummer in the early years of the twentieth century; the two volumes of *Vitae Sanctorum Hiberniae*, (Oxford 1910) comprise a great many of the extant Latin lives; and the two volumes of *Bethada Noem Erenn*, (Oxford 1922) contains the majority of lives written in Middle Irish. In these, Druids are frequent figures, almost always portrayed as the enemy of Christianity, doing their best to thwart the missionary saints. Vehement Druidic opposition to Christianity is recounted in the Lives of St Declan, St Fintan of Dun Blesci, St Lasren (also called Molaisse), St Berach, St Ciaran, St Germanus, as well as in the *Vita Tripartita* of St Patrick. Plummer, who had a great interest in Druids, discusses them at length in his introduction to Volume I of *Vitae Sanctorum*, which forms a significant and valuable resource for any contemporary student of Druidry. One of the most vivid accounts, and certainly the earliest, is in a seventh-century life of St Patrick by an Irishman, Muirchu:

> *There was in those days a great king, a fierce Pagan, and his royal seat was at Tara ... He had around him his wisemen and Druids, fortune-tellers and sorcerers, and the inventors of the secret craft, who, according to the custom of Paganism and idolatry, were able to know everything before it happened. Two of them prophesied that a new way of life was about to arrive from overseas, with an unheard-of and burdensome teaching, which would overthrow kingdoms, kill kings who resisted it, banish all the works of their magic craft, and reign forever ...*

The Patrician Texts in the Book of Armagh, L. BIELER, (1979)

When St Patrick arrived, these two disputed with the saint 'and the Druid Lochru provoked the holy man and dared to revile the catholic faith with arrogant words'.

Patrick looked at him as he spoke and said to the Lord, 'O Lord, who art all powerful, may this man be cast out and perish'. At these words the Druid flew up into the air and fell down again; his brain hit a stone and was smashed to pieces, and he died. After a few more *contretemps*, culminating in a Druid being burnt alive, the king summoned his remaining Druids and announced, 'It is better for me to believe than to die.'

In prayers, too, some traces of Christian-Druidic antipathy are found. One extremely famous eighth-century Irish prayer for protection is attributed to St Patrick. Usually called 'Patrick's Lorica', it involves affirming the orthodox teachings of Christianity and seeking Christ's protection against all evil:

> *against the incantations of false prophets*
> *against the black laws of Paganism*
> *against the false laws of heretics*
> *against the grip of idolatry*
> *against the spells of women and smiths and Druids*
> *against all knowledge forbidden to the human soul.*

Modern Druids, even Pagan ones, leave this material untouched: although it forms part of the relevant historical record, it does not form part of the relevant identity or the perceived history of modern Druidry. Much more popular with today's Druids are the writings of some 300–400 years later, when Christian Irish writers composed many texts expressing a positive, even syncretic, understanding of their Pagan past. The literature of the eleventh and twelfth centuries includes many Pagan tales and sagas, and saints' lives such as that of Brendan the Voyager. Because they show that the Christian Irish of this era felt there was spiritual concordance between the old and new religions, these texts can, I believe, show a vision of harmony between Christian and native Celtic traditions which can inspire Christian-based seekers today.

Wicca – A Different History

Wicca, as practised in Britain today, is a nature-reverencing path in which fertility is celebrated and in which the feminine and masculine elements of divinity are venerated as Goddess and God, the latter being most often portrayed as horned. It is a magical religion, its adherents using magical practices for healing and for spiritual communion. And it is a mystery religion, featuring the elements of initiation, experience of inner mysteries and esoteric secrecy. I should add that after its transmission to America, Wicca evolved many variants from its original British form. In America, it is customary for all the newer forms to fall under the term 'Wicca', while in Britain evolutions such as Dianic, solo, and hedge-Witchcraft do not use the term Wicca. That term is normally used as a shorthand synonym for the older Alexandrian/Gardnerian path. Throughout this article I have followed British terminology, and my descriptions apply not to all Witches equally, but to the Wiccan (Alexandrian/Gardnerian) path.

For their sense of identity, modern Witches, like modern Druids, look to the past. They believe they can see evidence of their precursors' survival in a wide range of sources: paleolithic cave markings, classical texts, the Bible, folk custom, myths, Inquisition records, and medieval and early modern art. Unlike the Druids, who were a largely Celtic phenomenon, people designated as Witches are found across the full span of the Classical and European worlds. Furthermore, Witches see in many places and many sources the key thematic 'signs' of Witchcraft – magicworking, Goddess-veneration, a horned God, a tantric approach to sexuality, and initiatory processes. Wherever these are found across the span of Europe and Britain, from the paleolithic to the nineteenth century, Wiccan initiates have interpreted them as traces of their religion.

Like Druids, Witches are selective in their use of the historical record. Proponents of the idea that Wicca was the universal 'old religion' have ignored important indicators in the source texts which demonstrate that it was not. Almost certainly, some elements of the old religion were carried on quite openly at the level of the peasantry, such as the ritual of maypole dancing and simple spell-casting. But the belief that *the whole* of the religion was kept alive, in secret, by the few who practised their rites secretly and passed them on from generation to generation, has now been disproved by academics. Early in this century, writers such as Margaret Murray and Robert Graves promoted this theory, which unfortunately was then adopted uncritically by most Witches of succeeding decades, even after the deep flaws in these works had been uncovered by historians.

Modern Wiccans are on stronger ground in perceiving Christianity as historically hostile towards the Pagans they identify as their spiritual forebears. In Wiccan folk history, the arrival of Christianity marks the moment when their religion was cast outside the walls of the polis, outside the walls of acceptability. Rather than imagining, as Druids do, that the wisdom of the old Pagan religion was accepted by the new faith, they imagine that it was demonized by the Church. Witches have often cited as proof of Christian antagonism to Pagan religion, a passage from Bede on the conversion of Britain, in which Pope Gregory instructs Abbot Mellitus:

> *that the temples of the idols amongst the people should on no account be destroyed. The idols are to be destroyed, but the temples themselves are to be aspersed with holy water, altars set up in them and relics deposited there. For if these temples are well built, they must be purified from the worship of demons and dedicated to the service of the true God.'*

History of the English Church and People, BEDE

Witches say their forebears were demonized because they practised the Pagan religion even though they were beneficent and spiritual people. And, because the old religion – its magic, its Gods and its Goddesses – was outlawed, its adherents perforce became social dissidents and religious infidels. Witches look for evidence in such early English sources as the decree of Alfred the Great (849–899 AD), which ordered the death penalty for Wiccans, (noting that the term 'Wicca' is actually used in the document). The *Liber Poenitentialis* by Theodore, Archbishop of Canterbury from 668–690 AD, advises penance for those who: 'sacrificed to devils, foretold the future with their aid, ate food which had been offered in sacrifice, or burnt grain after a man was dead for the well-being of the living and of the house.'

According to Wiccan folk history, the monopoly of Christianity does not in itself fully explain the reason why Witchcraft became anathema to the Christians. Simply, theological incompatibility was also an important factor. Wicca is a fertility religion, rather than one with an ethos of sexual sin. Its deity is not Yahweh but a Pagan Goddess and God. In Wicca, divinity is found within nature rather than outside it. Its priesthood is as much female as male. It does not promote Job-like passivity in the face of ill fortune but has instead a strong tradition of practical magic. I shall explore some of these features in turn, considering how modern Witches frame them within a historical precedent.

First, and perhaps most important, is the attitude towards the body. In Wicca, each person is believed to have a natural magnetic energy which is part of their birthright; a masculine or feminine force, depending on whether they are male or female. One author, Wiccan priestess Lois Bourne, put it thus:

> *I believe that there is a great residual force within the human body, it possesses an energy far in excess of its everyday requirements, and this force can be released by concentrating and stilling the mind. I believe this force to be motivated by emotion, by the desire to receive it and by the seeking of a state of grace. It can be used to fulfil some purpose in our own lives, or in the lives of others, for healing or transcendental experience.*

Witch Amongst Us, (SATELLITE, 1979)

A central mystery of Wicca is the interweaving of the male and female energies. At the heart of Wicca is the image of the God and Goddess joined in love as one – an image similar to that found among the Eastern tantrics. It should be said that in Wiccan rites the sex act is celebrated in private, but a joyful and respectful appreciation of the beauty of the male and female is found in all ceremonies. Wicca cultivates a certain holy sensuality, which Doreen Valiente, noted Witch and author, described as:

> *the capacity to respond to the senses, especially the sense of touch; the feel of another person's naked body, the colour of a flower, the music of a waterfall, the flow of air, the earth under one's feet, the slow rhythm of movement, the scent of sandalwood and musk ... All the universe is a sex act; to take part in sex is to partake of the nature of the universe in its deeper sense, beyond time and form.*

Witchcraft for Tomorrow, (HALE, 1978)

The Wiccan mythos asserts that Christianity's mistrust of the body and of natural sensate energy has made the Craft a target for abuse from Christianity throughout the centuries. Historical sources of the Witch persecutions, written from a Christian perspective, usually describe Witches' meetings as being orgiastic in some way. Modern Wicca's folk history however, states that these accounts actually describe meetings of Witches, not orgies – they argue that a Tantric-like, sacred religious rite could only be understood by a Christian as an 'orgy'. One such account describes how in 1022 in Orleans, France, a group of people were accused of holding sex orgies at night in a secret place. Apparently, the members were holding torches and chanting, hoping to raise an evil spirit. The 'devil' here, say many modern Witches, would have been a priest who had the Horned God of Wicca invoked upon him, and who would probably have been wearing a horned head-dress. However, scholars now believe there is no evidence for the survival of a self-proclaimed Pagan priesthood practicing Witchcraft rites, and that documents such as the one cited most likely, in fact, describe activities the participants themselves would not have considered Pagan.

The visual arts are as important to Wicca as ancient texts are to Druidry. Modern Craft books, from the 1920s onward, have been replete with reproductions of old woodcuts, in the same way that Druidic works are packed with quotations from Bardic poetry. Many modern Wiccans are emotionally moved and inspired by these sixteenth and seventeenth century illustrations of Witches; some say their initial pull toward Wicca came from seeing such images as a child or teenager. Walk into a Witch's house and you are likely to see several reproductions of old Witchcraft woodcuts, perhaps in formally framed prints or on photocopies sellotaped to the refrigerator. Wiccans place these images in their environments so that, when contemplated, they help open the channel between everyday consciousness and supra-reality, between the present and the past, between the heirs and their ancestors. The poetic primitiveness of the style captures the imagination; the images populate their interior, archetypal landscape. Thus, though largely unconsciously, Witches use these woodcuts as spiritual icons.

In these old pictures of Witches one sees nakedness, spell-casting, ecstatic dancing, rites, feasting and suchlike. A Witch takes these images as evidence for the survival of a tradition of Wiccan practice, for much of the activity looks somehow similar to modern practice. Looking at the artwork 'through' the distortions of time, the modern Witch sees in the nakedness the still-current custom of 'skyclad' working, sees in the spellcasting the long lineage of healing spells, and sees in the ecstatic dancing the familiar technique of raising power for spiritual transcendence. In short, the Witch sees the continuity of the tradition.

Wicca's attitude to the body, to sexuality and to emanating erotic spiritual power has made it almost impossible for it to be conventionally acceptable. Unlike Druids, Witches believe that when Christianity arrived they did not have the option of integrating with the new religion. Wicca would have had to renounce its central premise if it were to have even tried. But Druidry does not see an incompatibility between itself and Christianity, with regard to the body and sex. In Druidry, sex is more sublimated, more metaphorical, if it is present at all. This can vary from order to order. But overall, as Philip Carr-Gomm has put it, Druids emphasize the product of fertile union rather than the act of union itself. Thus Druids stress the notion of the divine child and other creations such as the Bardic arts of poetry, song, and music and, as discussed earlier, their perception of history reflects this.

The Goddess

Wicca is pantheistic; it reveres the feminine essence which runs through all women and through all of Nature, as well as the force of masculinity. In this sense it is 'gendered' much more strongly than any monotheistic religion. One of its most prominent features is the reverence of the Goddess, the Queen of Heaven, the Lady of the Moon, she who is the beauty of the green earth, the laughing maiden, the passionate mother, the ancient crone. Wicca says she has a thousand faces, and has been known in her many aspects throughout the ages. Western civilization, Witches note wryly, has long taken a dim view of Goddess worship. It cites instances such as that in the Biblical book of Jeremiah, where the prophet cursed the people of Judah for persisting in the worship of the Great Goddess. The women of the city, the officiants of the rites, were boldly unrepentant and replied:

> We will certainly continue to burn incense unto the Queen of Heaven, and pour libations unto her, as we have done and our fathers have done, and our kings and our princes, in the cities of Judah and in the streets of Jerusalem. For then we had plenty of food, and were well, and experienced no evil. But since we have left off burning incense to the Queen of Heaven and pouring libations to her, we have wanted in all things, and have been consumed by the sword and by famine.

Jeremiah 44:17–18

To this day, modern Witches make libations of wine and offerings of sweet-smelling incense to their Goddess, and call her, amongst other names, the Queen of Heaven. Like the people of Judah, they seek her blessings for health, harmony, peace and abundance. And like the people of Judah, they too experience no evil in doing so. Modern Witches assert that Witches have always worshipped the Goddess, and quote sources such as the very early tenth-century Canon Episcopi to support this: 'the Witches attend the sabbat with the Pagan Goddess, Diana and untold numbers of women riding on beasts; they traverse the open spaces in the calm night, obedient to her orders …'

Historical episodes are cited as evidence of the survival of Goddess-worship. For example, in 1133 a monk of St Trond related how people in the Rhineland built a wooden ship on wheels, which represented the ship of the Earth Goddess Nerthus. Having wheeled it to Aix-la-Chapelle:

> *under the twilight of dawn crowds of matrons, having cast away all feminine shame, loosened their hair, leapt about clad in their shifts, two hundred dancing round the ship shamelessly. You might see one hundred thousand people of both sexes celebrating into the middle of the night. When that execrable dance was broken off the people ran hither and thither making a noise as though they were drunk.*

QUOTED IN *Witchcraft from the Inside*, R. BUCKLAND, (LLEWELLYN, 1971)

What of the Goddess' place and history amongst Druids? Most modern Druids give some space to the feminine principle of divinity in their rites, though the form and extent of this varies greatly from order to order. Nonetheless, one may safely generalize by saying that however it is represented, female divinity in Druidry is cooperative. Druidic Goddesses are usually viewed as Goddesses of the land, who work in harmony with the rulers of the society, providing those rulers are just and righteous. The Druidic path brings out the presence of the feminine, but does so in a way unthreatening to the norm; thus the Druids' Goddess figures acknowledge and fit into the dominant structures; I believe this tendency reflects the wider inclination of Druids to seek accord between their doctrines and those of the prevailing social order. This is particularly noticeable amongst the more traditionalist orders. Some Druids of the 1990s, mostly Pagan-oriented ones, have been making an effort to bring the Goddess into a more central position. The traditional Universal Druid Prayer, which begins with the line 'Grant, O God, thy protection ...' is some-times now started with 'Grant, O Goddess' or even 'Grant, O God and Goddess, thy protection ...' In addition, the Goddesses of the Celtic pantheons are being explored and enlivened in research, writing and ritual.

But the female principle in Druidry will probably never have the same bold centrality it has in Wicca, as Druidic cosmology is not gender-based in the same forceful way that one finds in modern Wicca.

God

What then of the God, the male principle of divinity? If one were to find a similarity of essence, or historical perception, between Wicca and Druidry, one might well expect to find it in its formulation of the male divinity.

As has been seen, for eighteenth and nineteenth century Druids, the Druidic concept of God was consonant with that of Christianity, albeit a Deist, mystic, gnostic or esoteric Christianity. The precise formulation, of course, varied from generation to generation, and from order to order. Druidry conceives the male principle of divinity through a central image: that of the king. This may.be seen in the symbols of the oak tree and the sun, and through the historic personage of King Arthur. Many have seen the Druidic sun as the Logos, the One, the original source. When it comes to tree lore, about which most Druids are extremely conversant, the oak is seen as the royal tree, the tree of kings. Another constant theme is the solar imagery; for example, Stonehenge is aligned with the rising Midsummer Sun, as New Grange in Ireland is aligned with the rising Midwinter Sun.

Contrary to popular belief, the God in Wicca is highly conceptual-ized and deeply experienced. This fact has its roots in Wicca's histor-ical mythos. Many people forget that two of the most influential books on Witchcraft focussed not on the Goddess, but on the male God and the male priesthood: Frazer's *Golden Bough* was about the God of nature, and Margaret Murray's books on Witchcraft treat the survival not of Goddess worship, but of a Pagan God cult. The images and texts of many Gods informed the work of Murray and Gardner: Faunus, Sylvanus, the Celtic Cernunnos, John Barleycorn, and other vegetation Gods. In modern Wicca we find applied to him the images of king, tree, oak and holly, and his cycle is mirrored in that of the Sun.

So, is the God of Wicca really a re-working of the God of Druidry? One male Wiccan symbol, the most important one, surely dashes any speculation of this kind: the horns. Modern Witches look at the archaeological remains of Europe, from the Stone Age through the medieval period, and see their God in the myriad male horned figures to be found in the paleolithic cave drawings of Caverne des Trois Frères and Fourneau du Diable, on the Gundestrup Cauldron, on the stone altar found beneath Notre Dame in Paris. And they find traces of him in the British legends of Herne the Hunter, who supposedly rides near Windsor, and in the Staffordshire Abbots Bromley Horn Dance, which is practised to this day.

Pan in the Seventeenth century
(from *The Roots of Witchcraft*, Michael Harrison)

Witches also find him in classical mythology, in the horned God Pan, who is one of Wicca's most vitally inspiring God images. Pan's attributes permeate the Wiccan Horned God, and Witches believe that he is one of their God's expressions. As described in historical sources, he resonates deeply with familiar Wiccan concepts: he is manlike above and animal below, showing that his sexuality is unshorn. But at the same time his higher faculties also flourish, and he plays the panpipes, the music of the spheres, the tune that is the original sound of Beauty and Love. Wicca finds in Pan the perfect harmony between the primal drives and sublime elevated spirituality; it is the best of both forces interweaving freely. Furthermore, Pan is playful and celebratory, he is a dancing God; playfulness and dance are an important part of Wicca. He was worshipped by the people of the countryside and even in Greek religion was something of a nonconformist. It is no surprise then, that he is such an important archetype for the male Wiccan God.

Wiccan mythos says that the horned God was demonized by the new social order, and so, while he is profoundly inspiring, he is not a God of social acceptability as long as we live in a world where self-restraint, self-control and self-repression define what is 'acceptable'. Christianity demonized all the versions of the horned God, including Pan, for wild nature anywhere is the enemy of orthodox Christianity. Within, it is ecstasis and sexuality, without it is the untamed woods and hills. And as for his survival, medieval ecclesiastical sources can be quoted. For example, Witch author Raymond Buckland recounts that in 1282 a village priest at Inverkeithing was reprimanded for leading his parishoners in a dance around a phallic symbol.

Some Druids who mix socially in the Pagan community have looked at Wicca and, seeing the strong lunar imagery and the prominence of the Goddess, imagined that Wicca might be a feminine 'yin' completing the more masculine 'yang' quality of Druidry. But those Druids who see only the feminine when looking at the Craft are making a profound oversight, as profound an oversight as those who think that Wicca's God and Druidry's God are the same, or even similar.

Druids in Society Today

In general, Druidry seems to promote acknowledgement of rightful authority, social respect, and assistance in the proper ruling of the land. Though unconsulted by modern governments, today's Druids wear the psychic mantle of that noble and esteemed past. However

Druidry envisions its contribution to society today, it is now framed as a contribution which takes place outside the formal halls of power.

Nevertheless, that contribution does go on, and the particulars of its focus vary from order to order. The ancient Druidic eminence in the areas of research into astronomy, astrology and magic is the focus of the work of the Stargrove Druid Order. The cause of governmental justice is pursued by, among others, the British Druid Order. Action to protect the environment is a central concern of the Order of Bards Ovates & Druids. *Aisling,* the journal of the Druid Clan of Dana, promotes the Bardic arts, from ancient Celtic poetry right through to Pagan rock & roll. And most modern Druids value a role, taken by their ancient predecessors: that of the well-spoken, courtly ambassador, mediating between differing theologies and spiritual groups.

It is interesting to note that Druids – especially Pagan-oriented ones – may be found speaking out against government policies they consider unjust, as was the case in 1994, when a group marched in a rally against the Criminal Justice Bill. How does this sort of activity fit in with the underlying philosophy of Druidry? There are several parts of Druidic history to which a Druid subconsciously hearkens when taking an anti-establishment position. Defence of the realm is one such notion. Druids today remember that they have in the past defended the realm against hostile forces. In the first century AD Druids helped defend Britain against the invading Romans and Boudicca, queen of the Iceni Britons, defended her people against the Roman invaders using Druidic skill. Later on, medieval stories tell of the Druidic advisor Merlin, who served King Arthur in the struggle against the invading Saxons in the fifth and sixth centuries. Today's Druids can see themselves as defending their sacred realm against hostile invading forces, even if those forces come from within the realm.

Equally important is the notion of the Druid as the arbiter of true sovereignty. Historically, it was Druids who tutored kings and sat as judges in pre-Christian Celtic society. If a king was dishonourable, a Druid could depose him. The loyalty of the Druid is to the true sovereign, the true king – and the principles thereof. To this day, the Druid takes a stand for the principles of wisdom and justice.

King Arthur remains an important symbol of this, for according to modern lore he was the archetypal rightful king, the very embodiment of just rulership. He is 'the once and future king', who can and will be revived; his Druid, Merlin, with him. The mythology of Arthurian sovereignty is shared amongst most, if not all, modern Druids. I have been to several Druidic ceremonies in and around the

South of England, which have aimed to revive the spirit of King Arthur and/or Merlin; a particularly beautiful one was a winter rite performed by the Stargrove Druid Order at Conway Hall, under the auspices of the Pagan Federation. And at a lecture by the head of the Secular Order of Druids, when the question was posed, 'What royal authority do you acknowledge?', a chorus of Druids in the audience simultaneously and lightheartedly began chanting 'Arthur, Arthur!' A Druid sitting beside me chimed in with 'The One True King!'

Wicca In Society Today

Modern Witches are suspect of rulers. Their historical mythos has taught them to be cautious. Believing that their forebears were themselves outlawed for daring to worship according to their conscience, today's Witches carry a subliminal memory of what it can be like when 'the system' turns against one.

And yet their mythos, say the Witches, dared to be naked, dared to be sexual, dared to be out of doors at night, dared to perform magic, and dared to fly. The flying is deeply significant, for it is a metaphor for freedom of the spirit, for soaring above the delimiting social structures, even if one had to do so at night, and in secret. So too is the nudity. As the Goddess says in a possibly nineteenth-century Italian version of the Charge, a standard part of Wiccan liturgy:

> And ye shall be freed from all slavery, and so ye shall
> be free in everything; and as a sign that ye are really
> free, ye shall be naked in your rites, both men and
> women also ...

> Gospel of the Witches, C. LELAND

Witches still worship naked, or 'sky clad' as they call it. Their very religious 'dress' is a testament to a value they hold sacred, that of the sacrality of the body and the spirit, its personal integrity and its freedom of conscience. Over the past thirty years, a number of Witches have been very outspoken about the values and spiritual aspirations of Wicca, even though what it holds sacred can sometimes be difficult and challenging for society to accept. When Wicca interacts with the modern social order, it speaks as an alternative voice, as a voice of the 'Other', who can easily be scapegoated. After all, the naked human body is still shocking. Sex is still linked more with sin than holiness. Women are often treated as sex objects.

Female deity is still heresy. The notion of female religious leaders still provokes bemusement.

I spoke with a male Witch who works full time as an environmental activist, asking him about how he understood his work in relation to Wicca. He replied that in many respects our whole society has become 'a terminal grey culture in which everything is run along straight lines. It's male energy gone astray, male energy pulled away from the female energy. I feel that as Witches we're trying to bend those straight lines, curve them.' I remind him that the term 'Wicca' originated from an Anglo-Saxon root meaning 'to bend'. 'Yes, yes – of course, that's it exactly!' he replies. On what authority does he draw for his activities? 'A higher authority than that of this government – the Great Goddess, the Earth Mother'. (I also ask him about true kingship, and the archetype of the sacred sovereign. 'Pardon?' he asks bemused. I try again. 'King Arthur?', I suggest hopefully. He gives me a blank look.)

Our Histories, Past and Present

This article was originally conceived as a contribution to the comparative histories of Wicca and Druidry. The very idea of such a comparison is a relatively new concept, and a rather unusual one, for the histories of Witchcraft make little mention of Druidism, nor do the histories of Druidry or Druidism give much time or space to coexistence with Witchcraft. As this article has demonstrated, their dichotomous spiritual identities make any emergence of a synthesized folk history of Druidry and Wicca an unlikely, even fanciful, suggestion.

Yet two Druids of the modern age have expressed an interest in the project of a comparative history between the two paths. The first was Ross Nichols, an acquaintance of famous Witch Gerald Gardner. Nichols claimed that Druidry was the surviving universal 'old religion' of Britain and Europe, the same thing modern Witches had long been claiming about Wicca. (*The Book of Druidry*, especially pp. 76–95, Aquarian, 1990.) Philip Carr-Gomm, Nichols' spiritual heir, has recently carried on this line of enquiry, but in a more overtly comparative way. In *The Druid Way*, Element, 1993, he quotes a theory that in ancient times, and through the Dark and Middle Ages, those who followed the universal pre-Christian religion used no special name either for themselves or for their religion. Carr-Gomm wonders if perhaps only recently we have distinguished ourselves as either Witches or Druids … if only recently our identities have become distinct.

In spite of the vastly different histories told by their modern adherents, did the two traditions, in fact, meet in the past? Were they once the same thing? Academic history sheds critically important light on these questions. Thanks to the historical, ethnographic, anthropological and archeological research of the past thirty years, we now have answers based on evidence rather than speculation. It is now indisputable that Europe has never had a single, unified, pre-Christian religion. The history of pre-Christian religion is one of immense diversity; even within a relatively small geographical area there were vast differences in belief and practice.

It is also becoming clearer that Pagan survival in Europe and Britain after Christianity's arrival was much less articulate than was believed by Murray and Gardner – and, indeed, by Nichols. Those special people who believed in their local spirits, who cultivated psychic or magic powers, who told and retold their ancient myths, who cast spells and performed divinations, who dressed in animal skins – almost all considered themselves Christian once Christianity had arrived and established itself, although in rural areas this may have amounted to no more than a nominal Christianity. In simple terms, Pagan survival through the Middle Ages was largely subconscious, and most, if not all, of its adherents called themselves Christian.

Thus it is inappropriate for modern Pagans to speak of a single or a surviving 'old religion'. Threads of old Witchcraft practice and of Druidic traditions did unmistakably survive, but we must be aware that these are strands rather than whole cloth.

Today's Druids and Witches have rewoven ancient strands, picking up ones which have been lost in the passage of time, and consciously enlivening those which have survived. But, as this article has tried to show, they have not all chosen the same threads to re-weave into their respective cloths. Some are common to both, yes, but many of the important ones are different. And what of the pattern? The two modern cloths show two very different pictures, equally beautiful in their own way, but remarkable for their profound difference.

As academic research into Pagan religions and Witchcraft reveals more about ancient practices and survivals, (or lack thereof), the origin myths of both Druids and Witches will have to change to take these developments on board. Academics almost universally herald this as 'a good thing', as they view the origin myths of esoteric groups as examples of bad history. But, in learning history from academics, both Witches and Druids must be careful lest we lose a most precious thing, something which our origin myths have preserved and transmitted: the awareness that we are heirs to our own tradition whose life has traced its way through the centuries. In Wicca this is often called 'the current of the Craft', which in the present day is passed through certain magical acts in initiations, as well as through training. Amongst Druids I have heard it called 'the golden thread' of Druidry. It is my sincere hope that in the centuries to come, Witches will still feel the Wiccan current in medieval woodcuts, and that Druids will forever feel the golden thread of their tradition as they greet the sunrise at Stonehenge.

Suggested Reading

There are many original Irish texts referring to Druids, only a few of which I can mention here. For Patrick's tale of conflict with a Druid, read Muirchu's *Life of Patrick,* which is translated into English in two books: L. Bieler, *The Patrician Texts in the Book of Armagh* (Dublin Institute for Advanced Studies, Dublin 1979) and A. Hood, *St.Patrick: His Writings and Muirchu's Life* (Phillimore, Chichester 1978). I recommend also the collections of eleventh and twelfth-century Irish Saints' Lives, which were written by Christian authors during the phase of revived interest in the Pagan, Druidic past. The Lives in Latin are printed, untranslated, in C. Plummer, ed., *Vitae Sanctorum Hiberniae,* 2 vols. (Oxford 1910). The introduction to volume one discusses all the Druidic references in all the Saints' Lives, both the Irish and the Latin. The Lives written in Irish are (translated into English) in C. Plummer, *Betha Noem Erenn* (Oxford 1922). Tales and sagas, also written in a Christianized Ireland but referring to the Pagan past, are easily available in J. Gantz, *Early Irish Myths and Sagas* (Penguin Classics, 1981).

On the Witchcraft side, there are fewer texts. For a good collection of the old woodcuts, I recommend Ken Radford's *Fire Burn: Tales of Witchery* (Satellite, London 1989). For a contemporary understanding of early Witchcraft, see Dr Ronald Hutton's book *The Pagan Religions of the Ancient British Isles* (Blackwell, Oxford 1991); his forthcoming book on Witchcraft will cover the issue of survival in greater depth. Those interested in learning more about modern-day initiatory Wicca (what Americans call 'British Traditional Wicca') should attempt to correspond or meet with people initiated into it, for it is largely an oral tradition and very little about it can be learned via books. Nevertheless, those who want to read might try Doreen Valiente's *ABC of Witchcraft* (Hale, London 1973; reprinted in paperback 1994), Lois Bourne's *Witch Amongst Us* (Hale, Isleworth 1979; reprinted in paperback 1995) and Vivianne Crowley's *Wicca: The Old Religion in the New Age* (Thorsons, London 1996, paperback).

Contact addresses for initiatory Wicca:

1. *The Pagan Federation*, BM 7097, London WC1N 3XX. A pan-Pagan umbrella network which provides information. In addition to other Pagan contacts (including Druid ones) it has links with Gardnerian/Alexandrian Wiccan groups across Britain and Europe. Their magazine, *Pagan Dawn*, also often runs Wiccan-related articles: it costs £8 a year in UK (or send $25 in cash to receive it airmail in the US).

2. *The Wicca Study Group*, BM Deosil, London WC1N 3XX. Has contacts with Alexandrian/Gardnerian groups across Britain and Europe, and offers an introductory correspondence course.

3. American seekers may write for referrals and information to the *New Wiccan Church*, which is a network of Alexandrian, Gardnerian and other forms of 'British Traditional' Craft. PO Box 162046, Sacramento, CA 95816.

4. Readers may also write to me, and I shall be glad to provide what information and referral I am able. Christina Oakley, c/o Pagan Dawn Editorial Address, BM 5896, London WC1N 3XX.

Christina Oakley is a medieval historian with a specialism in the Celtic and early Middle Ages. The daughter of a United Nations geologist and a herbalist healer, she spent her childhood in rural West Africa, throughout which time she attended the rites and ceremonies of the local tribal community. It was from this era of her life that she gained her respect for initiatory mystery traditions and for those who walk between this world and the world of the unseen. Her early teens were spent in Burma, and it was at a remote pagoda in Mandalay she first saw a Buddhist monk levitate during meditation. Convinced that her own British heritage somewhere contained the remnants of its own magico-spiritual tradition, she eventually located a coven of witches in the Southeast of England who adopted her. She now heads a coven with her partner, and edits *Pagan Dawn* magazine.

Mara Freeman

THE CONNECTING THREAD:
Deep Ecology And The Celtic Vision

When holy were the haunted forest boughs,
Holy the air, the water and the fire.[1]

To contemplate the flowing curves and spirals of Celtic art, the pouring out of forms in vigorous, organic swirls, is to get a glimpse into the way the early Celts perceived the web of life. The astonishing interweaving patterns, whether on vellum page or stone cross, reflect a world filled with the endless delight of movement, a perfect, precarious balance between the orderly and the unbounded.

Interlacing designs speak to us of dense thickets in the deep forests that covered the length and breadth of Britain and Ireland, before later ages turned them into ships, or charcoal for smelting steel. Here and there an animal or bird appears out of the tangle of knotwork, as if from the shadows of trees. Human forms intertwine with animal, both joined by twisting and turning filaments that connect the whole tapestry. Sometimes a form that starts out as human may end up as beast or bird.

This rhythmical interpenetration of forms can be seen as a reflection of the interconnectedness between human beings and the natural world found in the Celtic wisdom tradition, which is the subject of this exploration. But before examining this relationship more deeply, it is important to note here that we have no actual body of lore that might be said to constitute a systematized wisdom tradition within Celtic culture. The Celts preserved their teachings orally, and what words we have were recorded by Christian scribes, writing long after the demise of the native Druidic orders. To use the forest as a metaphor, it might be said that as we stumble through the dense undergrowth of the past we too can only catch the glint of what appears to be an ancient earth-based spiritual path, as we emerge into occasional sunlit clearings. Our guides are poetry, legend and folk-lore.

What is clear from early literature is that the Celts believed themselves to live in an animate, ensouled universe. The pre-Christian Celtic world was peopled by a pantheon of gods and goddesses who inhabited, or personified, different localities. Ireland itself was seen as a great goddess, one of whose names, Eriu, gives us the country we know as Eire. Her body was the land itself: in County Kerry, two hills like great breasts are named the Paps of Anu, another of her names. To become an Irish king involved a ritual marriage with the land in the form of a goddess known as Sovereignty. Cavernous earth chambers built by earlier races, like New Grange in the Boyne River valley, were regarded as entrances to her womb, where the spirits of the ancestors dwelt. Lakes, wells and springs were sacred to goddesses, their waters bestowing healing and nourishment; in Wales, a creamy curd-like substance that issued from certain springs was seen as milk from her breast. The sea was the province of Manannan mac Lir, King of the Land-Under-Wave.

Trees, too, were ensouled, each having distinct qualities and attributes: the bright berries of the rowan afforded protection from evil, the nuts of the hazel bestowed wisdom.The sacred tree stood at the centre of each tribe's village, while the Druids worshipped in temples of oak groves.

Animals were regarded as powerful spiritual beings that could connect humans with the unseen realms, or Celtic Otherworld. The white hart beckoned to the hunter whose prey was not flesh, the boar drew him on into the darkness. Seers would know the future from watching the movements of birds and translating their cries. The Tuatha De Danaan, the supernatural race that lived in the hollow hills, often appeared to mortals in bird or animal form. (Time stops. White wings and a woman's smile. CuChulainn must follow.)

Under the influence of Christianity the sacred places still remained, only the names were changed. The living, speaking universe was still glorified as the creation of God. Mary or St. Brigid now guarded the holy wells, and even Jesus himself was spread against the heavens:

Son of the Dawn
Son of the clouds
Son of the stars
Son of the elements ... [2]

Gaelic prayers and hymns collected in Scotland as late as the nineteenth century invoke the power of the animals, as in the blessing:

> *Wisdom of serpent be thine,*
> *Wisdom of raven be thine*
> *Wisdom of valiant eagle …*[3]

So, to Pagan and Celtic Christian alike, the natural world was viewed
as a bridge that spanned and connected the worlds of Earth and
Spirit. The tree at the centre of the tribe was the earthly manifestation of the Otherworld tree that stood at the centre of the universe.
The source of the local sacred well was the Otherworldly Well of
Wisdom. The Celtic monk believed that the bird which sang contin-
uously to him as he built his church was an angel sent from God. To
relate to the natural world, then, was to be connected spiritually to
the deepest and most numinous powers of the universe.

When we take a closer look at this connection, three different
kinds of relationships emerge between those in human form and the
non-human – or, as David Abram, the philosopher and ecologist,
calls it, more-than-human – world. These might be described as first,
the familiar position where a human being relates to Nature as
perceiver to perceived, both discrete entities, the identity of each set
firmly within its own boundaries. Because within this relationship
Nature is seen as of intrinsic and equal value with the human, I am
calling this the *I-Thou* position. The second, less common relationship, I call here the relationship of *communion,* where the perceiver
begins to assume the identity of the perceived, and boundaries begin
to blur. In the third relationship, a kind of symbiosis takes place in
which human and other-than-human forms are interchangeable.
This occurs through a process of metamorphosis, and I call it the
transformative relationship.

The I-Thou position, where Nature is beheld as the object of
human experience, is to us the most familiar kind of relationship. It
is the subject of a number of poems written by people who lived a
simple ascetic existence in the wilderness. Some of these were
Pagan, visionaries and shamans known as *geilt* – the Wild Ones;
others were early Christian hermits and anchorites, possibly
members of the mysterious order of the Early Celtic Church known
as the Culdees, Companions of God, who may have been Druids
embracing the new religion while preserving the older teachings
within it.

These forest-dwellers lived in huts made of wattles, or even caves or trees; the walls that circumscribe our modern lives, cutting us off from intimacy with Nature, were fragile or non-existent. To live like this is to see oneself in perspective; small, in a huge and teeming world. In one poem, a seventh century hermit describes his dwelling:

> *I have a shieling in the wood,*
> *None knows it save my God:*
> *An ash-tree on the hither side, a hazel-bush beyond,*
> *A huge oak-tree encompasses it.*
>
> *Two heath-clad doorposts for support,*
> *And a lintel of honeysuckle:*
> *The forest around its narrowness sheds*
> *Its mast upon fat swine.*[4]

The clarity and detail of his descriptions are typical of Celtic Nature poetry, springing as it does from lived experience. Unlike the later medieval poetry of European courts, where Nature has become a pale allegory of abstract qualities, these verses carry the fresh immediacy of everyday life. The sheer variety of natural phenomena in each poem provides for us, living as we do at a time when we have decimated so many species, a window onto a world that teems with the bio-diversity of life:

> *Glen of the sleek brown round-faced otters that are pleasant and active in fishing; many are the white-winged stately swans, and salmon breeding along the rocky brink.*[5]

Celtic Nature poets evoke an existence where all the senses are involved. We who have banished ourselves from the rich banquet of the natural world, preferring the empty calories of 'virtual' realities and consumer items, can sense how it must have felt to our ancestors to be satisfied by the natural abundance of things:

> *Ale with herbs, a dish of strawberries*
> *Of good taste and colour,*
> *Haws, berries of the juniper,*
> *Sloes, nuts ...*
>
> *When brilliant summer-time spreads its coloured mantle,*
> *Sweet-tasting fragrance!*
> *Pignuts, wild marjoram, green leeks,*
> *Verdant pureness.*

> *Swarms of bees and chafers, the little musicians of the world,*
> *A gentle chorus:*
> *Wild geese and ducks, shortly before summer's end,*
> *The music of the dark torrent*[6]

The vividness of the imagery recalls Blake's famous phrase: 'If the doors of perception were cleansed, everything would appear to man as it is – infinite'. And indeed, in the Pagan Celtic wisdom tradition, poetry was regarded as a central skill of the seer and mystic. According to the old tales, the poet-seer received divine illumination by eating a sacred substance from the Earth's body, most often the Salmon of Wisdom that came from the well at the heart of the Otherworld. When Finn mac Cumaill, a hero who shares many characteristics of the *geilt*, eats of the Salmon by the banks of the River Boyne and becomes enlightened, the first words he utters are a paeon of praise to the month of May, as if the taking-in of the magical fish has opened his eyes to the wonder of the world:

> *May-time, fair season, perfect is its aspect then; blackbirds sing a full song ...*[7]

In every poem, the poet's relationship with the natural world is specific and intimate. In the twentieth century we tend to talk about trees, not to them, or we may expand our consciousness so far as to 'hug a tree'. But in the following poem, the poet addresses individual animals, plants and trees, revealing an authentic *I-Thou* relationship with each:

> *Little antlered one, little belling one, melodious little bleater,*
> *sweet I think the lowing that you make in the glen ...*
> *Blackthorn, little thorny one, black little sloe-bush; watercress, little*
> *green-topped one, on the brink of the blackbird's well ...*
> *Apple-tree, little apple-tree, violently everyone shakes you; rowan,*
> *little berried one, lovely is your bloom ...*[8]

The personal life of the poet is hardly mentioned in these poems. Only occasionally do we get a touching glimpse of a few domestic details, and then only in the poems about winter when the poet is confined inside: '*Cosy is our pot on its hook,*' begins one verse of a poem known as 'Winter Cold', but this line is there only to serve as a contrast with the plight of wild animals:

The wolves of Cuan Wood get
Neither rest nor sleep in their lair,
The little wren cannot find
Shelter in her nest on the slope of Lon.[9]

The scarcity of details of individual life highlight its relative insignifi-
cance compared to the huge drama being enacted outside. The poet
makes himself transparent so that he can relate to Nature from a
deeper level. The German poet Novalis called this place 'the seat of
the soul', which he located as 'where the inner world and the outer
world meet, and where they overlap, it is in every point of the
overlap.' And, in becoming transparent, these long-dead poets have
enabled us to participate in that relationship just a little, to taste air
fresh from the morning of the world.

Turning from the poems to a look at some of the lives of the
dwellers in the wild, we become aware particularly of their relationship with the living creatures of the forest. More than one Celtic
scholar has pointed out the etymological correspondence of *geilt*
with a word meaning 'to graze', referring to their vegetarian diet.
Although hunting was an obvious option in this plenteous land, many
geilt lived on a diet of roots, cresses, fruit and nuts. Could this have
been motivated by the desire to live in closer communion with the
wild animals? There are indeed many descriptions, both of Pagan
heroes and Christian anchorites, that illustrate such fellowship. In
the story known as 'Finn and the Man in the Tree', Finn mac Cumaill
comes upon one of his band that he has been seeking. He finds him
sitting in a tree surrounded by creatures:

> ... *a blackbird on his right shoulder and in his left hand a white*
> *vessel of bronze, filled with water in which was a skittish trout and*
> *a stag at the foot of a tree. And this was the practice of the man,*
> *cracking nuts; and he would give half the kernel of a nut to the*
> *blackbird that was on his right shoulder while he would himself*
> *eat the other half; and he would take an apple out of the bronze*
> *vessel that was in his left hand, divide it in two, throw one half to*
> *the stag that was at the foot of the tree and then eat the other half*
> *himself. And on it he would drink a sip of the bronze vessel that*
> *was in his hand so that he and the trout and the stag and the*
> *blackbird drank together.*[10]

Equal concern for the well-being of a wild creature was shown by the
Irish anchorite, Kevin of Glendalough, who lived in solitude by a
lake, existing only on nettles and sorrel. One Lent, as he lay fasting

on the grey flagstone that was his bed, a blackbird hopped upon his outstretched palm and built her nest there. The saint kept his hand in that position while she built her nest in it, laid her eggs, and then hatched her brood.

However, in many stories of the Christian hermits, a subtle difference enters the kind of relationship they have with the animals. Whereas the above examples illustrate human beings serving animals, legends of the Celtic saints more often portray animals as subordinates. In the story of St. Ciaran of Clonmacnoise, a fox carried the psalter while the lesson was read, and the monk would use the horns of a visiting stag as a book-rest! Where Pagan mythology portrays animals as numinous messengers from the spirit world, the monks relate to them more as pets or servants. This parallels the gradual 'move indoors', where, under the new religion, the Druid groves were replaced by walled churches, the sacred spring by the inside font.

So, as might be expected, practitioners of the deeper kind of relationship with Nature that I call here the relationship of communion, were the *geilt* rather than the Christian anchorites, and I will look more closely here at who they were. Like their Christian counterparts, these dwellers in the wild left civilization to follow a spiritual call. Often this came as a reaction to the horrors of war. In Ireland, the most famous of these was Suibhne Geilt, a warrior king who in the midst of battle was struck with revulsion and terror at the carnage, and fled for refuge into the wilderness. There he sought peace and solitude and became a prolific Nature poet.

In Britain, the same tale is told of Merlin, who fled the nightmare of battle for the solitude of the Caledonian Forest. Not all forest-dwellers were refugees of war; but for all, the call of the wilderness was a call from spirit. To dwell in the forest was to live between the worlds and to learn how to traverse the unmarked paths and perilous ways of the Otherworld. It was to start to merge with wild Nature itself. Suibhne and other *geilt* were said to have grown feathers, like birds, upon their bodies. With the typical ambiguity of Celtic literature, some texts tell us they could fly like birds; others that the feathers grew only to protect them from the fierce frost and cold, but that they 'run along the trees almost as swiftly as monkeys or squirrels'.[11] Did they really grow feathers, or were they garbed in feather cloaks that made them look like strange huge birds glimpsed between the branches on a dim evening? If these were cloaks, were they really for protection against the elements, or were they for the flight of the soul into the Otherworld? The feathered cloak used in

shamanic practices worldwide was certainly known in Celtic tradition: we hear tell of the great Druid Mog Ruith whose 'skin of the
hornless, dun-coloured bull was brought to him then and his
speckled bird-dress with its winged flying, and his Druidic gear
besides. And he rose up, in company with the fire, into the air and the
heavens ...'[12]

The legendary Finn mac Cumaill, and his warrior band of Fianna,
share characteristics with animals. Conan McMorna, one of his
men, had the fleece of a black sheep on his back instead of skin. The
mother of Finn's son, Oisin (or 'Fawn'), bore him while in the shape
of a doe.

Suibhne Geilt was said to have run with the herds of wild deer,
riding upon a fawn, living, like the deer themselves, on wild plants
and water. Merlin is also described as living as one of a herd of stags
'like a wild animal.' I am reminded of the extraordinary image on the
silver panels of the famous cauldron found in a peat-bog in
Gundestrup, Denmark, where a male figure wearing antlers sits in
ecstatic trance, surrounded by a forest of animals. This relationship
of communion with wild animals drew these men into the borders of
the Otherworld: both Suibhne and Merlin developed the supernatural powers of prophecy and shape-shifting.

And what are we to make of these other ambiguous figures, half-
men, half wild creatures, known in medieval Britain as the Wodwo or
Wild Men? While few words were written about them, they have
been extensively depicted in tapestries and church carvings. These
beings were in human form, but covered completely with hair. They
wore no clothes but were frequently garlanded with flowers and
leaves. They are shown riding upon various animals, some of them
fabulous: stags, bears, unicorns and gryphons. They have never been
conclusively identified as mythical figures akin to the satyr, or as a
remnant of a forest-dwelling people. Their presence as motifs on the
fine furnishings of the rich bespeak a fascination with the archetype
of wildness in an over-civilized milieu. They were certainly considered real enough by many, including Charles VI of France, who spent
a lifetime searching obsessively for them and was rewarded when one
joined in a charivari at a wedding-feast.

In the relationship of communion, the boundary between human
and wild animal is blurred; in the transformative relationship it
dissolves altogether. This is the province of the great seers who
were masters at walking between the worlds. By daring consciously
to undergo egoic death, they were able to expand individual

consciousness to identify with the experience of other-than-human forms, and, in that other reality, to spend many lifetimes as elements or creatures of the wild. Through living in the skins of other-than-human beings, they attained the wisdom of a self that identified itself with consciousness, not form; a fluid consciousness that could become universal by flowing into the myriad aspects of life in the natural world. This was the highest form of initiation in the Celtic Mysteries undergone by the most daring of poet-seers and heroes. Before Finn's birth, it was prophesied:

He will be in the shape of every beast,
Both on the azure sea and on land,
He will be a dragon before hosts at the onset,
He will be a wolf of every great forest.

He will be a stag with horns of silver
In the land where chariots are driven,
He will be a speckled salmon in a full pool,
He will be a seal, he will be a fair-white swan.[13]

Wales' greatest bard and seer, Taliesin, was initiated into the mysteries of the goddess Ceridwen through a shape-shifting sequence, in which he turned respectively, into a hare, a fish, a bird, and finally a grain of wheat. Each of these forms represented one of the four elements that constitute life: the hare as earth, the fish as water, the bird as air, and the sun-ripened grain of wheat as the spark of fire.

The poet-seer would often 'state his credentials' in incantations that ring with numinous authenticity. Taliesin declaims:

I have been a blue salmon,
I have been a dog, a stag, a roebuck on the mountain …

The seer Amergin, (in what I like to think was a voice that sent ripples of fear through his listeners), said:

I am the wind which blows over the sea;
I am the wave of the deep;
I am the bull of seven battles;
I am the eagle on the rock;
I am a tear of the sun;[14]

Where it could be said that these experiences might be no more than inner visions, other stories of metamorphosis with the wild things of earth have a definitely 'lived' quality, and recount all the terrors and marvels of the journey of transformation. In the narrative poem known as *The Hawk of Achill*, an ancient seer named Fintan converses with an aged hawk on the lonely island of Achill, off the west coast of County Mayo in Ireland. They find out they are exactly the same age – 6515 years – and both have lived through the early history of old Ireland, witnessed its many invasions, lived under numerous kings, and suffered many losses and deaths. For five hundred years Fintan was a salmon, for fifty he was an eagle, and finally, for one hundred years a falcon, before returning to his original human shape. He recounts the bitter cold of winter from the salmon's perspective:

> *I passed a night in the Northern wave,*
> *And I at Asseroe of the seals,*
> *Never felt I a night like that*
> *From the beginning of the world to its end.*
>
> *I could not stay under the waterfall,*
> *I took a leap, but it did not help me,*
> *The ice came like clear blue glass*
> *Between me and the falls of Mac Moduirn ...*[15]

Another shape-shifter and time-traveller was Tuan O'Cairell, an old seer discovered by the monk Finnian of Moville, to whom he recounts his history of transformations. Tuan O'Cairell describes the wretchedness of old age as an exhausted old man, and the joy of renewal as he is transformed into a stag, the first of many metamorphoses:

> *At last old age came upon me, and I was on cliffs and in wastes, and was unable to move about, ... hairy, clawed, withered, grey, naked, wretched, miserable. Then as I was asleep one night, I saw myself passing into the shape of a stag. In that shape I was, and I young and glad of heart ...*
>
> *Then there grew upon my head*
> *Two antlers with three score points,*
> *So that I am rough and grey in shape*
> *After my age has changed from feebleness.*[16]

Tuan, like Suibhne and Merlin, becomes the leader of the stag herds of Ireland, before taking the shape, in turn, of a boar, a hawk and a salmon, and finally a man again. Every time he wearies with age, he returns to a certain cave where he fasts for three days, the period favoured by Celtic seers for mantic journeys. Like Fintan, he undergoes intense hardships that ring with all the authenticity of lived experience:

> *I passed into the shape of a river salmon … was vigorous and well-fed and my swimming was good, and I used to escape from every danger and from every snare – to wit, from the hands of fishermen, and from the claws of hawks, and from fishing spears – so that the scars which each one of them left are still upon me.*[17]

Tuan's life as a salmon is brought to an end when fishermen of the chieftain Cairell catch him and serve him to his wife, who eats the whole fish herself. She becomes pregnant with Tuan, who remains conscious while in her womb, fully aware of who he is and of everything that is happening in Ireland. So, in a mysterious reversal which serves to highlight the magical interplay of human and non-human forms in the Celtic tradition, the man that eats the salmon to become a seer, turns into the salmon who is eaten so that a man can be born.

The spiritual intent behind these extraordinary initiations is best summed up by the seventeenth century Welsh writer, Iolo Morganwg, in his *Barddas*, a work, he claims, of ancient Druidic teachings:

> *And as there is a special form of knowledge that cannot be had in another, it is necessary that we should go through every form of existence before we can acquire every form and species of understanding, and consequently renounce all evil …*[18]

Although these ancient ways have vanished, along with the great forests of Northern Europe, even today in modern England traces of the old communion with the wild things survives in folk-custom and festival. Every September in Abbot's Bromley, Staffordshire, the Horn Dance takes place, with dancers wearing reindeer antlers; on May Day, in the small fishing town of Padstow, Cornwall, the townspeople take turns to don the costume of the 'hobby horse', and cavort wildly through the town, personifying the wild and untamed power of a new spring.

These ancient echoes remind us all to clearly that we have cast ourselves out of the Garden, journeyed far from the place where we knew our own Name. As we wandered to the edges of our separate-ness, we allowed the twin 'Thou Shalt Nots' of Church and Reason to shut down our perceptions, until our only reality was filtered through the thin and querulous cry of 'Cogito Ergo Sum'.

But, as is hinted by that most ubiquitous of Celtic symbols, the spiral, every journey is circular. This means that when we reach the furthest point from our beginning we have no choice but to return. Ken Wilber, the foremost theoretical psychologist in the field of transpersonal and spiritual studies, has shown how, as individuals, we develop by first following the outer arc of the circle, where we grow from unconsciousness into an awareness of our own individu-ality, the 'skin-encapsulated ego' that seems to be the extent of who we can ever be. But it is at this apparently most triumphant moment of separate selfhood that the boundaries begin to dissolve, and consciousness is free to expand into a wider, more inclusive sense of Self. Now we set forth upon the journey, on the inward arc of the circle that leads us back to our sense of oneness with all life, but this time with a more conscious, deeper apprehension of what that means. As one of the founding parents of the Deep Ecology move-ment, the American poet Robinson Jeffers puts it:

> A little too abstract, a little too wise,
> It is time for us to kiss the earth again,
> It is time to let the leaves rain down from the skies,
> Let the rich life run to the roots again.[19]

The signs are that, collectively, we have begun the Great Return on the inward arc. It is as if we are finally becoming aware of the numerous sentient forms of life that hover about us in unguarded moments, pressing against the windows of our dreams, waiting patiently for that simple act of recognition that can come like light-ning, or as quiet as leaf-fall. As modern ecological consciousness grows, fostering a thirst for an abiding relationship with the natural world, this ancient and all but dried-up river is being fed with fresh springs.

Whether we call these streams Druidry, NeoPaganism or Deep Ecology, their waters come pouring forth from the Well of Wisdom that has its source within the soul, so that we may reclaim our birthright as a natural part of all life. What matters most is that these are living streams for today, not content merely to run between the banks of the past, but vigorously engaged in recarving old patterns into vital traditions for modern lives. Like Fintan and Tuan O'Cairell, we too have been given the opportunity of experiencing a different, *deeper* way of perceiving life, by looking through the eyes of our ancestors. Now, like them, we know we are being called to effect nothing less than the transformation of the modern collective psyche, and the joyous renewal of the web of life.

NOTES

1. This quotation heads an article in Folklore vol. iv, no. iv, December 1893 by Gertrude M. Godden, entitled, 'The Sanctuary of Mourie.' Unfortunately she doesn't reference the quote.
2. Bamford, Christopher and Marsh, William Parker. *Celtic Christianity*, Massachusetts: Lindisfarne Press, 1987.
3. *Carmina Gadelica*, Alexander Carmichael, Lindisfarne Press, Floris Books, 1992.
4. Meyer, Kuno. *Selections from Ancient Irish Poetry*, London: Constable, 1959.
5. Jackson, Kenneth Hurlstone. *A Celtic Miscellany*, Middlesex: Penguin Books, 1973.
6. Meyer, Ibid.
7. Jackson, Ibid.
8. Jackson, Ibid.
9. Meyer, Ibid.
10. Ross, Anne. *Pagan Celtic Britain*, London: Routledge and Kegan Paul, 1967.
11. Chadwick, Nora. *Geilt*. Scottish Gaelic Studies, Vol. V., Part II. Oxford: Blackwell, 1942.
12. Ross, Ibid.
13. Meyer, Kuno, trans. *The Voyage of Bran*, Felinfach: Llanerch, 1994.
14. Ford, Patrick. *The Mabinogi*, California: University of California Press, 1977.
15. Hull, Eleanor. *The Hawk of Achill or The Legend of the Oldest Animals*, London: Folk-Lore, Vol 43, 1932.
16. Matthews, John. *Taliesin*, London: The Aquarian Press, 1991.
17. Matthews, Ibid.
18. Matthews, John. *A Celtic Reader*, London: The Aquarian Press, 1991.
19. Jeffers, Robinson. From *'The Return'* in *Selected Poems*. New York: Vintage Books, 1964.

Mara Freeman M.A., is a writer, teacher and storyteller of the British Mystery Tradition. Originally from England, she moved to California's central coast in 1979 where she lived close to nature in a mountainous wilderness area for twelve years. With degrees in English Literature and Psychology, she is also a transpersonal psychotherapist with a private practice in Carmel-by-the-Sea, California. Mara lectures and gives workshops and storytelling performances internationally.

For information and details of **Mara Freeman**'s audio-cassette series of Inner Journeys and Celtic stories contact: Mara Freeman, P.O. Box 3839, Carmel, CA. Email: chalice@redshift.com

RESOURCE GUIDE

Groups

There are now so many Druid groups it is not possible to list all of them. For details of many of the esoteric, as opposed to cultural, Druid groups, see Philip Shallcrass *A Druid Directory – A Guide to Modern Druidry and Druid Orders* from The British Druid Order, PO Box 29, St-Leonards-on-Sea, E.Sussex TN37 7YP. Write to the same address for details of *The Gorsedd of Bards of Caer Abiri* – an informal gathering of those interested in Druidry, and Druids from many different groups, who meet at festival times at Avebury and share an irregular newsletter.

Information on French Druid groups can be obtained from Michel Raoult, La Pommeraie-Avalon, 29252 Plouezoc'h, Bretagne, France.

The two largest Druid groups in America are Keltria, PO Box 33284 Minneapolis MN 55433 and ADF, PO Box 516, E. Syracuse, NY 13057–0516. Information on these, and other American groups is available in *American Druidism: A Guide to American Druid Groups* by Daniel Hansen from CSC, 27013 Pacific Hwy S. 315, Kent WA 98032 USA. (Both *A Druid Directory* and *American Druidism* are also available from The Oak Tree Press, PO Box 1333 Lewes E. Sussex BN7 lDX. Email: office@obod.co.uk)

The largest group, worldwide, is The Order of Bards Ovates & Druids, which offers a distance-learning programme using monthly mailings, audio-cassettes, and a personal mentor programme by correspondence or email. The Order's links with the literary world are maintained by the role of 'Presider' which has included Lewis Spence, Charles Cammell, John and Caitlín Matthews, and John Michell. The current Presider is Melita Denning. There are summer-camps in England and America, a retreat on Iona, and a monthly

journal, with groups meeting in many countries. Details from
OBOD, PO Box 1333, Lewes, E.Sussex BN7 lDX. Email:
office@obod.co.uk (website:http://ww.obod.co.uk/obod/)

Archives

The International Druid Archives holds the largest publicly-
accessible assembly of documents from modern Druid movements
worldwide. To consult, contact Carleton College Archives (re
Druid Archives) 300 North College Street, Northfield, Minnesota
55057 USA.

Magazines

Aisling PO Box 196, London WClA 2DY
The Druid's Voice PO Box 29, St.Leonards-on-Sea, E.Sussex
TN37 7YP
Keltria Journal of Druidism PO Box 48369, Minneapolis
MN 55448 USA
Druids Progress PO Box 9420 Newark DE 19714-9420 USA
Metrodruidz Nuz GM Grove, PO Box 3495, Jersey City,
NJ 07303 USA

Audio-Cassettes

Since Druidry was an oral tradition, audio-cassettes offer an ideal
medium for study. The following organizations offer relevant
cassettes:

Mara Freeman, PO Box 3839, Carmel, CA 93921 USA
John & Caitlín Matthews, BCM Hallowquest, London WClN 3XX
The Oak Tree Press, PO Box 1333, Lewes, E. Sussex BN7 lDX
Robin Williamson Productions, BCM 4797, London WClN 3XX
Sulis Music, BCM 3721, London WClN 3XX
Talking Myth Publications, 29B Grosvenor Avenue, London
N5 2NP

Divinatory Systems

Using the following sets, which draw on the Druidic and Celtic
wisdom traditions, can sometimes provide experiences of these
traditions in deeper ways than book study:

The Arthurian Hallows - works with the Arthurian & Grail mysteries to create a path of self-discovery. John & Caitlín Matthews, Aquarian, 1990.
The Celtic Oracle, The Ancient Art of the Druids – Nigel Pennick & Nigel Jackson, Aquarian, 1992
The Celtic Tree Oracle – works with the sacred trees of the Celts and Druids and the Ogham, Liz & Colin Murray, Rider, 1989.
The Druid Animal Oracle, Philip & Stephanie Carr-Gomm, Simon & Schuster, 1995, (USA). Connections, 1996, (UK).
The Merlin Tarot – a book and card set by R. J. Stewart, Aquarian, 1988.

Druids on the Net

Erynn Laurie

The Internet and other computer networks are an ever-expanding part of many people's lives. Druids are an active part of this growing network, participating in fascinating discussions, building Web pages, debating the nature of Druidism and building friendships all around the world. If you have a computer and a modem, you can join in this aspect of the Druid renaissance through local bulletin boards, commercial online services like Compuserve or America OnLine, or local Internet service providers.

When entering online discussions, observe for a while before you make your first post. This will help you to get some idea of how the conversation flows in each place, and the personalities of some of the more frequent posters. If you don't see discussions on topics of interest, try posting a message with a question, a book review, or a few paragraphs about your interests. This will often bring responses. Remember that discussions about religion often bring up strong feelings for people. Where strong beliefs are held, emotions can run high and sometimes tempers flare. People often type things that they would never say in person. Always read over your messages before you post them. Intentions can be easily misunderstood, and something that you think is funny may be taken as deadly insulting to the person reading it. Keep your sense of humour when reading messages, and try not to take things personally. Always remember that there is another human being reading your messages, and treat other people with the respect you would wish to receive. Your interactions on the net should be as civil as your face to face meetings. Be prepared to encounter a wide spectrum of ideas and emotions when you venture out onto the net. You will inevitably find challenges to your most sincerely held beliefs. If you are willing to defend and expound upon your views in a civil manner, you will find many fast friends all over the world.

Because of the nature of the net, these lists are not and cannot be comprehensive. They are merely meant as an entry into the world of Druidism online. Net resources come and go without notice. Although these sites and lists were active at the time this book went to press, some may no longer be available when you try them. Listings here are almost entirely English language resources, along with a few for the Celtic languages.

Local BBS Access

Local Pagan bulletin boards are often part of regional or world-wide networks. Many of these boards provide free access, or access for a low monthly fee. You can generally find their phone numbers in your local computer publications or by asking other Pagans with computers. Discussion areas are set up as 'echoes,' which means that you post messages on your local bulletin board. This board transfers messages to a node where other local bulletin boards call to send their messages and receive those sent by other boards. Your messages may take several days to a week to receive a response. Some discussion echoes of interest to Druids and Celtic Pagans include:

PODS (Pagan Occult Distribution System) US, Canada and a few boards in England:
PODS Celtic – Celtic religions and culture
PODS ADF – ADF and other Druidic groups
PODS Wicca – All forms of Wicca including Celtic Wiccan traditions
FIDO is available on BBS systems worldwide:
FIDO Magick – All magickal systems including Celtic magick. Religion is not usually discussed here.
OPEN (Occult Pagan Esoteric Net) Australia, New Zealand, Netherlands, England and a few US boards:
OPEN Druid – Druidism and Celtic Paganism
OPEN Celtic - Celtic religions and culture

Commercial Services

Commercial services provide structured forums on a number of topics including many forms of Paganism. Most services charge a basic monthly rate for a certain number of hours' access, and then an hourly rate above that. When you sign up for a commercial service, look for Celtic and Druidic discussions under general topic areas like Religion, Lifestyles, Paganism or New Age.

Usenet Newsgroups

Usenet is a part of the Internet that allows subscribers to participate in open discussions on thousands of topics. Some newsgroups get hundreds, or even thousands of posts every day, and you may receive responses to your posts within minutes. Most Usenet newsgroups are completely uncensored. You will need to sort through messages offering get-rich-quick schemes, ads for telephone sex services, and anti-Pagan messages urging you to give up 'Satanism', in order to find the interesting and useful posts. There are newsreader programs available to help you in this filtering process. Here are a few Usenet newsgroups that may include discussions of Celtic mythology, Celtic Paganism or Druidism:

    alt.mythology
    alt.pagan
    alt.religion.druid
    soc.culture.celtic

Mailing Lists

Mailing lists are privately maintained discussion lists conducted through email. All you need to participate in these discussions is an email account. You do not need full Internet access. Email lists vary in size, some having just a few members, others having several hundred. The number of messages you receive in one day will vary with the size of the list and the activity of its members. Some lists have a 'digest' option which allows you to receive all new messages to the list as a daily or weekly single message to your mailbox. As a member of an email list, you are the guest of the listowner, and may be subject to rules concerning topicality, language, or civil behaviour. Some lists of Celtic interest are:

Celtic-L: send email to listserv@irlearn.ucd.ie with the message subscribe Celtic-L <yourname> General discussion of all things Celtic.

Gaelic-L: send email to listserv@irlearn.ucd.ie with the message subscribe Gaelic-L <yourname> Gaelic-language list for learners and users of the language. Includes posts in Irish, Scots Gaelic and Manx.

Welsh-L: send email to listserv@irlearn.ucd.ie with the message subscribe Welsh-L <yourname> Welsh-language list for learners and users of the language. Includes posts in Welsh, Cornish and Breton.

Nemeton-L: send email to majordomo@io.com with the message subscribe Nemeton-L <yourname> Celtic reconstructionist Pagan and Druid discussions. Does not include discussion of Wicca or shamanism.

Shaman-L: send email to listserv@listserv.aol.com with the message subscribe Shaman-L <yourname> The listowner of this list is a Celtic shaman. Discussion of Celtic shamanism is welcome here.

World Wide Web Pages

The World Wide Web is accessible through your local Internet service provider and through some commercial services, with software like Lynx or Netscape. Here are some sites that are accessible through the Web that may be of interest to Druids and Celtic Pagans. These sites include information about Druidism or things of Celtic interest including but not limited to illustration files, humour, bibliographies, FAQ's (Frequently Asked Question files), language files, and information files. Each site may link you to more sites that the site builder finds interesting. These links build the Web and will take you to thousands of interesting places all over the world.

ADF Web Page
http://www.adf.org/

Anders Magick Page
http://www.nada.kth.se/~nv91-asa/magick.html

Bibliographies of Interest to Mythologists
http://www.the-wire.com/culture.mythology/mythbibl.html

BUBL Information Service: Religions of Ancient Peoples
http://www.bubl.bath.ac.uk/BUBL/ReligPre.html

Celtic Culture Page
http://www.pic.net/~callahan/celtic.htm

Celtic, Germanic & Nordic Culture Page
http://ukanaix.ce.ukans.edu/~eickwort/cu/hrd_main.html

Celtic & Viking Art Files
http://www.tardis.ed.ac.uk/~feorag/paganlink/gallery/celtpics.html

Ceolas Celtic Music Archive
http://celtic.stanford.edu/ceolas.html

Dalriada Heritage Society
gopher://gopher.almac.co.uk/11/scotland/dalriada

DrOOP Home Page
http://www.pixelations.com/users/pixelations/drphome.html

Lysator Pagan Files Directory
http://www.lysator.liu.se/ftp/pub/religion/neopagan/index.html

Myths & Legends
http://pubpages.unh.edu/~cbsiren/myth.html

Nemeton-L Home Page
http://www.speakeasy.org/~mimir/nemeton.html

Order of Bards Ovates & Druids Home Page
http://ww.obod.co.uk/obod/

Pagan Resources Page
http://www.ssc.org/~athomps/pagan/paganres.html/

Rowan Fairgrove's Home Page
http://www.crc.ricoh.com/~rowanf/rowanf.html

Brief information on Druid groups is available in the United States by telephoning 1-800-DRUIDRY.

Email information via the Internet on the larger Druid groups is available from:
ADF@aol.com   Keltria@aol.com   OBOD@aol.com